The New Managerialism and Public Service Professions

The New Managerialism and Public Service Professions

Change in Health, Social Services and Housing

Ian Kirkpatrick,
Stephen Ackroyd

and

Richard Walker

First published 2005 by
PALGRAVE MACMILLAN
Houndmills, Basingstoke, Hampshire RG21 6XS and
175 Fifth Avenue, New York, N.Y. 10010
Companies and representatives throughout the world

PALGRAVE MACMILLAN is the global academic imprint of the Palgrave Macmillan division of St. Martin's Press, LLC and of Palgrave Macmillan Ltd. Macmillan® is a registered trademark in the United States, United Kingdom and other countries. Palgrave is a registered trademark in the European Union and other countries.

ISBN 0–333–73975–2 hardback

This book is printed on paper suitable for recycling and made from fully managed and sustained forest sources.

A catalogue record for this book is available from the British Library.

Library of Congress Cataloging-in-Publication Data
Kirkpatrick, Ian, 1965–
    The new managerialism and public service professions :
change in health, social services, and housing / Ian Kirkpatrick,
Stephen Ackroyd, and Richard Walker.
        p. cm.
    Includes bibliographical references and index.
    ISBN 0–333–73975–2 (cloth)
        1. Public welfare administration–Great Britain. 2. Social work
administration–Great Britain. 3. Health services
administration–Great Britain. 4. Public housing–Great
Britain–Management. I. Ackroyd, Stephen. II. Walker, Richard M.
III. Title.

HV245.K57 2005
362.941'068–dc22   2004053756

10   9   8   7   6   5   4   3   2   1
14   13   12   11   10   09   08   07   06   05

Printed and bound in Great Britain by
Antony Rowe Ltd, Chippenham and Eastbourne

Contents

List of Tables

List of Abbreviations

AHA	Area Health Authority
ALMO	Arms Length Management Organisation
BMA	British Medical Association
CCETSW	Central Council for Education and Training of Social Work
CHA	Community Health Authority
CHI	Commission for Health Improvement
CIH	Chartered Institute of Housing
CIPD	Chartered Institute of Personnel Development
CCT	Compulsory Competitive Tendering
DGA	District General Hospital
DHA	District Health Authority
DoE	Department of Environment
FE	Further Education
GDP	Gross Domestic Product
GNP	Gross National Product
GP	General Practice/Practitioner
HIP	Housing Investment Plan
HT	Health Trust
LSVT	Large Scale Voluntary Transfer
MBA	Master of Business Administration
NFHA	National Federation of Housing Associations
NHS	National Health Service
NICE	National Institute for Clinical Excellence
NPM	New Public management
OECD	Organisation for Economic Co-operation and Development
Ofsted	The Office for Standards in Education
PSO	Professional Service Organisation
PSS	Personal Social Services
RHA	Regional Health Authority
SSD	Social Services Department
SSI	Social Services Inspectorate
TOPSS	Training Organisations in the Personal Social Services

Preface

This book is about change in the management of public services – how much of it and what consequences. For over two decades the goal of restructuring welfare provision has been at the heart of UK government policy. Under the Conservatives the focus was on controlling expenditure and re-organising services to make professionals more accountable for resource decisions. In health, education and social care, the objective was to install a system of managed provision heavily influenced by the practices of private firms. After 1997, New Labour accelerated this process under a different banner of modernisation. Today perhaps even more so than a decade ago the dominant image projected by politicians and the media is of a public sector in crisis. This is manifested in a constant barrage of critical reports highlighting performance failure and the limited availability and uneven quality of services. Root and branch change, it is argued, is both highly desirable and unavoidable.

In this book our purpose is to chart these developments but also raise questions about how they have been understood. In a good deal of the literature it is taken as given that management in UK public services has been transformed. New forms of organising are said to be firmly established, while, across public services, more subtle shifts in professional identities and commitments are under way. To be sure it is often recognised that this process is contested and uneven. But for most observers the longer term trajectory or direction of change is assumed to be clear and beyond dispute. Indeed one gets the distinct impression that the debate has moved on. Few practitioners or academics today appear willing to challenge the idea that public services are now 'managed services'. Fewer still question the assumption that management reform itself is a good thing or that progress has been made in terms of improving the effectiveness of services.

In this book our aim is to develop a quite different account. We do not deny that change has occurred or that, in some areas, professional practice has been altered beyond recognition. But for us it is important to question the idea that policy goals have been fully translated into efficient new public sector services or even that they will be in the long term. The attempt to reshape the management of welfare professionals, we argue, has been far more contested and problematic than many assume. In our approach the public sector organisation is not taken to be a passive instrument of policy. It cannot be assumed that whatever new policies were deemed necessary were simply translated into new patterns of action as was required by policy makers.

To develop these arguments this book presents a detailed review of the published research on management change in three key sectors: health care, housing and social services. In doing so our aim is to draw attention to the uneven nature of restructuring and to marked variations in the way professional groups received and responded to the reforms. Our intention is also to emphasise the wider costs and unintended consequences of this process. Even after two decades of reforms, few would argue that there are no problems left, or that there is little more to be done.

Some readers no doubt will be aware that this book has been a long time, perhaps too long, in the making. The original idea for it was first floated by one of us (Stephen) in a paper presented at Cardiff Business School back in 1994. The arguments put forward then, about the need for a more comparative and sober evaluation of the new managerialism struck a cord. It seemed to us that the literature was crying out for a more critical appraisal of the reforms, one that took seriously the ability of the professions to resist or mediate change. But, despite our initial enthusiasm it was some time before we approached a publisher (then Macmillan) and even longer before we embarked on the project. Over this period much has changed, not least the transition to a New Labour government. This required us to devote some time updating our material and keeping abreast (if that is possible) with the torrent of new policy initiatives and directives. However, we remain convinced that the ideas formulated back in 1994 are as relevant today as they were then. In our view there is still a pressing need to take stock of the new managerialism and look critically at the process and consequences of reform. It is our sincere hope that in what follows readers will agree that we have at least come close to meeting that need.

In the course of writing this book we have received help and encouragement from a number of sources. First we should thank various people at Palgrave Macmillan, including, Sarah Brown, Zelah Pengilley, Catlin Cornish and Jacky Kippenberger for their support and, more importantly, patience over the past five years. We got there in the end. We would also like to acknowledge the assistance of colleagues who over the years supported this project and offered invaluable advice on how to develop and improve it. Special thanks goes out go to Ray Bolam,

Keith Soothill, Martin Kitchener, George Boyne, Robyn Thomas, Miguel Martinez-Lucio, Sharon Bolton and Daniel Muzio. Finally Richard Walker would like to acknowledge the support of the ESRC/EPSRC Advanced Institute of Management Research under grant number 331-25-006 for this research.

Ian Kirkpatrick
Stephen Ackroyd
Richard Walker

1
Introduction

...one of the key problems of studying the new public management [NPM] is a degree of confusion about its status. Many examinations of the NPM conflate politics and practice of public service reform treating the NPM as though it has been installed as the only mode of coordination in public services. They also conflate the descriptive and normative aspects of the concept treating the claims of NPM advocates as though they describe new realities...Nevertheless, it seems overstated to treat this as an unequivocal, and completely accomplished, change in the co-ordination of public services. We would suggest that the impact of these ideas has been more uneven, contested and complex than can be accounted for in a view of a simple shift from public administration to New Public Management... (Clarke et al., 2000: 7).

Sometimes one can 'take a horse to water but not make him drink' (Pollitt and Boukaert, 2000: 274).

A distinctive and enduring feature of the welfare state in Britain is the central role played by organised professions. In the post war era groups such as doctors, teachers and even social workers became active partners in the development of public services. Their 'influence on the kind, pace and structure of provision' was 'often crucial, if not... decisive' (Perkin, 1989: 344). Such influence manifested itself in a number of ways. Through their collective organisations the professions played a key role in shaping policy, in some cases defining both problems and solutions. At the level of service delivery itself, within broad financial and legal constraints, professional groups exercised considerable *de*

1

facto control over both the means and (sometimes) ends. All this was underpinned by a degree of trust in the ability of the professions to provide services in the public interest. The autonomy and independence of these expert groups was considered not only to be unavoidable, but also to some extent desirable.

From the late 1970s these institutions and their underlying assumptions became the target of sustained and relentless attack. Increasingly governments saw public services as inefficient and the professions as incapable of regulating their own practice. This, in turn, spurred attempts to weaken the autonomy and power of the welfare professions. Extensive legislation was introduced prescribing the goals and sometimes methods through which services were to be provided. Alongside this were moves to increase the accountability of professionals to their users and the establishment of more judgemental and controlling approaches towards regulation. However, what stands as the most radical and far-reaching change was the attempt by the state to reform the management arrangements of professional work itself. Public services, it was argued, needed to adopt not only the practices of private sector management but also its central and narrow concern with the goal of cost efficiency (Rhodes, 1996). First under the Conservatives from 1979 and, after 1997, under New Labour, this objective has been pursued with great vigour. Across the UK public services, the demand for change has been 'continual, often intense, and sometimes harsh' (Pollitt and Boukaert, 2000: 274).

In much of the literature the assumption is that these management reforms have already substantially transformed professional work. This view is especially prevalent in practitioner focused accounts (OECD, 1995). Here the tendency is to assume that 'major changes in form and legitimising ideology are inevitable' (Greenwood and Lachman, 1996: 568). Developments in the UK and elsewhere constitute a paradigm shift (Osborne and Gaebler, 1992) or 'clear-cut movement…away from outmoded traditional ways of organising and conducting public business towards up-to-date, state-of-the-art methods and styles' (Hood, 1998: 196).

Although far less sanguine about the desirability of the new managerialism, in much of the critical literature, one is also presented with the idea that professional organisations have been or soon will be transformed. Exworthy and Halford (1999a: 6), for example, suggest: 'calls for managerialisation in the public sector posed such a fundamental challenge to established practice that the professional paradigm might really be threatened'. Others go further, articulating this process in terms of a shift in design archetypes, with public services moving inexorably towards 'more corporate and managerial modes of organisation' (Powell et al., 1999: 2; Kitchener, 1998; Ferlie and Fitzgerald, 2000). Finally are accounts that point to the way in which professional work is steadily being colonised by management ideology and subject to more rational modes of top down control and surveillance (Cutler and Waine, 1994; Lloyd and Seifert, 1995; Broadbent and Laughlin, 2002). Change, it is argued, has been driven by a new cadre of 'commercialised' professionals, actively seeking 'management assets' and strongly identifying with government policies (Hanlon, 1998: 50; Causor and Exworthy, 1999).

In this book our goal is to develop a different kind of account of change in UK public services. This is not to deny that major restructuring has occurred or that, in some areas, professional practice has been altered beyond recognition. Nor do we fundamentally dispute the claim that a new 'hierarchy of legitimation' has emerged in which discourses of 'managerialism and business' are now hegemonic (Clarke and Newman, 1997: 104). Rather, our objective is to argue that the project of management reform has been far more uneven, contested and problematic than is often recognised. For us there has been no 'unequivocal, and completely accomplished change in the co-ordination of public services'. Such a view, we suggest, is misplaced for at least two reasons.

First it fails to account for the robust nature of the institutions against which management reforms are directed. In our approach, unlike much writing on public choice, the public sector organisation is not taken to be a passive instrument of policy. It cannot be assumed that whatever new policies were deemed necessary were simply translated into new patterns of action as was required by policy makers. Indeed, we think that because social services are provided by particular forms of organisation within which there are identified groups of people – people who are organised for co-operative activity in particular ways – the effects of policy themselves can be quite varied. In particular, it will be our argument that because public services have been, and to a considerable extent continue to be, provided by professionals within specific forms of organisation in which they hold key positions, the effects of change have been not always what were expected. The capacity of these groups to negotiate or 'capture' reform in ways that minimise disturbance to their day-to-day activities should not be under-estimated (Ackroyd, 1996; Pollitt et al., 1998). Nor should the potency of established values and assumptions that inform practice. Even amongst senior professionals – the supposed vanguard of the new management – one might question how far marked shifts in commitments have occurred.

Second is the uneven application of management reform. This has taken different forms at different times and has been pressed home with varying degrees of vigour. It can even be argued that elements of the policy are internally contradictory, which, at a minimum, leads to ambiguity over the path of change. According to Clarke et al. (2000: 7) there is a tendency in much of the literature to present a 'rather over-unified or over-coherent view of the NPM as a form of co-ordination'. In reality, under both Conservative and New Labour governments, public organisations were faced with a succession of inconsistent (Boyne et al., 2003) and sometimes competing and even irreconcilable demands (Lowndes, 1997; Pollitt and Boukaert, 2000). This, in turn, may have greatly problematised attempts to translate policy goals to local levels. For example, at the same time as professional groups have been asked to improve management practice, they have faced pressures to cut costs and remove 'needless administration' (Ackroyd, 1995a: 8).

Arising from these concerns this book therefore aims for a more mea-sured assessment of developments over the past twenty five years. Our aim is to consider just how far there has been continuity and persis-tence of older modes of organising. It is also to analyse the sources of continuity and inertia. If change has not occurred, then how might we explain this?

A further objective of this book is to evaluate some of the wider con-sequences of management restructuring. In doing so we question the assumption made in the policy literature that change was necessary to 'modernise' public services or that it is 'broadly beneficent and to be welcomed' (Hood, 1998: 196). For us this idea is problematic in two main respects. First it ignores how moves to reform public services were driven, at least initially, by political and ideological considera-tions. As we shall see, the period of gestation for the new approach to policy was highly truncated. There was very little attempt to analyse what was routinely achieved by the old system, what the sources of the strengths it undoubtedly had actually were as well as getting clear sight of the problems. In fact, there was very little attempt to think through what needed to be done by way of reform or to evaluate the likely con-sequences. Rather, in the UK the tendency was for policy to combine 'ideology and rhetoric with minimal evidence' (Wistow et al., 1996: 12; Pollitt, 2000).

A second set of reasons for questioning the desirability of manage-ment restructuring are the numerous costs (either directly or indirectly) associated with it. In much of the literature this issue is rarely discussed. But for us it is essential to draw attention to the wider consequences, especially those that are unintended. Efforts to induce change have now lasted more than two decades, and the human and the financial costs have been large. One might point for example to the stultifying effect of new management systems for controlling and monitoring practice (Audit Commission, 2002d). Also of concern is the trend towards work intensification in many areas, rising levels of stress, staff demoralisation and employee turnover (Guest and Conway, 2002). In the long run, these and other developments may undermine the quality of services, producing what Hoggett (1996: 10) describes as a 'high output/low commitment public sector workforce'. As such one should draw attention to the reverse consequences of the new public management (Hood, 1998). This is not to deny that restructuring did lead to some improvements (these will be discussed in Chapter 7). Rather it is to emphasise the fact that change has not been cost free. Even after two decades of reforms, few would argue that there are no problems left, or that there is little more to be done. Despite the upbeat assessments of policy makers the new public management is far from being a 'doctrine beyond question' (Power, 1997: 92–3).

In summary this book seeks to assess both the nature of change in professional public services and the wider consequences of it. In what remains of this introductory chapter we now set out our approach towards addressing these concerns. We then provide an outline of the book and describe its contents.

Our approach

Our approach to the recent changes in the public services in this country differs from many others that are available now or are being undertaken. Unlike many previous studies the focus here is not exclusively on the individual professional and the experience of managing or being managed (Dent and Whitehead, 2002; Lleywellyn, 2001; Thomas and Davies, 2004). Nor is it primarily concerned with the strategies of professional groups as collective actors (Evetts, 2002; Ackroyd, 1996; Dent, 1993; Crompton, 1990). Rather our central concern will be with the *modes of organising* through which public services are made, in health, in social care and more generally. Specifically, we focus on the forms of organisation that the professional groups within the different services we examine have developed for themselves. We then consider how these have affected the broader patterns of relationships and, in particular, how these typically affected decision-making processes and service delivery. Following Clarke and Newman (1997) our idea is also to show how professional groups were embedded within a wider institutional regime. This regime both maintained a highly autonomous, producer controlled, mode of organising and was reinforced by it.

A key objective of this book is to describe this mode of organising and, more importantly, to consider what has been done to it. The plan of governments in the UK, we suggest, has been to move from administered services, in which the professionals are basically in control (and decide on what to do for patients and clients on the basis of their professional judgement), to managed ones (in which professional priorities may be overridden on grounds of inefficiency and/or cost). These objectives have been pursued relentlessly over the past two decades. However, as mentioned earlier, it is far from clear what change has been achieved. To address this we examine what was actually done to these professional services after 1980 in terms of changes in the law, overarching institutions and policy expedients.

The need for a comparative analysis

A further characteristic of our approach is the emphasis on comparative evaluation. The aim is to depart from the polarisation of much work on the public sector which either analyses public services as separate cases – usually in order to emphasise particular problems – or focuses on the same general trends in them all. Our objective is to look at specific conditions in particular areas and to come up with a more subtle account. The book will therefore attempt to calibrate, more precisely than is commonly attempted, the different degrees of new management developed in chosen areas of public services. For us, it is centrally important to examine the ways in which policy unfolded in different services and how change itself has, to some extent, been path dependent. To achieve this we cast our net wide and look at three substantial areas of public provision: social services, hospital care and housing (both local authority and voluntary).

The rationale for selecting these three services is partly their size in terms of levels of expenditure. Together they account for just under one third of total UK welfare expenditure.[1] Table 1.1 reveals that by far the largest share is taken by health, with total spending estimated at around £54 billion in 2000/1, followed by the personal social services and housing. Combined expenditure on these services accounts for a significant proportion of national gross domestic product (GDP), just below 8 per cent in 2000/01 (Table 1.2).[2] Looking at trends over time it

Table 1.1 Total UK Managed Expenditure on Health, PSS and Housing (£ Billion)

	1984–85	1990–91	1995–96	1996–97	1997–98	1998–99	1999–00	2000–01 (estimated)
Health [1]	16.6	27.5	39.4	40.8	42.7	44.7	48.7	54.2
Personal Social Services	–	–	9.4	10.1	10.7	11.35	12.5	12.9
Housing	4.6	4.9	5.0	4.6	3.7	3.7	3.0	3.5
– Local authority share	–	–	2.2	1.9	1.5	1.65	0.9	1.3

Source: Stationery Office (2001) *Public Expenditure: Statistical Analysis 2001–2002*, Cm 51a), London: Stationery Office.
[1] Includes central health administration and other services.

Table 1.2 Expenditure on Health, PSS and Housing as a Proportion of UK Gross Domestic Product (%)

	1984–85	1990–91	1995–96	1996–97	1997–98	1998–99	1999–00	2000–01 (estimated)
Health [1]	5.0	4.9	5.4	5.3	5.2	5.2	5.4	5.7
Personal Social Services [1]	0.9	0.9	1.3	1.3	1.3	1.3	1.4	1.4
Housing	1.4	0.9	0.7	0.6	0.5	0.4	0.3	0.4

Source: Stationery Office (2001) *Public Expenditure: Statistical Analysis 2001–2002,* Cm 51a), London: Stationery Office.
[1] Approximate figures only.

can be seen that both health and the personal social services experienced a marked increase in managed expenditure in real terms over the
past two decades (Table 1.3). Health spending, for example, almost
doubled in real terms from £36 billion in 1984/5 to an estimated
£66 billion in 2000/2001. This trend is also reflected in the growing
share of these services as a proportion of GDP (see Table 1.2).

The three services under consideration are significant in employment
terms as well. Put together they account for well over a third of total
UK public sector employment of around 5.3 million in 2002 (Black
et al., 2003). Table 1.4 reveals that health continues to be a large
employer with numbers rising from approximately 1.15 million in
1979 to 1.36 million in 2002. Local authority run personal social services are also significant in employment terms with numbers increasing slowly over the same period to about 367,000. Comparative figures
for housing are much harder to calculate given the number of organisations, both public and voluntary, involved in this area. Our estimates suggest that in line with shifts in expenditure mentioned above
the trend here has been towards a decline in public sector employment
from approximately 58,000 in 1979 to 35,000 in 2002. However
employment including the private and voluntary sector has increased
from around 13,000 to 48,000 over the same period.

Crucially from the perspective of this book it is important to note
that a large proportion of those employed in each of the three sectors
claim professional status. This is most obviously the case in health
(Harrison and Pollitt, 1994). In 2002 it was estimated that there were
603,077 professionally qualified clinical staff in the NHS, including
103,350 doctors, 367,520 qualified nursing, midwifery and health visiting staff (including practice nurses), 116,598 qualified scientific, thera-
peutic and technical staff and 15,609 qualified ambulance staff. Added
to this were also 86,292 general practice staff (excluding practice nurses)
and 32,294 managers and senior managers (www.publications.doh.
gov.uk/public/staffinthenhs2002.htm). In the personal social services
a large (albeit smaller) proportion of the workforce also claims professional status. One recent survey found that in England local authorities employed a total of 52,650 qualified social workers and 2,244
Occupational Therapists, not to mention a growing number of aspiring
professional groups such as social care organisers (Eborall, 2003).

The level of professionalisation in housing is generally lower than in
health and social care. There are approximately 15,000 members of the
Chartered Institute of Housing (CIH) based in Britain. Walker (1998)
has estimated that in the mid-1990s that 10 per cent of all housing

Table 1.3 Total UK Managed Expenditure on Health, PSS and Housing in Real Terms (£ Billion)

	1984–85	1990–91	1995–96	1996–97	1997–98	1998–99	1999–00	2000–01 (estimated)
Health and Personal Social Services [1]	36.1	43.2	54.6	55.1	56.0	57.4	61.2	66.0
Of which: Health	30.7	36.1	44.0	44.1	44.8	45.8	48.7	53.3
Housing	8.4	6.4	5.6	5.0	3.9	3.8	3.0	3.4

Source: Stationery Office (2001) *Public Expenditure: Statistical Analysis 2001–2002,* Cm 51a), London: Stationery Office.
[1] Includes central health administration and other services.

Table 1.4 UK Public Sector Employment in Health, Social Services and Housing 1979–2002 (Thousands)

	1979	1985	1990	1995	2000	2002
National Health Service [1]	1,152	1,223	1,221	1,182	1,246	1,360
Social Services [2]	344	376	417	412	386	367
Local Government Housing	58	55	52	49	41	35
– Other Housing:	13	14	19	27	45	48

Sources: Figures for NHS and social services adapted from: Black, O., Herbert, R., and Richardson, I. (2003) *Jobs in the Public Sector, June 2002*, Economic Trends, No. 598, Sept. Figures for Housing based on the Audit Commission (1986), Wilcox (1999) and data from the Housing Corporation's Regulatory Statistical Return.
[1] Figures include NHS jobs in central government and jobs in NHS trusts (after 1991). In 2000 the central government figure was approximately 79,000.
[2] Figures cover only local government social services. The total social services workforce as traditionally defined is much larger. In England this stood at approximately 929,000, including local authority social services staff, residential, day and domiciliary care staff, agency staff and some NHS staff (Eborall, 2003).

staff were members of the profession, a proportion that is likely to have increased in recent years. Housing management is also associated with a range of other professional groups, including engineers, surveyors, architects and social workers that make up a large part of the remaining 400,000 (excluding education and social services) local government workers who are not directly employed in housing services.

The rationale for focusing on health, social care and housing is therefore their importance as employers and providers of public services that are mediated by professionals. However, there are more specific reasons for why it is useful and informative to compare developments in these three areas. First, they are illustrative of historically distinctive patterns of professional service organisation. Social services and housing have traditionally been more bureaucratic and 'managed' settings than health care. In health (especially within hospitals), the emphasis, at least until the early 1980s, was on passive or consensus administration and professional self-regulation (Webb and Wistow, 1986). Such differences, as we shall see, are crucially important for understanding the variable impact of management reforms. Generally speaking change has been more extensive in those settings where, in the past, the professions were less well organised and more closely managed.

Second is the fact that the process of management restructuring itself followed a different path in each of these service areas. One aspect of this is the development of a separate (general) management cadre in health but not elsewhere. Also important were differences in the extent to which services were re-organised in the 1990s to create single purpose organisations with management boards. As we shall see in health and (to a lesser extent) housing, radical shifts towards a devolved and semi-autonomous form of management occurred. By contrast social services remained under local authority control with fewer additional management functions or powers being devolved.

Of course, when engaging in comparative research of this kind some compromise between breadth and depth of coverage is necessary. It would be ideal if we could consider the impact of change on every area of public provision. Studies that cover everything run the risk of (and in our view often succumb to) a lack of adequate analysis. Either it is just not there, or it fails to be consistently applied by the contributors. By contrast, studies written by subject experts often do go into considerable detail; but, if they aspire to be more than a review of a particular area of provision, they are usually biased by the peculiarities of the service with which their authors are most familiar. It is certainly true that particular areas of social provision will mislead if what has happened in them is taken as symptomatic of change in other areas. However, because we want to make our approach both broad and insightful, we have restricted our consideration to the impact of public policy on our three chosen areas of provision. These three areas will be thoroughly considered and the details of the way in which public policy has affected them will be analysed carefully. We have also used a common analytical approach – which will be set out below – in order to ensure that precise comparisons can be made between otherwise diverse areas of provision.

The long view

To evaluate change in these three services we have made a choice to consider a relatively long time period. The decision to examine the experience of the British public services over the last twenty five years of the century was made in the light of recognition that 1979 was a significant date (Rhodes, 1997a). This is not to deny that certain preconditions of a new policy were in place before the Thatcher government was formed in

1979. However, key policy changes were then developed and consolidated by that government and its successors, and these have not been significantly changed in the intervening period. The last twenty years then marks a period in which change has been proceeding in a consistent direction. The attempt to evaluate the consequences of policy during this period therefore has a clear general rationale.

Following this logic it is assumed here that important continuities exist between the policy goals of the 1979–97 Conservative governments and those of the current New Labour administration (Clarke et al., 2000: 5–6). This is not to ignore shifts in the tone and content of policy after 1997 (Colling, 2001; Newman, 2000). Under Labour, as we shall see, the emphasis has been on a broader agenda of 'modernising' public services, on consulting stakeholders, with less emphasis on markets and the wholesale privatisation of services. In some areas there has also been a more generous level of financial support. But, at the same time, these shifts in policy should not be exaggerated. Concerns about professional under-achievement, lack of accountability and so-called producer power remain central (Laffin, 1998a). In many respects the attitude of denigration towards the social services and the professionals, has lingered on. Beyond this is a continued focus on the objective of management reform and on the goal of controlling public expenditure. This is notable in the government's Public Service Improvement strategy which is predicated on national performance standards, devolved, delegated and flexible management practices, incentives and consumer choice (Office for Public Services Reform, 2003). Hence, it might be argued: '1997 marked the end of a chapter, not a new book, as the "plot" has continued' (Corby and White, 1999: 20). The New Labour approach, it seems, 'is developing within a discourse which is familiar as NPM, rather than a radical departure from it' (Dawson and Dargie, 2002: 43).

A UK focus

Most observers would agree that public management reforms are a global phenomenon (Flynn, 2000; Pollitt and Boukaert, 2000; Hebdon and Kirkpatrick, 2004). Originating in the Anglo Saxon world (mainly in the US and UK) these ideas spread more widely, including to countries with strong traditions of state administration such as Sweden and Denmark (Flynn and Strehl 1996; Hood, 1995). During the 1990s national governments engaged in very similar programmes of management restructuring, a process supported and fuelled by consultants and international agencies, such as the OECD. Hence one should not assume that public management reform is unique to the UK. That said, it can be argued that the UK represents a particularly interesting and informative case study of this kind of policy change. Two main reasons can be given to support this.

First is the nature of the welfare service organisations against which change was directed. In the UK, groups of highly specialised professionals were able to exert far greater control over the nature of service provision than was the case elsewhere. Unlike France and Germany, in the UK, professions were loosely incorporated in the state bureaucracy and retained some distance from the administration (Dent, 2003). These differences can be attributed to distinct patterns of historical development of the professions in each country (Siegrist, 1990). In the UK, as we shall see, the professions had some success in achieving occupational closure and negotiating with the state the terms and conditions of their involvement in public services. This was especially true of more powerful groups such as doctors. By contrast, in continental Europe the professions were more dependent on state patronage and did not achieve the same level of control over the process of service delivery (Crompton, 1990). Here, as Macdonald (1995: 97) suggests, 'knowledge-based services...remained in the ambit of the state, restricting the success of the professional project'.

Differences in the level of professional control can also be attributed to the nature of welfare regimes. Comparative analysts like to distinguish universal systems of welfare provision (such as the British or Scandinavian) with different kinds of insurance-based systems, such as those found in continental Europe (Esping-Anderson, 1990; Ferrara, 1998). Within the latter – which typically have limitations as to the extent of state subsidy meaning that certain groups are wholly or partially excluded from the system – the costs of provision are partly borne by revenue streams generated directly from users. Insurance companies and other parties are involved in monitoring costs. They therefore have clearer mechanisms for rationing scarce resources and do not rely so fully on doctors or other groups exercising professional judgement about what needs to be done for users. By contrast, in systems such as the British, which are financed out of general taxation, historically a main mechanism for rationing has been the professions exercising judgements over what is appropriate. Professions in this context have accordingly acquired considerable influence over the standards and types of services provided.

A second reason for focusing on the UK is the radical nature of reform that was planned and implemented. According to Pollitt and

Boukaert (2000: 93–94) it is possible to identify contrasting visions of desired future arrangements that were expected to follow from public service restructuring. In the UK, the emphasis was on achieving revolutionary change, dismantling existing structures and moving towards a minimalist or 'night watchman state'. However, in continental Europe, concerns about the so-called deficiencies of the welfare state were (and remain) far less pronounced (Kickert, 1997). In Europe, the focus has been more on modernising public services (for example, in Sweden) or, as was the case in Germany, seeking only to maintain the status quo while making it work better.

Comparative research also suggests that management reforms were implemented most fully in the UK. According to Bach (1999a: 14): 'public service reforms in Britain have the greatest claim to the epithet "transformation"'. One reason for this is that governments have faced less effective opposition from administrative elites and unions than was the case elsewhere (say in France). Added to this is the fact that in the UK, fewer constitutional and legal barriers stood in the way of reform (Hood, 1995). The German constitution, for example, affords civil servants a degree of legal immunity from interference by politicians, making it hard if not impossible, for government to impose change unilaterally (Rober, 1996). By contrast, central governments in the UK have found it far easier to legislate or impose restructuring using crown prerogative and other executive powers (Bach and Winchester, 2003).

Theoretical models

Much of what follows draws heavily on organisational theory and, in particular, that branch of it concerned with professional organisation (for a historical review see Powell et al. (1999)). Under this heading is subsumed a variety of different strands. These include the work of early functionalists (Blau and Scott, 1963), contingency theorists (Pugh, 1987) and studies that draw on the tradition of symbolic interactionism (Strauss et al., 1963; Bucher and Stelling, 1969; Friedson, 1994). The work of these authors leads to a similar conception of professional organisation, usefully described by Mintzberg (1993) as a 'professional bureaucracy'. This is held to be a mixture of different organisational principles. On the one hand there is a weakly developed administrative structure, while, on the other, professional services providers – the operating core – are present in numbers, with extensive autonomy largely outside the direct line of administrative control. Essentially what this amounts to is a decentralised form of organising within which service delivery itself is largely defined and controlled by qualified experts. Such organisations, many argue, are appropriate under certain conditions, for example, when services are complex – requiring discretion – but are also standardised.

Recently there has been a growing emphasis in the literature on using archetype theory to describe this form of professional organisation (Powell et al., 1999; Kitchener, 1998; Pinnington and Morris, 2002; 2003; Mueller et al., 2000). These ideas originate in the work of C.R. Hinings and Royston Greenwood (Hinings and Greenwood, 1988; Greenwood and Hinings, 1988; 1993) who for twenty years and more have been at the centre of a consistently active group of organisational researchers based at the University of Alberta. Central to archetype theory is the notion that professional service organisations (PSOs) – such as law and accountancy firms – may be understood as coherent design archetypes. This suggests a holistic view of an organisation as 'a set of structures and systems that consistently embodies a single interpretative scheme' (Greenwood and Hinings, 1993: 1055). Organisational structures and practices are said to both influence and be shaped by deeper, underlying values that are shared by organisational members. These values in turn relate to how organisations define their domain (or primary task), principles of governance and criteria for evaluation (Greenwood and Hinings, 1988: 295).

A further characteristic of this approach is the link with mainstream institutional theory. Important here is the idea that particular design archetypes (or interpretive schemes) are not free standing but originate from wider organisational fields (DiMaggio and Powell, 1991). Different modes of organising, such as the partnership model in accountancy firms, may therefore be strongly reinforced by prevailing institutions in a field and may persist for some time (Greenwood and Hinings, 1996: 1026). Indeed, in professional fields it is assumed that the forces for conformity will be especially powerful as both coercive and normative isomorphic demands combine to maintain legitimate modes of collegial organisation (Greenwood et al., 2002). Emphasis is therefore placed on the importance of normative or cultural blueprints in shaping organisation building and evolution. Particular structures, routines and ways of working may persevere, because of path dependent patterns of development in which initial choices preclude future options.

For us this approach has considerable value. It draws attention to the historical formation of professional organisations, their embeddeness in particular contexts and capacity for inertia. Archetype theory also enlarges the role allowed to the activity of individuals and groups in shaping organisational change. Pressure for change is seen as originating from organisation fields as new archetypes emerge and become dominant. An important role is assigned to groups and interests within organisations who might succeed in deflecting or mediating these demands (Greenwood and Hinings, 1996).

Notwithstanding these strengths, in this book we depart from archetype theory in our conceptualisation of professional organisation. While the theory allows for the possibility of effective action by agents, it does so only when this helps to bring about an organisational reconfiguration that is more functional for the organisation in its new situation. Hence, although the theory finds a place for collective agency, in the end, this is dependent on its supposed functionality in much the same way assumed by classic contingency theory.

A further problem with this approach is that arguments have been formulated with the example of accountancy and law firms centrally in view. This has led to assumptions about the forces acting on organisations and the scope for independent action by key groups of professionals that are inappropriate in other contexts. The image conjured up by archetype theory is of a professional service organisation as a semi-autonomous entity, dominated by professional interests and concerns and free to respond to its environment. But while this may be appropriate for some private sector firms it is less clear how far it applies to professional services in the public domain. These organisations, as we shall see, are structurally subordinated with more limited scope for independent action (Brint and Karabel, 1991). Although professionals are able to exert control over service provision, their ability to do so remains heavily circumscribed by rules, budgets and policy regulations.

Also problematic are assumptions made about how change takes place in professional organisations. In archetype theory emphasis is on how new ideas about organising emerge from processes of negotiation within fields and how professional groups play a key 'entrepreneurial role' (Powell et al., 1999). But, once again one might question how far this is appropriate in the context of public services. Here, as we shall see, it is more likely that new models of organising are formulated independently of the professions (by central government) and imposed regardless of professional interests and concerns. In archetype theory the dynamics of more coercive change are rarely discussed or fully explained.

These limitations, we suggest, are sufficiently serious to point to a need for alternative ways of theorising professional organisation. Elsewhere

(Kirkpatrick and Ackroyd, 2003a; 2003b) we have argued that a useful starting point for this are insights of the strand of social theory which deals with the relationship between agency and structure, developed in the last twenty years (see, for example, Giddens, 1984; Archer, 1995). This approach offers a quite different account of the nature and origin of organisational forms – one that suggests that agency is always central and not only when it is conducive to positive adjustment to the environment. From this perspective, professional modes of organising are seen as emerging from a process of negotiation between contending parties and groups. While the emergent structures do have to be at least minimally functional in most circumstances, their functionality is not their raison d'être.

These ideas can be further developed with reference to the sociology of professions (Johnson, 1972; Larson, 1977; Abbott, 1988; Collins, 1990). Professional organisations, it might be argued, are structures that are to some extent produced and reproduced by members of the profession. The sociology of professions is helpful for understanding this by providing an account of the relationship between general processes of professionalisation and the particular modes of service organisation that emerge in different circumstances. From this we can also discover much about the relative capacities of professional groups to act within organisations. Only quite few among the traditional professions (some doctors and some lawyers) as well as a number of 'new model professions' (such as accountants and architects) have also developed and maintained ownership and control of the formal organisations in which they work. But this is a special case, rather than the normal one. Indeed, for many sociologists, the connection between professionalism and the organisational forms such occupations adopt is seen to be a contingent rather than determinate. Johnson (1972) for example, differentiates between 'collegiate professions', which control their own organisations, from 'state mediated professions', which, typically, do not. By contrast, archetype theorists assume that professional groups will find a place within similar patterns of formal organisation, no matter what their power or their status in the wider community.

In combination, ideas drawn from agency/structure theory and the sociology of the professions, constitute a useful way of understanding professional organisations and processes of change within them. They lead us to view such organisations as emergent, contested and not necessarily functional. More importantly the focus is on the variable capability of groups of professionals to establish control over formal organisations. Some groups (for example, 'free standing' collegiate professions (Johnson, 1972), such as accountants, architects and lawyers) have been relatively successful in this respect. By contrast, in the case of less well-organised professions in the public domain (for example, teaching, social work or nursing) a different pattern has emerged. Here, as we shall see in Chapter 2, the professions were strongly dependent on state sponsorship to maintain degrees of occupational closure (Cousins, 1987). The result has been a form of organising that, while subject to negotiation, also places significant constraints on the autonomy and collective aspirations of key professional groups. Hence this approach allows us to build on neo-institutional theory while avoiding some of the pitfalls associated with it.

Methods

Finally it is useful to say a few words about methods. The literature and evidence on public management reform and changes to the professions is fragmentary. There are no longitudinal datasets on the adoption of new management practices and their impact on the public sector professions. There is, however, an abundant range of secondary sources. For each service area (health, social care and housing) reference will be made to academic studies of management restructuring that have been conducted. Included in this list are studies that we ourselves have been involved with, for example, relating to health (Ackroyd, 1998; Ackroyd and Bolton, 1999), social services (Whipp et al., 2004; Kitchener et al., 2000; Kirkpatrick et al., 1999) and housing (Walker, 1998; 2000; 2001; Walker et al., 2003; Walker and Williams, 1995). In addition we draw on material from the extensive practitioner and policy literatures. Here the focus is not only on academic studies, but also on various published reports conducted by (or on behalf of) central government departments, regulatory agencies (such as the Audit Commission and Social Services Inspectorate), employer's organisations and professional associations.

Of course this approach is not without its limitations. The detailed sources described above are often ad hoc studies into specific aspects of service provision or snap shot surveys of the current state of management in a professional domain. Consequently, there is not a systematic or comparative baseline from which we can measure change – change has been introduced in a piecemeal way at different rates and in different combinations in our three areas of study. Furthermore, other influences have affected the professions beyond government sponsored programmes of reform. Varying social economic circumstances, changing demographic trends and policy measures in other public domains are all likely to influence outcomes. In addition to these technical evaluation issues some of the studies we draw upon are now dated (for example the last comprehensive study of social housing was undertaken in the early 1990s (Bines et al., 1993)). While we are fortunate to draw upon a wealth of practitioner and policy reports these studies are funded for a particular purpose, and often answer politically motivated questions. Therefore we do not seek to formally test the extent to which management reforms have impacted on the professions or to undertake a meta-evaluation. Rather our purpose is to interpret these diverse sources to construct a rich picture of the kind of changes that have occurred and to analyse the consequences of these changes and assess their costs and benefits.

The organisation of the book

This book has been structured in such a way as to reflect the goals and themes described above. Chapter 2 sets out to describe the main features of professional service organisation that emerged in the UK during the post war era. In doing so it is argued that these structures must be understood in terms of a broader institutional regime, founded on an 'organisational settlement' or bargain struck between state and professions (Clarke and Newman, 1997). Attention will then turn to the nature of these arrangements and the distinctive forms of custodial administration that developed and were sustained at local levels.

Chapter 3 then turns to how, from the early 1980s, attempts were made to dismantle and re-shape the institutions described above. It is argued that in this period governments in the UK sought to substantially undermine the power and autonomy of professional groups and that one aspect of this was a drive to implement new management practices. A description of these reforms is provided, as is a discussion of the processes through which government attempted to implement change. Finally in this chapter we focus on the question of what change has occurred and the likely obstacles to management reform.

The next three chapters, 4 to 6, focus specifically on developments in each service area: health, social services and housing. In each case similar themes and issues will be addressed. All three chapters begin with an overview of the policy context and the main factors that drove management reform. Following this each chapter presents evidence of how far change occurred, focusing on three main dimensions: the development of management roles and functions, shifts in the nature of control over front line work and changes in values and orientations.

This analysis begins in Chapter 4 focusing on what has been happening in the NHS in recent decades. The chapter starts with a brief overview of the history of the development of medical services in Britain. The main changes since 1983 are then summarised, together with their implications for management. Following this evidence is presented from research on the impact these changes are actually making on the NHS and the responses of professional groups, notably doctors and nurses. This review points to the radical nature of restructuring in this sector and the shift towards qualitatively new forms of organisation. However we raise questions about how far new management practices have colonised the professions and displaced older ways of working, and argue that the improvements in efficiency and effectiveness have been limited as well as very costly.

In Chapter 5 we assess management change in local authority social services departments (SSDs). As in health, over the past two decades considerable effort was made to reform practice in this area. Our review of the evidence suggests that important changes occurred, most notably with the establishment of a mixed economy of care and the management of budgets. However the analysis also reveals some opposition to restructuring and limits on the extent to which it has been possible to develop more strategic approaches to provision. Certain costs of change are also noted, most of all those associated with rising stress and turnover amongst professional social workers.

Chapter 6 turns to the provision of social housing. In comparison to health and social work this sector is characterised by a number of differences that help explain why management reforms have taken a stronger hold here. Differences include the involvement of a number of professional bodies beyond housing managers, competing methods of provision by local authorities and housing associations and economic exchange embedded in the model of service provision. These features, together with the weak professional basis of housing work, lead us to conclude that in social housing significant change has occurred.

Finally, in Chapter 7 we return to some of the big questions and themes raised in this book. The chapter begins by comparing the three sectors in terms of the nature and extent of change. The analysis suggests that, overall, professional practice was not transformed, although some areas (notably housing) adopted the new management more completely than others. Following this the chapter looks at how we might explain variable and limited change and seeks to assess the wider costs and benefits of restructuring.

2
Professions and Professional Organisation in UK Public Services

> In the modern world, the professions are increasingly the arbiters of our welfare fate; they are the key holders to equality of outcome; they help to determine the pattern of redistribution in social policy (Titmuss 1965 – in Perkin, 1989: 352).

The purpose of this chapter is to describe the main features of professional service organisation that emerged in the UK during the post war era. We argue that the institutions of the state became sites that the professions colonised and gradually developed over much of the last century. This process gathered pace with the founding of the welfare state after the Second World War. Professions occupied public services with different motivations: either, as in the case of medicine, by moving into them somewhat reluctantly; or, as in the case of social services, because they provided the opportunity for significant development of an occupation. In so doing, however, public organisations were thoroughly adapted to the orientations and practices of the professions that colonised them. The result was a particular kind of institutional regime, founded on an 'organizational settlement' between professions and the state (Clarke and Newman, 1997). This 'settlement' was neither entirely stable nor conflict free. But it did ensure that, within the confines of the welfare state, professional groups were able to secure varying degrees of occupational closure and institutional autonomy (Evetts, 2002; Flynn, 1999). It also reinforced a unique form of 'custodial' organisation at local level. As we shall see a key feature of this mode of organising was that – within broad constraints – welfare professions were able to exert considerable *de facto* control over both the means and (to some extent) ends of service delivery.

To consider these issues, this chapter contains three main sections. First, space is devoted to a discussion of core concepts and ideas. Following the arguments made in chapter one, we point to the usefulness of the sociology of professions literature for understanding the subject under investigation. In section two our attention focuses upon the more specific development of professions in the public domain and the notion of a 'regulative bargain' between state and professions. Finally, in the main body of the chapter we turn to a description of the characteristics of the organisational settlement that emerged in the UK and the pattern of custodial administration that was associated with it.

Understanding the professions

Early discussions about the nature of professions and professional organisation were dominated by what Saks (1994) refers to as the 'taxonomic approach' (Carr-Saunders and Wilson, 1962). A key feature of this approach is the delineation of characteristics, or traits, that are held to constitute a profession (Raelin, 1991). Greenwood (1957), for example, famously identified five 'distinguishing attributes of a profession': systematic theory, community sanction, authority, an ethical code and professional culture. An additional feature of trait theory is the concept of the semi-professional. This label is used to designate certain occupational groups (including some of which are the focus of this book) that have not acquired the status or necessary traits associated with 'full' professionalism (Goode, 1957; Etzioni, 1969; Bills et al., 1980).

Problems with this trait model of professions are widely documented (see, for example, Abbott and Meerabeau, 1998) and need only be summarised here. One difficulty has been identifying agreed traits that constitute a profession. More serious is the problem of the status of the traits that are associated with professionalism. The perspective encourages us to assume that traits such as service ethos are fixed assets rather than statements made by an aspirant group seeking to define itself as professional. As Hugman (1998: 180) argues, the trait model has 'served to reproduce aspects of the professions' own ideologies within the findings of social science enquiry'.

These limitations of traits theory have led in more recent times to the dominance of radically different sociology of professionals drawing on the classical theories of Marx and Weber (Friedson, 1994; Johnson, 1972; Larson, 1977; Collins, 1990; Abbott, 1988). Here the central concern is not with the identification of archetypal features of a profession, but with the range of ways in which professions, as particular kinds of occupation, conduct themselves. Emphasis is on what Macdonald (1995) described as the 'professionalisation project', or on the strategies pursued by occupations as collective social actors to acquire the rewards and cherished status of a profession. Johnson (1972), an early and influential exponent of this approach, argued that professionalism does not so much describe privileged occupations as identify the characteristics which certain of them have developed to organise and control themselves. From this perspective then 'professionalisation' is defined as 'a peculiar type of occupational control rather than an expression of the inherent nature of particular occupations' (Johnson, 1972: 45).

In more recent accounts a potent concept used to good effect in aiding the exploration of these processes is social closure (Parkin, 1979; Murphy, 1988). According to Parkin (1979: 44) 'social closure' can be defined as a 'process by which social collectivities seek to maximise rewards by restricting access to resources and opportunities to a limited circle of eligibles'. From this perspective, professionals are seen as interest groups seeking to achieve 'internal occupational control' through an active strategy of exclusion (Witz, 1992: 46). When successful this leads to numerous benefits for the occupational groups involved. For example, in the short term it might ensure opportunities for income, job security and other privileges such as the capacity to control work and resources within employing organisations (Larson, 1977). In the long term, closure may be associated with upward 'social mobility' of particular groups (Armstrong, 1986). Important here is the link between professionalisation and the relative position of expert groups as members of a broader service class (Savage et al., 1992; Hanlon, 1998).

The conditions under which these professionalisation projects might be said to be successful are obviously multiple and complex. Most accounts emphasise the role of abstract knowledge (Wilensky, 1964; Abbott, 1988). Torstendahl (1990: 2), for example, suggests 'knowledge (and/or skill) is used by its owners as a social capital and not only for purposes connected with…immediate problem solving'. Professionals, it is argued, are able to legitimate their privileged position by merit of their knowledge and claim of 'cognitive superiority' (Larson, 1977: 48). The extent to which this strategy is effective may depend on the nature of the knowledge itself. Jamous and Peloille (1970) argue that a successful profession must be able to maintain equilibrium between technical aspects of tasks, which can be routinised, and the indeterminacy that is necessarily a feature any knowledge base. The greater the former the more susceptible professional work becomes to processes of bureaucratisation and external control.

Although abstract knowledge is a central resource used by professions to achieve occupational control it by no means guarantees it. One must also consider professionalisation projects more broadly as historical processes involving negotiations between professions and other actors, such as clients, competing groups and the state. These projects are enacted simultaneously in both the 'economic' and 'social' orders (Macdonald, 1995: 29–34). In the economic order the emphasis is on how far 'the possessors of specialist knowledge set about building up a monopoly of their knowledge and, on this basis, establish a monopoly of the services that derive from it' (ibid, xii). Important here are collective efforts (by occupational associations or other bodies) to gain control over the process of knowledge production and over training and education of new entrants. Also important are moves to achieve a 'regulative bargain' with state agencies to ensure legal protection (such a licensing or registers) for professional monopoly. Effective action in the 'economic order' therefore follows when a profession acquires legal control over the 'production of producers' (Larson, 1977) and, in the process, the ability to regulate both the quality and supply of expert labour.

Turning to the social order, the emphasis is more on the strategies used by professions to justify and defend their special influence and privileged position. A variety of validating claims may be made to achieve this goal. For example are claims about the 'technical competence' of professionals and the superiority of their specialist expertise, credentials and training (Collins, 1990). Closely related to this are claims about the trustworthiness of professions, stressing their capacity to self regulate and monitor their own work (Hanlon, 1998: 45). Finally are discourses rooted in notions of a service ethic or 'ideology of service' (see Wilding, 1982: 77–79). According to Hugman (1994: 6) 'the concepts that professions are defined by an ethic of service to the wider society and by their inherent trustworthiness can be explained in terms of occupational bids for service and privilege'. As we shall see, such claims are crucial in the public domain, both in shaping practice and as a justificatory rationale to support particular modes of organisation.

Finally it is important to emphasise how these professionalisation projects are in constant flux and transition. Looking at the historical record, over the last four centuries, periods of widespread professionalisation can be noted, and periods of remission when even established professions have struggled to hold their own (Ackroyd, 1996). In sum, the ability of a profession to hold onto a given jurisdiction of knowledge indefinitely cannot be assumed. Much will depend on shifting technology, relationships with the state and challenges posed by other occupations with competing jurisdictional claims (Abbott, 1988). As Macdonald notes (1995: 33) 'a profession does not merely mark out its domain in a bargain with the state', but must 'fight other occupations for it, not merely at the time, but before and after as well'. Put differently, professionalism must be understood as a shifting rather than a concrete phenomenon.

Professionalisation projects in UK public services

These ideas are extremely useful for the study of UK public services, which has been a prime site for the development of professions (Halmos, 1973; Perkin, 1989). They draw our attention to the wide variation in professionalisation projects and the extent to which different groups have been able to organise effectively to attain degrees of occupational closure. To illustrate this we look briefly at the emergence of professions in the three sectors under consideration in this book: health, social services and housing.

Health

At one extreme is medicine, the archetypal case of a successful free standing or 'collegial' form of professionalisation (Ackroyd, 1996). In the early nineteenth century medicine was highly fragmented and made up of various groups with separate and mutually antagonistic organisations: physicians, surgeons, apothecaries and general practitioners. However, by 1858, with the passing of the Medical Registration Act some degree of unification (albeit uneasy) was achieved. With the creation of the General Medical Council and state-sponsored register of qualified practitioners, the profession was also granted an effective legal monopoly over the training and supply of expert labour (Parry and Parry, 1976).

In the twentieth century medicine was successful in retaining considerable independent control of its own affairs, despite increasing state involvement in health care regulation and provision. Even the formation of the NHS in 1946 did not significantly undermine this (Cousins, 1987: 109). The expansion of state funded, national provision greatly increased the demand for medical services by a population that was hitherto unable to access such services sufficiently.

Despite considerable initial resistance to direct involvement with state organisations, especially on the part of senior professionals, incorporation did not at all reduce professional control over processes of knowledge production, education or the mode of service delivery. In Britain, doctors have to be state registered and there is a detailed administrative machinery surrounding registration. Among other things the state has severely restricted the number of training places for doctors, thus helping to limit the supply (and raise the market value) of qualified practitioners. The self-regulatory character of doctors is also enhanced by the role of such things as the Royal Colleges and their faculties, and pre-eminently the British Medical Association. Only in recent years has there been a shift towards greater state intervention in professional training and regulation although, as we shall see (in Chapters 3 and 4), it is not yet clear what impact this will have. The effective closure of the profession to external control has, until recently, been complete.

Since the early part of the present century nursing also has been a highly organised occupation and nurses have attempted to protect their social standing through various periods of change since then. Promoters of nursing have, with varying degrees of explicitness, taken the profession of medicine as their model and, among other things, insisted on high levels of training and formal qualifications for their members. Academics differ in the extent to which they think that nurses have achieved professional organisation and standing (Jolley, 1989; Melia, 1987; Witz, 1995) but few argue against the idea that the pursuit of high levels of formal qualifications and, through this, limited control of labour markets, is the goal. Qualified nurses, who make up the largest number of staff responsible for patient care in British hospitals, therefore achieved a degree of occupational closure (Walby and Greenwell, 1994). However, in many ways their closure is much weaker than that achieved by the doctors. Any claim that high levels of skills (tested by qualifications) are necessary to all nursing work is difficult to defend if not implausible much of the time. There is much fairly menial work involved in the care of the sick, and for this reason it is has been easy to expand the supply of recruits, weakening the bargaining position of nurses. There are also care assistants who are not recognised as nurses. Hence, while one might argue that nursing represents a successful professionalisation project it is also tenuous. The problem for nurses is it is difficult to show that high levels of nursing skill are always essential, and the skills required for basic care are not scarce.

Social services

The professionalisation project of social workers stands in stark contrast to the early consolidation of professional power in medicine and public health. The origins of this profession date back to the nineteenth century and to a number of diverse strands of activity linked both to state-run and voluntary sector organisations (Clarke, 1993). Unlike medicine, attempts to merge various groups and develop a specific professional identity or unifying knowledge were markedly unsuccessful (Younghusband, 1978; Walton, 1975: 154). Only in the 1950s was some degree of consolidation achieved following major central government legislation, the Children Act 1948 and the National Assistance Act 1948. These Acts, as has been noted elsewhere (Glennerster, 1998), initiated a system of local provision of social care within national policy guidance. They established three main areas for professional employment of social work: the probation service, local government children's departments and Health and Welfare Departments. However, it was not until the Seebohm Report (1968) and the formation of local authority social services departments (SSDs) that professional 'Balkanisation' finally came to an end (Webb and Wistow, 1987: 49). This led to the development of generic social work loosely based on social science knowledge. It also assisted the formation of a unified national association (the British Association of Social Work) (Payne, 2002). Nevertheless, social work today remains a weakly organised occupation both in terms of its ability to influence knowledge creation (which is dominated by academics) and to control the supply of expert labour. Training and education has, since the early 1970s, been tightly regulated by government quangos; first by the Central Council for Education and Training of Social Work (CCETSW) and, after 1997, a General Social Care Council and employer-based Training Organisation in the Personal Social Services (TOPSS). Until recently, with the introduction of registration, it was not even necessary to be qualified in order to practice as a social worker.

Housing

Finally, housing officers represent a group that has faced perhaps the greatest difficulty in its attempts to professionalise. As with social work, the origins of this group date back to the late nineteenth century and, in particular, the actions of various philanthropists and voluntary organisations in the middle of the century and with moves by local authorities to fund and administer social housing from the 1880s onwards (Malpass, 2000). By the early 20th century two main bodies had emerged claiming to represent housing workers in public, private and voluntary sectors. First was the Institute of Municipal Estate Managers, registered in 1938. This grouping represented (male) local government employees and was focused on an idea of professionalism linked to technical and financial skills of administration. Second was the Society of Women Housing Estate Managers, registered in 1932. Membership of this body was based mainly in the voluntary sector and drew on the social reform ideas of Octavia Hill, stressing the welfare aspects of housing administration (Clapham, 1992). These organisations remained in competition until 1965 when, in the context of the post war housing boom, they merged to form the Institute of Housing Managers. From this time there was also an expansion in employment opportunities for housing professionals, especially following the 1974 reorganisation of local government and the establishment of large housing departments. However, the profession remained relatively weak, representing only a minority of employees within the housing sector (public and voluntary) and making little headway in terms of developing a core professional knowledge or skill base. Professional development, as we shall see, was also hampered by competition from other groups (notably architects, engineers, lawyers and planners) involved in the process of housing decision-making (Proven and Williams, 1991). Despite this the profession continued to grow in the 1980s and 90s, achieving chartered status in 1984 and increasingly seeking to upgrade training and education.

These brief accounts reveal something of the diversity of professional projects in the context of UK public services. They point to important distinctions in the form of professionalism, between free standing and organisational professions (Ackroyd, 1996). The former (represented by medicine) were largely successful in achieving closure and self-organisation at an early point in their development. Other groups, such as social workers, housing officers and nurses, have been far less successful in this respect.

Professionalisation and the state

What emerges from the previous discussion is the key role of the state in supporting professionalisation projects. While some groups (such as doctors) were successful in achieving a high degree of formal organisation and closure prior to the expansion of state welfare functions this was much less in evidence in other areas (social work, teaching, housing). For the latter group of occupations, the growing involvement of local and central government in the administration of public services was not only a major boost to professionalism but, one might argue, a pre-condition for it (Larson, 1977: 179). As Wilding (1982: 67) suggests, these occupations were effectively the 'offspring and the beneficiaries of welfare state policies'.

In Britain this process of welfare state expansion can be traced back to the early nineteen century with the establishment of local boards of guardians to oversee the provision of services. But since that time the emergence of a public sector has been surprisingly slow and ad hoc when compared to other European nations (Burrage, 1992; Ackroyd, 1996). Broadly speaking one might identify two main phases of development: a period spanning roughly from about 1870 to 1950 referred to as 'local public administration', followed by an era of 'centralized welfare state provision' (Ackroyd, 1995b). The first period dates roughly to the establishment in 1871 of the Local Government Board and attempts to create a national system of local authorities (Griffiths, 1976: 4). From that point on were piecemeal efforts by local authorities to develop portfolios of various services (policing, health, education, housing) which, it was judged, required professional training and expertise (Laffin and Young, 1990). From the turn of the 20th century, these local authorities also began to acquire responsibility for education and, increasingly (especially in urban areas) the provision of hospital services (Perkin, 1989: 344–347). This led, by the end of the second war, to a patchwork of locally administered services in areas where there was insufficient provision by 'voluntary' or charitably organised institutions.

The second phase of 'centralized welfare state provision' (Marshall, 1977) commenced roughly from 1950. Prior to that, central government was involved in regulating and, increasingly, offering direct financial support for welfare services (for example, through the system of national health insurance). However, in the aftermath of world war two this involvement escalated with legislation creating national systems for the provision of education, health and social security (Glennerster, 1998: 18; Osborne and McLaghlin, 2002: 8). These services were provided partly by the municipalities (education, child care), partly by new bodies at regional level (health) and partly by the national administration (unemployment benefits). After 1950 the system of uniform public service provision grew rapidly. By 1975 local authority current spending in England and Wales stood at £12,253 million compared with £2,161 million in 1930 (Stoker, 1989: 149).

During that time a variety of new services were created, most notably the local authority run social services departments (also see Chapter 5).

A key point to make is that it was largely as a consequence of this gradual process of state involvement in the administration of public services that various professional groups were able to consolidate their position. This was most obvious in terms of expanding employment as the professions 'colonized the new bureaucracies' that were created by the local and national state (Laffin, 1998: 4). As we shall see, the new structures were also locales in which professional groups were able to exert considerable *de facto* control over the process of service delivery. However, prior to looking at this it is useful to return briefly to debates within the sociology of professions literature. Specifically we focus on how one might understand these organisations as a product of a wider 'regulative bargain' between the state and the professions.

State-professional relations: a regulative bargain

A useful starting point for such an analysis is the classic work of Johnson (1972). This centres on a typology of professions based on the different kinds of clientele they are able to maintain, despite their similarities of status. Hence, 'corporate patronage' professions (a classic example being modern accountancy) are groups who deal with clients (such as large firms) that have a large degree of scope to determine their own needs (1972: 46). By contrast public service professions are in a situation where the nature of relationships with clients is mediated by a third party, or more specifically, by the state. According to Johnson this leads to a situation in which 'the state intervenes in the relationship between practitioner and client in order to define needs and/or the manner in which such needs are catered for' (77). In the extreme this can take the form of professional services being provided directly by a state agency: 'which is the effective employer of all practitioners who have a statutory obligation to provide a given service' (ibid).

In developing these ideas others have focused on how 'state mediated' forms of professional organisation emerged over time from a 'regulative bargain' negotiated between different occupational groups and the state (Macdonald, 1995). Wilding (1982: 11) for example, refers to how professions and government agencies represent 'power blocs' that had negotiated a 'truce'. More generally, the focus has been on understanding this process in terms of a corporate relationship in which professions exchange their expertise and cooperation for favourable policies and resources (Cawson, 1982; Johnson, 1977). According to Cousins (1987: 106) 'as functional groups, professional provider groups are drawn into a specific relationship with the state in order to formulate and implement public policies'. This in turn means that they are granted 'structurally determined privileges'.

A key feature of this approach is that it points to advantages that accrue both to state agencies and professions from greater co-operation. The former is understood to require professional expertise primarily in order to deal with areas of risk and uncertainty. This is especially the case when administrators 'lacked clear criteria on which to make decisions regarding the provision of welfare services' (Cousins, 1987: 108). More generally the state may seek professional involvement on the grounds of expediency or as a way in which to 'legitimate state intervention in terms of expertise' (Hugman, 1994: 24).

So far as the professions themselves are concerned, an alliance with the state is also beneficial. Incorporation helps to reinforce occupational closure by establishing labour market shelters, or 'institutional settings which guarantee...a demand' for professional services (Larson, 1977: 181). Such guarantees, as we have seen, may be especially important in the case of many weaker occupations (such as housing and social work). For these groups, the very possibility of collective organisation and control over jurisdictions of work is premised on the fact that the state itself has chosen to monopolise a particular area of service provision (Savage et al., 1992).

To be sure, not all professional groups have been equally successful in terms of securing 'special privileges' from the state. As we saw in Chapter 1 there are important differences between the experiences of professions in the UK and elsewhere in Europe (Crompton, 1990). Even in the UK it should be noted: 'the mutual compliance and dependence between the state and professional providers has led to selective privileging and sponsorship of some professions...' (Cousins, 1987: 92). Groups such as doctors have been able to effectively define the terms and conditions of their collaboration with the state and in the process secure a high degree of autonomy and influence (Dent, 1993: 247). By contrast, housing managers, social workers and nurses have been in a far weaker position. These occupations were (and remain) less able to assert control over processes of training, education and determination of content of practice. As we shall see, they have more clearly taken on the status of 'managed' employees within state bureaucracies (Johnson, 1972: 83; Webb and Wistow, 1986).

Professional formation in the public sector is therefore inextricably linked to the expanding role of the state in funding and providing services. However, while it important to emphasise the 'mutual dependence' of professions and the state one should not also overstate the dynamic of accommodation and consensus (Hugman, 1994: 24). It is important to recognise that these arrangements are also unstable and may involve conflict as well as cooperation. Two main sources of such conflict can be identified. First are tensions between the interests of professions and state agencies. Second are ongoing struggles within and between the professions themselves.

The struggle for control

According to Wilding (1982: 65), while 'the state and the professions need each other' they also interact in an 'alliance at different times firm and precarious, explicit and implicit'. Implied by this is that the regulative bargain described above might be associated over time with costs as well as benefits for those involved. For state agencies the most significant cost is the loss of control that follows when professions are granted degrees of freedom to organise public services. This is most true in health where the professions have not only been able to control delivery, but also determine the broader shape taken by services (for example, organized around particular specialisms) (Perkin, 1989). As we shall see, in other public services the state also faces a problem of control, especially where resource allocation is concerned (Cousins, 1987: 98; Wilding, 1982: 39).

For the professions, although incorporation within the 'organisational framework of government agencies' (Johnson, 1972: 79) is unavoidable it is likely to be resented. Even in the case of powerful groups such as NHS doctors incorporation will mean some constraint on professional autonomy and freedom. Specifically it leads to what Derber (1982: 18) describes as 'ideological proletarianisation' or 'the worker's loss of control over decisions concerning the goals, objectives and policy directions of his work'. Related to this are more general tensions that emerge between the espoused goal of serving the client interest (as defined by the professions) and wider resource and policy constraints (Webb and Wistow, 1986). Through their incorporation in public organisations professionals become in effect 'agents of the state' and, as a consequence of this, are forced to engage in contradictory practices such as rationing provision and 'caring and controlling' (Hugman, 1994: 21).

Hence, while the state and professions are in a relationship of 'mutual dependence', this is neither entirely stable nor conflict free. In any context these relationships are characterised by 'continued struggles' around the nature and goals of public service provision (Hugman, 1994: 81). According to Flynn (1999: 22) there exists a:

> constant dialectic between autonomy and heteronomy, between independence and subordination: as professional occupations seek to maintain their own control over the execution of tasks and self-regulation, other external bodies attempt to exercise increasing control over their training and performance.

In the UK these 'struggles' became manifest at an early stage and were apparent even in the 1960s as central government sought to reign in expenditure (Dent, 1993; Cockburn, 1977; Ackroyd, 1995b). More recently, as we shall argue in the next chapter, this tension has been greatly intensified.

Inter and intra-professional conflict

The second source of instability associated with the regulative bargain is that which arises from divisions *within* the system of professions itself. In seeking to understand this it is helpful to note two main issues. First is the way the growth of public organisations has tended to reinforce demarcations between occupations. Second are processes of internal stratification within each professional group.

A major consequence of the emergence of public organisations was to formalise and accentuate divisions within and between professional groups. As Larson (1977: 180) suggests, 'a protective institutional barrier is erected around occupations...when the organisation itself asserts its monopoly over a given functional area'. In public services this process served to formalise divisions between the professions both horizontally and vertically. The former occurs when the functional division between public services (say between social care and health) also comes to reflect an inter-professional boundary. This can be noted throughout the UK public sector, especially in local government where the tendency has been for departments to be 'organized around professional skills rather than client needs' (Perkin, 1989: 348).

In a similar way, the growth of public service organisations also serves to reinforce vertical divisions between occupations (Larkin, 1983). Within these structures various groups may engage in what Cousins (1987: 109) defines as 'strategies of solidarism and exclusion'. In the UK these tendencies have been especially pronounced in the case of health, where a clear (albeit contested) hierarchy of jurisdictions emerged dominated by medicine with other groupings such as nurses, midwifes radiographers in a subservient position (Larkin, 1983). Elsewhere, strategies of exclusion focused mainly on divisions between professional and non-professional occupations. In the personal social services social workers went to great lengths to reinforce demarcations between themselves and less well qualified groups such as social care assistants (Abbott and Meerabeau, 1998). Similar examples can be found in the recent history of professions such as teaching, nursing (Abbott and Wallace, 1998) and librarianship (Kirkpatrick, 1999). Professional housing workers also demarcate themselves from wider, less qualified groups. However, this profession has sought to capture these less qualified groups, such as sheltered housing wardens, and bring them into the professional fold.

A second key source of conflict arises from processes of internal stratification *within* each occupational grouping. In the literature it is widely recognised that in all professions, despite the rhetoric of collegiality, there are 'hierarchical elements' (Friedson, 1994; Hugman, 1994). Larson (1977) notes how 'technobureaucratic' wings of a profession become increasingly prominent as a consequence of incorporation within organisations. In the public sector this applies to elite groups of professionals who take on responsibility for the running or administration of hospitals, departments of social services, education and so on. These groups, as we shall see, may develop interests and concerns quite different to their rank and file colleagues and this, in turn, represents a source of conflict.

Finally it is important to draw attention to the gendered nature of these processes of fragmentation and stratification. In the UK this has been particularly marked with the emergence of the so-called caring professions (nursing, social work, housing and remedial therapies), most of which continue to be dominated, in numerical terms, by women. Historically these professions found themselves in a subservient position within the hierarchy of jurisdictions described above. One reason for this is that their professionalisation projects were shaped and determined by the interests of more powerful, male dominated groups such as medicine (Witz, 1992; Davies, 1995, Abbott and Wallace, 1998). The subservient position of the caring professions was also accentuated by cultural stereotypes. Abbott and Meerabeau (1998: 12–13) note how the work of these groups is often: 'seen in relation to natural female abilities – women's ability to care and natural altruism – and as an extension of women's natural role as nurturers in the family'. Witz (1994: 39) also points to the way dominant stereotypes of care work are 'saturated with gender bias' and how this, in turn, means that such work is often 'systematically undervalued'.

The development of public service bureaucracies not only accentuated these tendencies, but also helped to create further gender divisions *within* the caring professions. Most notable is a very marked horizontal segmentation within professional hierarchies, which confines women to the lower levels. Men are in senior and managerial posts in nursing, social work and school teaching out of all proportion to their numbers in these occupations (Hugman, 1994, Abbott and Wallace, 1996). In social work, for example, women account for 78 per cent of the qualified workforce in England, but for only 65 per cent of junior and middle management grades and 22 per cent of social service director positions ((LGMB/CCETSW, 1997: 77). A similar story can be told where nursing and other groups, such as housing officers are concerned (Brion, 1994).

The organisational settlement in UK public services

In this section our aim is to describe the particular form taken by the state-professional relationship in the UK. Our concern is with the kind of 'institutional regime' (Ruef and Scott, 1998: 884) that emerged in the post war period and the modes of delivery and organisation that were associated with it. The main purpose of this exercise is to develop a clearer understanding of the institutions, which, as we shall discuss in Chapter 3, UK government sought to radically transform in the 1980s and 1990s.

When seeking to develop these ideas a useful place to start is with Clarke and Newman's (1997: 1) observation that the post was welfare state in the UK was 'legitimated and sustained by a range of settlements: political-economic, social and organizational'. Implied by the latter, or 'organizational settlement', was a high degree of consensus over the appropriateness of a particular mode of coordination, namely one rooted in the joint principles of bureaucratic regulation and professional expertise. According to Clarke and Newman (1997), acceptance of these principles was based on more than just expediency:

> the place of professionalism in the welfare state... was...an actively sought principle...Professionals...were indispensable partners in the great national task of reconstruction and, within limits, they were to be trusted and encouraged to apply their expertise for the public good (ibid: 7).

This 'settlement' in no way represented a perfect consensus or symmetry of interests (Glennerster, 1998). But at least until the mid 1970s broad agreement existed over the usefulness and necessity of professional regulation. The emphasis was on how professionals might assist in the more rational allocation of public services and how their expert knowledge could serve as an 'engine of social progress' (Laffin, 1998: 4).

This trust in professional self-regulation manifested itself in a number of ways. First was a willingness to accept a high level of professional involvement in the process of policy formulation (Perkin, 1989: 344). In the post-war years many professions acquired the status of 'autonomous sources of influence on public policy' (Laffin, 1986). This was achieved partly by occupying key positions in the relevant departments of state and, more generally, through the participation of various associations in tightly knit 'policy communities' (Laffin and Entwistle, 2000: 210). Through these and other mechanisms, the professions were able to exert considerable influence on how social problems were defined. They also influenced the solutions (the latter, more often than not, leading to some extension of professional control).

The nature and extent of this involvement varied, being most developed in the case of health (Larkin, 1995). Since the formation of the NHS in 1946 UK governments went out of their way to accommodate the interests of doctors whom 'to a large extent succeeded in defining certain areas as out of bounds to non professionals' (Klein, 1989: 57). But even less powerful groups were able to play a role in shaping the policy agenda (Webb and Wistow, 1986). Teachers, for example, were central to the development of public education 'based on a view of the curriculum as the province of "professional expertise"' (Clarke and Newman, 1997: 6).

A second feature of this regime was the hands off approach adopted by central government towards regulating professional practice. This is not to say there was no control. In the UK the professions operated within a framework of legislation and guidance and overall constraints on spending that became steadily more pronounced during the 1970s. But compared to other European states and to what came later, the level of government intervention in practice matters was minimal. The frameworks of law within which services were provided were, quite often, not very detailed so far as types and standards of provision were concerned (Webb and Wistow, 1986). This was especially true of health (Klein, 1995), but also of professional services (such as education and social care) located within local government. According to Greenwood and Stewart (1986: 40) in these areas the emphasis was very much on 'local choice within a national framework of (traditionally) broadly drawn legislation'. While overall budgetary and policy constraints clearly existed, they did not amount to a 'direct line of command from central government dictating...detailed policies to be implemented' (Harris, 1998: 845).

Central governments also adopted a relatively hands off approach towards monitoring and evaluation (Hallett, 1982; Day and Klein, 1990). While agencies were established to regulate professional practice – such as the Social Work Advisory Service (later to become the Social Services Inspectorate), Central Housing Advisory Committee and the Health Advisory Service – their work was characterised by 'a lightness of touch' (Harris, 1998: 845). As Henkel (1991: 121) suggests, practice was very much dominated by notions of 'professionally led, liberal and interactive evaluation' with the focus being on 'resource needs, inputs and on processes' (ibid, 122). This meant a regime in which the autonomy of professional groups to regulate themselves was largely preserved and where the role of external agencies was essentially 'advisory'. While central government did try to influence practice, the emphasis was on pursuing change through persuasion and 'rigorous argument rather than conclusive judgment' (ibid, 122).

But perhaps the most significant feature of this institutional regime was the control professions were able to exert over the process of service delivery itself (Evetts, 2002). The dominant mode of organising at local levels was one in which – within broadly drafted legal and financial constraints – producer groups were able to shape the means and (sometimes) ends of provision. This did not mean no limits were placed on professional freedoms and aspirations (Parry and Parry, 1979; Webb and Wistow, 1986). Rather, within the framework of state bureaucracy an informal system of organising emerged that, to a greater or lesser extent, was dominated by the concerns of practitioners. In what remains of this chapter we now describe this system in more detail and focus on some of the consequences of it.

The producer-driven organisation of public services

Prior to looking at how professional services were administered it is useful to identify some of the broad characteristics of the organisations in which these activities were located. In doing so it is important to note that these were not really 'organisations' at all. Hood (1995) describes public services as 'semi anonymised organisations', encapsulated within wider institutions of the state. Secondary education, social care and housing, for example, were incorporated within the framework of local government. As we saw earlier the emphasis was historically on local authorities (especially those of the upper tier) providing a multiplicity of services – each organised along professional lines – within a given geographical area (Hinings and Greenwood, 1988; Leach et al., 1994). Although regulated in policy terms by central government ministries, questions of management, resource allocation and the 'fixing of...priorities across services' (Greenwood and Stewart, 1986: 41) were a local matter. By contrast, in health, the decision was taken in 1948 to establish a national organisation administered and funded centrally. This however, only meant that provider organisations such as hospitals and clinics were located within a different kind of administrative structure, one made up (after 1974) of regions, districts and areas. At each level a nominal degree of local political oversight was introduced in the form of community health councils (Harrison and Pollitt, 1994).

These arrangements mean that, unlike the professional service firms described in much of the literature (Mintzberg, 1993; Powell et al., 1999), schools, hospitals and SSDs can not be viewed as autonomous organisations (Brint and Karabel, 1991: 353). Management processes tended to be 'dispersed' between professionals, senior administrators and a 'wide range of "functional" managers', located at higher levels in the hierarchy (Bach and Winchester, 1999: 33). This was most pronounced in health where policy decisions were made through a complex process of negotiation and bargaining between committees at hospital and district level. Even in local government, where more defined management roles existed within each department, many key decisions – notably in the areas of finance and personnel – were (and often still are) taken elsewhere (Keen and Scase, 1998: 41).

A further consequence of this encapsulated nature of professional services was the role of local politicians in policy and administration. In local government supervision by members committees diluted the authority of senior professionals and represented a major source of uncertainty (especially with regard to resources). But while this system made it hard to engage in long term planning of services it did not weaken professional control over the way services were provided. As we shall see, in practice much decision making was 'officer dominated' (Harris, 1998; Laffin and Young, 1990). According to Greenwood and Hinings (1993: 1064): 'The primary performance criterion is professional competence within each service area, and good performance is the best practice as defined by professionals'.

A second feature of these organisations was that middle and senior ranking positions within them tended to be dominated by qualified professionals. This was most straightforward in social services where a single professional group, social work, was able to monopolise the administration. By contrast, in health and housing the process was made more complex by the large number of competing groups of professionals involved in service delivery. This was especially true in the NHS where the tendency for professions to fragment into specialisms and separate occupations is widely noted (Ackroyd, 1995a). Not only is medicine itself divided into various 'craft committees', one finds below it 'a dozen semi-professional associations for physiotherapists, radiographers, midwives, health visitors, nurses and others' (Burrage, 1990: 170). In the context of hospitals, such divisions meant that control over the administration had to be shared between different groups. It also required that considerable time and effort was devoted to ongoing negotiation between groups to ensure co-operative action.

Thirdly, it is important to reiterate the fact that these 'organisations' were formally bureaucratic. This meant that work was governed to some extent by rules and procedures. In most instances there was also a hierarchical structure differentiating, in terms of power and status, between operational, middle ranking and senior professions (Hugman, 1994; Causor and Exworthy, 1999). These structures were especially developed in housing and social services. Here decision-making was subject to more detailed rules (for example, governing eligibility to various services) than was the case in health (Webb and Wistow, 1986; Howe, 1986). Added to this were differences in the nature of hierarchical organisation. In social care there existed a unified chain of command, made up of professionals. In this service, senior professionals tended to be more involved in routine administration. By contrast, in housing and health, one finds multiple hierarchies. Housing departments were characterised by fragmentation with key decisions about aspects of service provision undertaken within different local government departments by different professional groups. While this has changed to some degree, it remains a feature of council housing provision (Bines et al., 1993). Finally in health, at least until 1983, decisions were made through a system of committees or 'consensus' management teams at different levels. These teams, in turn, were made up of senior professionals (including medicine and nursing) and administrators, each drawn from a separate, parallel, hierarchy (Harrison and Pollitt, 1994). One consequence of this arrangement was that professionals, even at senior levels, were able to detach themselves from routine administration. In hospitals these two domains of work were often kept 'sharply distinct' (Denis et al., 1996: 676).

A fourth point to make concerns the geographically dispersed nature of service operations. Wilding (1982: 69) notes how, in many areas, professionals worked in 'decentralized settings' such as residential establishments, hospital sites, schools or area offices. One consequence of this was the emergence of strong sub-cultures and attachments to local communities and client groups (Pratchett and Wingfield, 1996). The dispersed nature of work also led to perennial difficulties of communication in these services between front line staffs and back room administrators located in central offices.

Finally, these organisations were characterised by distinctive cultures and values that shaped practice. Important here were strong cosmopolitan orientations and a relatively weak sense of identification with employing agencies (Pratchett and Wingfield, 1996: 642). This was especially marked in health with its highly developed occupational labour markets (Ackroyd, 1996), but was also present in local government (Greenwood and Stewart, 1986: 46). Clarke (1995: 46) for example, notes the emergence of a 'professional culture' within SSDs, based on a collective identification with 'social work' and a sense of 'professional (rather than organizational) loyalty and commitment'.

Also influential were wider notions of a public service ethos (PSE) (Pratchett and Wingfield, 1996; Hanlon, 1998; duGay, 2000). By the PSE is implied a number of values, including those stressing accountability to the political process, acceptance of bureaucratic norms of honesty, integrity and impartiality and an emphasis on the altruistic (rather than purely financial) motivations of public servants. According to Pratchett and Wingfield (1996) this PSE might be understood as a 'political institution', helping to ensure a degree of coherence and consistency of values amongst staff delivering a diverse range of public services. It also offered a distinct 'logic of appropriateness' that served both to legitimate and shape the behaviour of officials. As we shall see, appeals to the PSE were an important tactic used to defend the status quo and resist attempts by managers to exert control. But these same ideas also helped foster amongst front line practitioners a strong sense of vocation, commitment to service and, in some cases, a willingness to work beyond contract.

Custodial management

Despite the variations in structure noted above, our contention is that it is possible to generalise about a mode of organising that was present in all professional services, including health, housing and social care. Broadly speaking, this can be described as a system in which the producers of services were largely able to define and control what public services are given within legal and financial constraints. This in turn was underpinned by a distinctive approach towards administration, previously defined by one of us as 'custodial' (Ackroyd et al., 1989). Implied by the term custodial is that:

> management sees itself primarily as the custodian of standards of service provision. It is, in self-conception if not practice, management of the stable state...The custodial approach is, therefore, centred on existing services; focused on the necessity of maintaining minimum standards of provision, and almost invariably wedded to the conceptions of practice held by service providers themselves (Ackroyd et al., 1989: 613).

This approach resulted in a 'stable monopoly of service provision' (611) by practitioner groups. As we shall see, it also lead to a highly decentralised form of organising (what Mintzberg (1993) refers to as an 'inverse pyramid') that was both hard to control and resistant to change.

Two key factors contributed to the emergence of custodial management in UK public services. Firstly was the fact that managers (or senior professionals) in these contexts are required to oversee activities, which, as Friedson (1994) puts it, are 'inherently discretionary'. In most areas the delivery of services depended on a complicated process of evaluation as to the 'need' or eligibility of clients and the appropriateness of different treatments or interventions. Even when rules and procedures were laid down (for example in housing or social work) judgment and skill were needed in their application (Lipsky, 1980; Mintzberg, 1993). To be sure this did not mean that such work was immune to processes of commodification and de-skilling. Rather, at least until recent times, there existed obvious limits to these tendencies. Such change was also made difficult by the resistance of professions and their success in defending jurisdictions. In many cases the demand for autonomy was reinforced by a powerful service ideology or ethic (see above) instructing practitioners 'that only they – having the detailed knowledge of particular people and situations – are adequately equipped to decide on the appropriateness of different courses of action' (Ackroyd et al., 1989: 611). Added to this were discourses stressing the role of professional self-regulation as a mechanism for maintaining standards and ensuring that services were provided in the wider 'public' or 'commonwealth' interest (Johnson, 1972; Wilding, 1982; Pratchett and Wingfield, 1996).

A second factor contributing to the 'custodial' approach were the orientations of middle and senior ranking professionals charged with the administration of services. As noted, in most public services the tendency was (and in many cases remains) for higher-level positions to be attained only by people who have experience of the basic tasks involved in service delivery (Hugman, 1994). This system has numerous advantages. Ex-practitioners are generally more credible in the eyes of junior staff, and therefore more effective in mediating between competing interests (Causor and Jones, 1996; 116; Friedson, 1994). They were also less likely to be 'informationally dependent' (Power, 1997: 132) on their subordinates (although, as Pollitt (1990: 438) notes, 'professional experience, unexercised, is a decaying asset'). But while this system allowed for the routine administration of services, it also led to a situation in which senior professionals were generally unwilling to interfere directly in the work of junior practitioners. Because management 'has its origin in the practitioners' groups, it also tends to have and exaggerated respect for practitioner autonomy' (Ackroyd et al., 1989: 612).

To be sure this 'exaggerated respect' did not mean that there was no divergence of interests or values between junior and senior staffs. In many cases (especially in more managed settings) the tendency was for senior professionals to closely identify with agency goals and priorities (Flynn, 1999: 31). In SSDs, for example Clare (1988: 493) notes how managers adopted a 'different value system and set of priorities' to front line staff. Others refer to a 'Berlin wall' separating senior and rank and file professionals (Parsloe et al., 1981). This inevitably led to conflict in these organisations over the nature and extent of practitioner autonomy (Hugman, 1994: 77). But while this conflict was damaging it tended to occur within a context in which management's overall orientation was to preserve rather than fundamentally challenge practitioner control. Attempts to manage or influence this work (at least until the 1990s) were therefore indirect and focused more on nibbling away at professional autonomy rather than attacking it at its core.

The system of custodial administration therefore tended to reinforce the autonomy of practitioner groups. It also represented a highly decentralised approach to managing, one might say leaving the professionals to 'manage themselves'. All this did not completely negate the need for managers. At the very least there was a necessity for routine administration, mediation and keeping records of allocations between different groups of practitioners. Senior administrators also played an important brokerage role between providers and external paymasters (Mintzberg, 1993). And yet, while these functions were clearly important, they did not alter the basic fact that these organisations were essentially provider driven. 'Management' (even if labelled as such) tended to be a largely passive activity, focused on maintaining the status quo and customary patterns of service delivery as defined by professionals.

In what remains of this section we discuss in more detail some of the consequences of this mode of organising. Our attention will focus on three main issues. First are limits on how far managers and paymasters are able to evaluate staff performance and take action to influence standards. Second are obstacles to detailed financial control. Finally are problems associated with the implementation of policy change or strategic shifts in the nature of provision.

Performance evaluation

The mode of organising described above placed a number of limitations on the ability of external managers and paymasters to influence or evaluate the performance of front line staff. One reason for this, noted above, was the 'complex' and 'internally controversial' nature of much of the work in question (Power, 1997: 114). Not only did the ambiguity surrounding this work require a high level of discretion it made it hard to evaluate, especially by non-experts (Broadbent and Laughlin, 2002; Pollitt, 1990). Added to this was the lack of time and resources devoted to the activity of collecting information relating to practice. In SSDs, for example, a succession of reports noted the underdeveloped nature of formal record keeping systems and the sparcity of 'detailed forms and guidelines' (Parsloe, 1981: 60). According to Bills et al. (1980: 126), the tendency was for many aspects of social work practice regarded as 'professional' territory' not to be 'precisely defined' and 'frequently left in organizational limbo land'.

The 'problem' of performance evaluation was further compounded by the inadequacies of the formal hierarchy itself as a mechanism of control. This was perhaps most pronounced in the case of medicine where an explicit system of peer (or collegial) review existed (Wilding, 1982). Here the emphasis was firmly on the responsibility of professionals (through a variety of local and national committees) to regulate themselves. Managerial interference of any kind was (and is) strongly resisted (Pollitt, 1990). Elsewhere, in teaching and social work, systems of peer review were far less developed. In these areas greater importance was given to formal supervision and appraisal of lower level staffs. However, more often than not, supervision took on a form of *de facto* peer evaluation, with managerial concerns either downplayed or ignored (Hugman, 1994; Causor and Exworthy, 1999). The emphasis was on maintaining a 'fiction' of collegial equality, with the manager

(or 'first amongst equals') more concerned to support staff and influence practice than systematically evaluate performance (Friedson,
1994; Causor and Jones, 1996).

As a result of all this, to a greater or lesser extent, professional practice and decision-making remained 'invisible' to senior administrators
and politicians (Pithouse, 1989). This, in turn, meant that practitioner
rather than managerial definitions of service quality and standards
tended to dominate. The emphasis was on 'conformity, reliability and
a basic standard of services' (Ackroyd et al., 1989: 614), or more generally, prioritising the technical or process related characteristics of
service provision rather than measurable outcomes or outputs (Henkel,
1991; Hood, 1991).

Financial control

A further implication of this custodial mode of organising was for the
allocation and monitoring of resources. As noted earlier, in the UK
governments, especially since 1976, increasingly sought to control and
place overall cash limits on public services (see Chapter 3). However,
within this framework (at least until the 1990s) the ability of paymasters to define service priorities and control the way in which resources
were allocated has been severely limited. Wilding (1982: 35) notes how
'professional power in resource use is substantial and is often exercised
with few political or bureaucratic controls'. Two main reasons can be
given for this.

Firstly, was the lack of detailed information regarding the cost of
different services and professional treatments. This was due both to
the complexity of these services and the absence, in most areas, of
developed systems of financial monitoring (Tonge and Horton, 1996:
76–77; Farnham and Horton, 1996a: 29). Local managers and politicians relied heavily on professional judgments regarding resource use.
In most areas, incremental approaches to budgeting were the norm
(Greenwood, 1984) with allocations of resources linked to existing
patterns of provision and little or no 'extra professional analysis
of base budgets' (Hinings and Greenwood, 1988: 74). All this, in
turn, meant that resources tended to be deployed along 'customary
lines' and in accord with professional definitions of need and priority
rather than those of external paymasters or managers (Ackroyd et al.,
1989: 613).

A second factor weakening external control over resources was the
limited way in which professional decisions, at operational levels, were
informed by cost considerations. Often it was assumed that these

domains should be kept separate (Ackroyd, 1996). This was most marked in health where the tendency was for clinicians to prescribe treatments according to professional judgments of what was appropriate or expedient rather than cost (Klein, 1989). In social care and housing resource-based decisions were more closely supervised. But even here there existed a strong belief that services were universal entitlements and should be provided regardless of the gravity of need, cost or ability to pay (Lewis and Glennester, 1996). Of course in all areas a ceiling existed (especially from the mid 1970s) on the overall quantity of services that could be provided. This inevitably meant that professional groups were engaged in rationing. But crucially, this rationing remained implicit. It was professionals who were left to draw the rules about priorities rather than external managers and politicians.

Policy implementation

Finally, this custodial mode of organising presented major obstacles to those seeking to change practice or impose policy top down. One reason for this was the unwillingness of senior administrators to impose change in the face of staff opposition. More often than not the preference was for strategies of negotiation and dialogue with practitioner groups (Hinings and Greenwood, 1988: 112). There was also a tendency for senior professionals to adopt a brokerage role, attempting to reconcile external demands with local, pragmatic concerns and interests. As Friedson (1985: 30) notes in relation to the medical profession:

> Those in administrative positions in practice organisations balance the necessity to carry out the collective ends of a governing board... against the needs and desires of those who do medical work, thereby buffering the practice of medicine against the political and economic pressures of the environment.

These processes of negotiation ensured that, to a greater or lesser extent, top down policy initiatives and demands were subject to compromise and modification. What passed for policy in many instances was therefore likely to consist of 'the pragmatic resolution of controversy surrounding proposals to introduce new techniques or practices at the level of actual service provision' (Ackroyd et al., 1989: 614).

It was also the case that senior professionals (even assuming they were willing) were often unable to implement policy changes. Partly, this was due to the limited skill-base of managers and, in many areas, the under-developed nature of backroom activities associated with policy formulation and planning. Added to this was the fact that managers faced considerable uncertainty over resources, especially in the context of local government where policies might change according to shifting political priorities (Denis et al., 1996: 674). Finally, were characteristics of internal organisation that tended to work against change. As we saw above, many public services were geographically dispersed and 'organized according to professional skills and ideas rather than...client needs' (Wilding, 1982: 25–26). This led to the emergence of loosely coupled systems in which the task of co-coordinating different groups and interests around unified policy goals was extremely difficult. Under these conditions: 'the notion of a strategy – a single, integrated pattern of decisions common to the entire organization – loses a good deal of its meaning...' (Mintzberg, 1993: 200).

All this did not mean that change or innovation was impossible. Rather change was most likely to occur in incremental steps, 'within the terms and constraints of the professional frame of understanding' (Greenwood and Stewart, 1986: 48). Public service organisations, as we suggested earlier, were essentially conservative. Their focus was on the maintenance of customary modes of service provision as defined by practitioners. This meant a strong tendency to resist any change that was radical or which threatened dramatic shifts in the nature and mode of provision.

Conclusion

This chapter has outlined in general terms the main characteristics of the organisational settlement that emerged in the UK and its consequences for the welfare professionals. Attention focused on the nature of the organisational forms that emerged at local levels. These were seen to vary along a number of dimensions, most notably the extent to which professional work was managed and subject to formal bureaucratic controls (Webb and Wistow, 1986). However, it was suggested that in all contexts a distinct mode of custodial organisation and administration existed.

As we shall see in the next chapter this custodial system of organising services has been strongly criticised. Today it is assumed to be largely ineffective and outmoded. Yet it is easy to exaggerate those limitations. Contrary to popular opinion, public services in the UK were not fundamentally inefficient or wasteful of resources. Nor were they necessarily ineffective mechanisms for the delivery of public services to a minimum (often very high) standard (Glennerster, 1998;

Greenwood and Stewart, 1986). A desire to resist change and defend the status quo was a characteristic of these organisations. But so too was 'an ethos of public service, founded upon accountability, impartiality and commitment to communitarian values' (Colling, 2001: 600). As such, it is important to recognise certain strengths of this mode of organising and how, in many respects, it was well suited to the demands placed upon it. However, by the late 1970s, even assuming such 'strengths' were acknowledged, they were largely brushed aside in the clamour for radical change. It is to this development that our attention will now turn in the next chapter.

3
Dismantling the Organisational Settlement: Towards a New Public Management

> The welfare professions embodied many of the characteristics of the old world which the New Right were committed to cleansing. They saw the professions as a powerful vested interest, effectively accountable to no one – politicians, managers or consumers. They were inefficient, the inevitable result of their insulation from the bracing competitive stimulus of market forces. They were ineffective in achieving society's aims for particular services. Their claims for expertise were scarcely supported by experience and their claim to an ethic of service which legitimised their lack of normal accountability was dismissed as the most specious of special pleading. 'Professions' were seen as very much secondary to management as an instrument of effective social policy (Foster and Wilding, 2000: 146).

The aim of this chapter is to describe how, from the early 1980s, attempts were made to radically transform the institutions and practices of the post war organisational settlement. We argue that over this period there occurred a 'break with the interplay between the state and the professions' (Jepperson et al., 2002: 1564). This process weakened the influence and 'institutional autonomy' (Flynn, 1999; Evetts, 2002) of organised professional groups. Added to this, and of central concern to us in this book, were attempts to transform the management arrangements of professional services. According to Exworthy and Halford (1999a: 3–4), the new managerialism represented a 'strategic weapon with which to curb the powers of overly independent professionals'. Under both Conservative and New Labour governments, a primary goal of policy has been to move away from the custodial pattern of administration described in Chapter 2. The aim was to establish in these services a new and supposedly more effective 'managerial mode of coordination'.

To explore these issues the remainder of this chapter is divided into three main sections. First we consider some of the factors that drove governments in the UK to seek to dismantle the organisational settlement. Second, attention focuses on the broad implications of this change for the professions and their institutions. Finally, section three will consider in more detail the nature of management reforms that were attempted and their possible consequences. It will be argued here that while intense pressures have been generated for change one cannot assume that these have always been fully translated into effective reform or the effective delivery of services through a managed mode of delivery.

The broad context of change

Prior to describing the nature of change that was attempted it is pertinent to look at the broad context in which it occurred. Important here is the question of why governments in the UK sought change at this time? To understand this, we suggest, it is necessary to consider two key factors. First is how the reforms were partly (if not entirely) a response to broader economic conditions and an emergent fiscal crisis. Second is the way that shifting political and public attitudes towards the professions and their modes of organisation were important in driving and legitimating radical change.

Structural crisis

It is widely noted that moves to restructure the organisation of welfare states occurred in the context of more general shifts in the global economy (Flynn, 2000). A starting point for this kind of analysis is the pressure generated in the 1970s by world economic recession and oil price shocks. In most developed countries, these pressures emerged at a time when public expenditure was rising at a rate faster than the economy as a whole. In the UK, for example, between 1965 and 1975 (deflated) social expenditure grew at 5.9 per cent per annum while the growth rate of GDP was only 2.6 per cent (Pollitt, 1993: 29). Economic recession also coincided with a period of growing demand for certain public services – linked to rising unemployment and some unfavourable demographic trends (such as population ageing) (Pollitt and Boukaert, 2000: 29). All this resulted in what O'Connor (1973) describes as a 'fiscal crisis of the state'. Just as the demand for welfare services increased the capacity of governments to raise income from general taxation to meet welfare commitments was undermined.

Wider shifts in the global economy also created pressure for change (Ackroyd, 2002). It is argued that the globalisation of capital markets and the expansion of international trade reduced the room for manoeuvre of nation states. Governments enjoyed less freedom to pursue demand-led macro-economic policies, especially if these involved raising public expenditure through taxation (OECD, 1997). For many, this change implies nothing less than a radical shift in the role of the nation state (Whitfield, 2001; Burnham, 1999). Jessop (1994), for example, talks about the emergence of a 'hollowed-out neo-Schumpeterian workfare state' in which the focus is on a 'productivist reordering of social policy' (263). In such a state, government interest is said to shift decisively towards supply-side policies aimed at promoting national competitiveness. More emphasis is given to reducing the so called burden of welfare expenditure and improving efficiency.

These conditions, many argue, made some kind of restructuring of welfare states unavoidable. The nature and timing of such change varied between developed countries, but a number of common themes were evident.[1] All national governments faced growing pressure to control or even reduce levels of overall public expenditure (Hood, 1995). This, in turn, led to attempts to restructure the organisational forms through which public services were provided (including those dominated by professional groups). Bureau-professional regimes, which, in the past, had proven to be 'relatively weak institutional arrangements for the exercise of...financial discipline', became a key target of reform (Clarke, 1998: 237).

But while the conditions of financial crisis were evident across all developed countries few responded as quickly or as drastically as did governments in the UK. In part this can be explained by more fundamental weaknesses in the British economy and the spiralling inflation of the late 1970s. The radical nature of change was also a reflection of shifting political commitments and a growing tendency to question the value and necessity of a welfare state based on the principals of universal provision and incremental growth (Clarke and Newman, 1997). In the UK, structural crisis coincided with a more general breakdown in political consensus (albeit one that had previously been tenuous) (Glennerster, 1998). In the long run it initiated a shift from a 'welfare' state, focused on the principle of universal provision of services based on citizenship, to a more modest 'plural state' in which benefits were variable and means tested (Rhodes, 2000).

Initially, financial constraint was quite crudely applied under the tenure of the 1974–9 Labour government. Hyper-inflation and industrial unrest led this government to seek a loan from the International Monetary Fund, which, although provided, came along with conditions concerning the imposition of tight annual cash limits (adopted in 1976). With the election of a Conservative government in 1979, the 'reduction in public expenditure' was pursued even more vigorously and became a 'principal objective' of policy (Exworthy and Halford, 1999: 4). Tight cash limits were extended and imposed on departmental spending and national pay settlements (White, 1999). There were moves to reduce the size and scope of public services ('rolling back the frontiers of the state'), for example, through privatisation and compulsory competitive tendering.[2] Finally, a range of policies were introduced aimed at re-structuring the management and organisation of public services.

By the mid 1990s, it is clear that these policies had had a marked impact. While overall public expenditure increased in real terms, the rate of growth was substantially slower than in the 1970s (Shaoul, 1999) and below what was required to keep pace with changing needs (Wilding, 1992: 203–204). Since the mid 1970s the proportion of national income (or GDP) accounted for by public expenditure has been effectively contained (Glennerster and Hills, 1998: 330–1). By 1998 the UK was transformed from being one of the highest (in 1970) to the lowest ranking OECD nations in terms of the proportion of national income devoted to general government expenditure (Shaoul, 1999: 31).[3] Only time will tell how far more recent announcements of increased funding in health and education will significantly reverse this picture (Bach, 2002: 324).[4]

Moves to restructure public organisations were therefore driven, at least in part, by the necessity of governments to respond to broader economic conditions and a growing fiscal crisis. Yet, while this kind of explanation is important, it should not be exaggerated. There are risks of overstating the structural necessity of change and the choices available to national governments in how they responded to economic forces (Pollitt and Boukaert, 2000; Flynn, 2000). There is also a problem of ignoring the wider context of ideas that shaped the nature and extent of change. It is to this subject that we now turn.

Performance crisis

From the mid 1970s the institutions of bureau-professional control in the UK (and elsewhere) became the subject of a torrent of criticism. The origin and focus of this critique differed, but the overall effect was to weaken support for these institutions and to generate increasingly vocal demands for reform. Following Oliver (1992) one might usefully describe this as a process of deinstitutionalisation. Gradually, the legitimacy of established modes of professional organising was undermined, subject to 'challenge, reassessment or rejection' (Oliver, 1992: 564).

A major source of critique during this period came from academics, policy makers and practitioners both on the left and the right of the political spectrum. From the left, a radical critique emerged in the context of wider social changes (see Clarke and Newman, 1997) and focused mainly on the power wielded by the professions (Wilding, 1982). Feminists pointed to the nature of bureau-professional regimes as bastions of male privilege (see Chapter 2) and to the dominance of patriarchal ideologies that shaped relationships with clients (Hearn, 1982; Newman and Williams, 1995). Welfare professions were attacked for their limited engagement with issues of race discrimination and for their inability to recognise the special needs of groups such as the disabled (Hugman, 1994; Dominelli, 1997). The thrust of these attacks was to question the role of the professions as 'agents of social control' (Abbott and Meereabeu, 1998: 14). Despite their claims of neutrality and impartiality the welfare professions were, helping to produce and reproduce relations of power and inequality.

A quite different critique of originated from the New Right. By the New Right is meant an amalgam of different groups and academics composed of both libertarian and 'traditionalist' wings, broadly opposed to the post second world war welfare settlement (Kirkpatrick and Martinez-Lucio, 1995: 16–17). What these groups held in common was a deep-rooted cynicism regarding the nature and underlying values of public organisations. Public choice theorists, in particular, drew attention to the costs associated with state monopoly and how this tended to limit the choices of consumers (Niskanen, 1971). These arrangements ensured that service provision was inherently wasteful and inefficient. High costs followed from the 'producer driven' nature of pubic bureaucracies and the tendency for administrators (and professionals) to pursue their own interest of maximising budgets and defending restrictive practices (Alaszewski, 1995: 56–9, Crompton, 1990: 158).

From this perspective the professional claim to act as 'disinterested guardians of the public interest' was simply dismissed as a 'sham' (Burrage, 1992: 24).

A further critique developed by New Right intellectuals was of the knowledge claims of the welfare professionals. In particular were concerns about the promotion of what were seen as inappropriate liberal and permissive values. Some groups (for example, social workers) were arraigned for their failure to emphasise the responsibilities of individuals and for 'creating and maintaining a dependency culture' (Alaszewski and Manthorpe, 1990: 238).

In addition to these increasingly vocal critiques, other developments served to undermine public confidence in the professions. Most important was a series tragedies and scandals in education, housing, health and social services in which the professions were deeply implicated. Notable scandals in council housing included the collapse of the Ronan Point tower block in the late 1960s. In the personal social services abuse scandals date back to the Maria Colwell case in 1973 and have continued well into the late 1990s (Cochrane, 1993; Berridge and Brodie, 1996). These ran alongside high profile inquiries into the conduct of field social work teams and their tendency to intervene either too late (as in the Beckford case (1985)) or too early (as with the Cleveland affair in 1987 (Parton, 1991)). In health, attention was also drawn to a series of 'failures' in the care system (Martin, 1994), culminating most recently, in 1999, with the revelations of malpractice at Bristol Royal Infirmary.

These high profile tragedies and scandals raised questions about professional judgement in the care of vulnerable people. A succession of inquiries unearthed weaknesses in systems of professional supervision and self-regulation (Salter, 1999, 2001; Evetts, 2002). Wider concerns emerged about the accountability of the professions and the extent to which they could or should be trusted to manage public services independently of external control. As Foster and Wilding (2000: 145) put it: 'Accountability to themselves, to a professional ethic or to their professional peers was criticised as little more than a fig leaf on a naked unaccountable, unmanaged, unresponsive independence'.

Finally, more general trends towards a better educated, critical and (arguably) less deferential society served to undermine trust in the institutions of professional regulation (Dent and Whitehead, 2002). One indicator of this was the emergence, from early 1970s, of a number of consumer movements calling for greater transparency and public involvement in decisions regarding the planning and delivery of services. In social services, for example, Langan (1993: 58) notes how 'Many clients, from lone parents to homeless young people...repudi-ated the tendency of social workers to reinterpret their material needs in terms of personal inadequacy'. One might also point to wider shifts in public attitudes towards experts and their knowledge claims. According to Laffin and Entwistle (2000: 211) the uncertain and tenta-tive nature of knowledge in the late-modern period has meant that professional judgement is less likely to be accepted without question.

A wide-ranging critique of the welfare professions therefore devel-oped in the UK from the mid 1970s. This in turn was to substantially damage the credibility of the professions and weaken support, both amongst the public and politicians, for their modes of organising. Increasingly the professions were 'billed as self-interested, self-serving, inefficient and ineffective' (Wilding, 1992: 202). The institutional context in which the professions operated was transformed into one that was endemically hostile to and suspicious of their specialist exper-tise and claim to be working in the public interest (Reed, 2004).

Not surprisingly all this had some influence on policy, especially where the New Right were concerned. As the UK state faced a grow-ing fiscal crisis the New Right was remarkably successful in terms of framing political understandings of the nature and causes of such difficulties (Hutton, 2003). The professions were successfully cast as the villains, as 'part of the problem' and therefore a major target for any subsequent reform.

Re-negotiating the regulative bargain: some consequences

In this section we turn to the question of how, in the UK, both Conservative and Labour governments sought to re-structure the post-war organisational settlement described in Chapter 2. In doing so, our analysis will focus primarily on developments from the early 1980s. This is not to ignore that important changes took place prior to this. Rather, it is to argue that the election of a Conservative government in 1979 was an important juncture. After that a more concrete and radical policy agenda emerged and was not subsequently reversed.

When seeking to describe this radical policy agenda we also re-cognise that governments 'tempered ideology with pragmatism' (Alaszewski and Manthorpe, 1990: 238). A high degree of oppor-tunism was evident, especially with regard to the mechanisms used to implement various changes (Farnham and Horton, 1996a: 317). However, at the same time, our view is that developments over this period have been informed by common goals, or what Corby and White (1999: 8) refer to as an 'overarching ideology'. We agree with Foster and Wilding's (2000: 146) assessment that under both the Conservatives and New Labour a primary objective of policy has been to 'bring welfare professionals firmly under political and managerial control'. Since the early 1980s, governments in the UK have displayed much less confidence in professional expertise, competence and capacity for effective self-regulation. Increasingly the assumption is that politicians must play a greater role in establishing the priorities of welfare services and in regulating (or even prescribing) the way in which these are delivered.

Returning to the concepts discussed in Chapter 2 one might understand these developments as a shift in the nature of the regulative bargain between state and professions. However, this did not mean any reduction in demand for professional expertise. Nor has it implied a fundamental challenge to the basic institutions of occupational closure and professional regulation in public services. True, there has been a recurrent antipathy towards professional monopoly, especially from the New Right (Crompton, 1990: 158). There have also been piecemeal and largely opportunistic moves to downgrade professions such as probation workers (May and Annison, 1998), nurses (Grimshaw, 1999) and school teachers (Fergusson, 2000). But none of this represents a fundamental break with the past. On balance, the 1990s were a period in that saw increased calls for professional training and accreditation, for example in areas such as social work (Orme, 2001) and housing (Cole and Furbey, 1994). In many respects 'professionalism in the form of education and credentials remains an attractive route to career and status' (Laffin and Entwistle, 2000: 217).

It therefore seems inappropriate to talk about change in terms of deprofessionalisation or even a basic fracturing of corporate relations between state and professions. What has occurred instead, we argue, amounts to a 'reformation of structures and relationships in new alliances and divisions' (Hugman, 1994: 24; Johnson, 1993). Implied by this is a far more active supervisory role by government in determining both the ends and, more fully, means and of welfare provision. The professions remain key agents through which services are provided (and will continue to be so), but their semi-independent position as equal 'partners' in this process has been fundamentally challenged. The broad shift is therefore from 'professional self-regulation' to greater 'state control' (Burrage, 1992: 24), or, as Pollitt (1993) argues, to a system in which the professions are 'on tap rather than on top'.

In what remains of this section we describe some of the major impli-cations and possible consequences of this re-articulation of the rela-tionship between state and welfare professions. In particular we identify four main ways in which government policies over the past two decades moved away from the old organisational settlement. First concerns the role played by the professions and their associations in policy formulation. Second, is a shift towards greater political control. Third have been attempts to increase the power and influence of users. Finally, has been a sustained drive to transform the management and organisation of professional services.

Weakening of professional influence at policy level

In Chapter 2 we saw that a key feature of the post war organisational settlement was the influential role of the professions in framing both the 'problems' and 'solutions' of policy. However, since the early 1980s this situation has been transformed. Increasingly, 'Politicians from both the left and the right' have felt 'confident to implement major changes to welfare policies without gaining the agreement of...welfare professionals' (Foster and Wilding, 2000: 153). While the professions retain much influence, their once exclusive and coveted role in deter-mining and shaping policy has (in most cases) been lost.

A number of developments illustrate this change. In health, the BMA were effectively marginalised in discussions regarding the content and implementation of the Griffiths Report (1983) – in stark contrast to their earlier role in the formation of the NHS in 1948 (Hunter, 1998). Harrison and Wood, (1999: 757) also describe how the NHS review of 1988 (leading to *Working for Patients* and, ultimately, to the internal market in health care) was 'conducted informally, largely in secret and uninformed by expert opinion from the field'. In education, the story is very similar. According to Barber (1992: ix–x) 'The 1980s...saw a steady diminution of teacher union involvement in national policy-making'. This culminated in the decision by government to delib-erately exclude the teaching profession and unions from policy discussions prior to the 1988 Education Act (Ball, 1990). The teachers, it seemed, were 'a voice no longer heard or needed' (Timmins, 1996: 428; Quoted in Foster and Wilding, 2000: 146).

This account of declining influence does not apply equally to all professional groups. In some areas, for example the police (Loveday, 1998) and housing managers (Walker, 1998), professional influence may, relatively speaking, have increased over the past two decades. Nor should we assume that members of the professional 'knowledge elite' (Friedson, 1994) will not continue to exert some influence on the policy agenda for welfare services. Yet, it does seem that in the 1980s and '90s most professions 'lost ground'; few if any retained their old monopoly over policy advice (Laffin, 1998a). One should also note wider changes in the way governments formulate policy (Rhodes, 1997b). Increasingly politicians have come to rely upon a wider range of inputs from outside professional communities, such as from policy think tanks, academics, management consultants and even consumer organisations (Stone, 1996).

In many ways this story of weakening professional influence at the macro, policy level, continued under New Labour. Laffin and Entwistle (2000: 211) note that while a more 'consultative style' has been adopted, 'the professions have not reclaimed their role as framers of policy problems'. If anything, under the current administration the emphasis is on a more inclusive or multi-disciplinary approach towards policy formulation. As such, it might be argued that the professional role has been transformed from a partner to a (albeit important) participant. Increasingly the professions may be 'trailing rather than leading change' (ibid, 217).

Political controls and professional autonomy

A key feature of the post war organisational settlement described in Chapter 2 was the ability of the professions to exercise degrees of freedom and discretion within loosely drawn core legislation and guidance (Webb and Wistow, 1986). This also meant limited state interference in the area of professional education, training and accreditation. However, since the mid 1980s there has been a significant move away from this pattern of 'hands off' state supervision (Wilding, 1997). Governments sought to play a more active role and 'exert tighter controls over activities previously the province of professional judgement' (Newman, 2000: 51).

Three main developments testify to this growing centralisation. First is the tendency of central government to prescribe local practice through more tightly drawn legislation, departmental guidance and other mechanisms (Hoggett, 1996: 23; Broadbent and Laughlin, 2002: 103–4). In secondary education, the introduction of a national curriculum (after 1988) has had a marked impact on the autonomy of teachers at local levels (Fergusson, 2000). More recently state intervention is being extended into the domain of teaching methods – for instance with new rules prescribing a literacy hour in the daily timetables of primary schools. In the personal social services very similar trends can be noted. Major legislation – the Children Act 1989 – led to a proliferation of rules and, some argue, to the 'bureaucratisation' of social work decision-making (Howe, 1992, Bilton, 1998: 201, Whipp et al., 2004) (see Chapter 5). Even in health, the area where the state has been least willing to intrude upon professional freedoms, there has been some movement in this direction. In recent years the Department of Health and the National Institute for Clinical Excellence (NICE) (established in 1999) have become more active in specifying models for clinical practice. These models, derived from 'evidence-based' appraisals of clinical interventions, represent a move towards a standardised 'scientific-bureaucratic' approach towards decision-making (Harrison, 2002).

Greater centralisation is also indicated by changes in the nature and scope of the external inspection and evaluation. In Chapter 2 we saw how the approach of regulatory agencies tended to be interactive, advisory and essentially non-judgemental. But in the late 1980s this model was largely abandoned. The emphasis shifted to a form of evaluation focused on achieving conformity with national policies and on holding 'the inspected for account for what they had done, and how' (Day and Klein, 1990: 4). This meant a greater focus on evaluating the 'performance' of services in terms of processes and outcomes (Hoggett, 1996; Power, 1997). According to Henkel (1991: 122), the assumption was that 'complexities of provision could be broken down and objectively assessed on measurable indicators of performance according to nationally established standards'. Also important were changes in the style of inspection, becoming more judgemental and, in the case of Ofsted (the Office for Standards in Education), also more confrontational.

Under New Labour this new regime of inspection and audit has continued to evolve (Boyne, Day and Walker, 2002). There is now more emphasis on a 'stakeholder' approach towards performance measurement, on continuous improvement and broadening the range of indicators used to judge 'success' (Cutler and Waine, 2000; Sanderson, 2001: 302). However the general shift towards more judgmental forms of inspection was not reversed (Deakin and Parry, 1998). In many respects the current administration extended this logic even further (Webb, 1999), as seen with the proliferation of new 'performance targets' in areas such as health, education and the personal social services (Waine, 2000; Lagnan, 2000). There are also much stronger inducements for provider organisations to conform. Take 'for example' moves to publish comparative performance statistics, the purpose of which is to highlight and reward success (assigning 'beacon' status) and to 'name and shame' so-called 'failing' service providers (be they health trusts, SSDs, or even local authorities) (Audit Commission, 2002a). Judgements are now made about organisational performance and the management arrangements put in place by public agencies in regimes such as the Comprehensive Performance Assessment in English local government (Audit Commission, 2002b).

Finally there have been attempts by governments – both Conservative and New Labour – to intervene in the area of professional education and training. An early example of this was in the personal social services, where, in the late 1980s, politicians tried to influence the content of a new social work qualification (Dominelli, 1996). According to Jones (1999: 46) the intention was to 'appropriately socialise neophyte social workers', moving from 'education to training, to the acquisition of skills and competencies rather than knowledge and understanding'. A similar approach was seen in housing education following the Rayner Scrutiny, when government advanced proposals to alter the training of housing officers (DoE, 1994). In secondary education the trend has also been towards greater state control. This has been the case especially after 1997 with attempts to determine the content of training by linking funding for university-provided programmes to government priorities (McMahon, 1999). Finally, in medicine, while government has yet to intervene directly, it has placed mounting pressure on the profession to reform its own practice. In the wake of the Bristol inquiry a number of changes were agreed, including a periodic revalidation of doctors; state registration and compulsory formal appraisal of individual performance (Salter, 2001).

Taken together these developments suggest a more intrusive central government role in prescribing the goals and methods of professional practice. It seems that deep inroads have been made into areas, which, in the past, were regarded as belonging exclusively to the domain of professional self-regulation. However, as suggested earlier, it is unlikely that all this has (or ever will) amount to a process of de-professionalisation (Reed, 1996; Broadbent and Laughlin, 2002). The state will continue to rely on professional judgement in the delivery of services and – albeit within more tightly drawn frameworks of accountability and monitoring – on their capacity to self regulate.

Empowering users

At the heart of the organisational settlement described in the previous chapter was a degree of trust in the ability of the professions to manage service provision in the interests of clients. However, as noted above, from the late 1970s these assumptions were subject to considerable scrutiny. It was argued (especially by the New Right) that professionals could not be trusted to act in the public interest and that major reforms were needed. This in turn resulted in a series of policy initiatives both under Conservative and New Labour governments aimed at 'empowering' the users (or consumers) of public services and developing new forms of accountability.

When seeking to understand these developments it is useful to differentiate between policy initiatives that have focused on extending either the choice or the voice of users (Kirkpatrick and Martinez-Lucio, 1995). The former arose largely as a consequence of the New Right and it's unfavourable account of professional bureaucracy (see above). The emphasis was on creating 'consumer markets' for professional services (Hoggett, 1996: 12), either through direct fee paying arrangements (as in Dentistry) (Taylor-Gooby et al., 2000) or the wholesale restructuring of services. The latter has been especially pronounced in housing and secondary education with moves to develop league tables and encourage 'parental choice' (Gerwitz et al., 1995). By contrast, in other areas (such as health and social care) the focus has been more on professionals (such as general practitioners or care managers) acting on behalf of users as proxy consumers (Wistow et al., 1996).

Turning to the issue of voice one can note an even more diverse range of initiatives. Under the Conservatives, the most significant development was the introduction of the Citizen's Charter in 1991 and various service based charters (for example, in health and local government). A key objective was to codify user rights of complaint and redress and extend the use of performance indicators so that decision-making would be more transparent (Corby and White, 1999: 10–11). In addition were moves to directly involve user groups in the running of some professional services. For example, in secondary education a key reform was to delegate a range of executive powers to elected boards of governors. In housing attempts have also been made to extend user (or tenant) involvement since the 1970s. These gathered pace over recent years especially in those services that transferred out of local authority control to become housing associations (see Chapter 6).

After 1997 the government continued its 'attack on the "producer dominance" associated with monopoly forms of provision' and stepped up efforts to 'sharpen accountability to users and other stakeholders' (Newman, 2000: 46). Under New Labour, the focus shifted to wider notions of the 'citizen consumer' and to various forms of community based participation (ibid., 56). Examples of this can be found across public services. In local government the regime of Best Value stipulates that users and other stakeholders must be involved in the process of reviewing services (including those provided by professionals) and in the development of performance plans (Martin, 2000). In health there have also been moves to establish formal mechanisms of patent representation and involvement in hospital administration and at higher levels (such as primary care groups) (Dawson and Dargie, 2002: 37).

There has therefore been a sustained effort to increase the choice and voice of users in professional public services. This, in turn, led to the establishment of new forms of external accountability and scrutiny of the work of the professions. One might question how far these policies have (or will) enhance the power of users. But their introduction is important nevertheless. Increasingly the expectation is that the professions will consult with their users and that they will adopt (or at least appear to adopt) more 'want regarding' standpoints (Keat and Abercrombie, 1991).

Administrative reform

There have therefore been some important shifts in the nature of the regulative bargain between state and public service professions. But what we have yet to discuss is perhaps the most important development of all, namely attempts to reform the management of professional work itself. From the early 1980s demands for change in this area mounted against a backdrop of growing criticism of the professions and their system of organisation. As we saw, the New Right were especially vocal in this respect, drawing attention to problems of accountability and failure to control costs. More specific questions were raised about the effectiveness of these systems as tools for managing services and allocating resources. Professionals were criticised for allowing '"happenstance" to dictate the persistence of anachronistic patterns of service provision and staff allocation. ...' (Langan and Clarke, 1994: 75). They were thought to be blind to the ' to the need for change to meet changing problems', tending to limit rather than excite innovation (Greenwood and Stewart, 1986: 48).

To be sure, the 1980s did not mark the beginning of state sponsored attempts to reform public administration. According to Dunleavy and Hood, (1994: 10), 'many NPM innovations seem to be a delayed response to ideas originally developed in the 1960s'. Nevertheless, as we indicated earlier, 1979 did represent an important watershed. In part this is for the reasons already discussed – the deepening fiscal crisis and growing critique of professional institutions. But also important in the UK was the strong belief held by Conservative politicians in the superior performance and efficiency of private sector modes of management (Rhodes, 1997a). These convictions, combined with the growing influence of right wing think tanks, international agencies and management consultants led, at this time, to 'a widespread shift in the legitimacy of management in the public sector...' (Exworthy and Halford, 1999a: 3–4).

Since the early 1980s there has been a succession of initiatives aimed at implementing new management. Initially change was quite limited in scope (relatively speaking) with central government focusing on financial restraint and attempts to install management regimes within existing state bureaucracies. Typical of this was the Griffiths report (1983) on the NHS and Jarrett report (1985) in higher education. However, by the late 1980s, following a third successive Conservative victory, the pace of change began to accelerate (Colling, 2001). Attention shifted to the 'role, organisation, institutions and management' of the welfare state (Stoker, 1989: 157). Attempts were made to re-structure public organisations and to introduce new forms of market competition within and between services (Hoggett, 1996). Such policies were especially marked in health, following the introduction of an internal market, and in secondary education, with the local management of schools. In local government major restructuring also occurred with some professional services (such as polytechnics, further education colleges and, to a lesser extent, housing departments) being moved outside of local authority control.

Since 1997 there has been no real let up in the pressure from government to reform management. There continues to be '...an overriding conviction that the public sector has much to learn from private enterprise' (Geddes, 2001: 498). There have also been a number of new initiatives. Most notable is the policy of 'corporate governance' in the NHS – for the first time extending the control of general managers into the domain of professional self-regulation (Harrison and Ahmad, 2000). Also important in this respect is the strategy of Best Value in local government (Boyne et al., 2002) and moves to decentralise management decision-making in secondary education – for example, with the forced introduction of performance related pay (Waine, 2000).

This brief overview suggests that attempts to install management in public services have been ongoing over the past two decades. This, in turn, marks a further departure from the organisational settlement described in Chapter 2. However, while the broad nature of this change is well understood, it is far from clear how far these demands have been translated to organisational levels. Questions remain about the response of the professions and the extent to which their 'custodial' modes of organisation have been transformed. It is towards addressing these issues that our attention will now turn in the remainder of this book.

Towards a 'managed' professional organisation in UK public services

In this section we consider in more detail the nature of the management restructuring that was attempted in the UK. Three main issues are addressed. First is the question of what kind of change was sought. Secondly, we focus on the mechanisms used by governments to implement policy. Finally are questions about the outcomes and consequences of reform.

The nature of management change

A common point of reference for many recent accounts of change in UK (and other) public services is the concept of the new public management (NPM). Broadly speaking this refers to a cluster of doctrines and practices that are held to constitute a paradigm of management distinct from traditional modes of public administration (Osborne and Gaebler, 1992; OECD, 1995). Hood (1995) for example, asserts that the NPM can be distinguished from traditional public administration in two main ways. Firstly, NPM implies a convergence of public and private sector management styles. Under NPM it is assumed that the gap between the private and public sectors will be removed, with the public sector emulating many of the same structures and practices. The second fundamental change implied by NPM relates to the question of 'how far managerial and professional discretion should be fenced in by explicit standards and rules' (1995: 95). According to Hood, an NPM agenda means greater empowerment for managers, stressing the right to manage with fewer constraints such as those imposed by formal procedures and rules.

Recently, doubts have been expressed about how far the NPM can be taken to represent a coherent, international programme of reform. It is noted that while governments in developed countries pursued change, they did so for quite different reasons and followed distinctive trajectories (Pollitt and Boukaert, 2000; Flynn, 2000; Kickert, 1997). There are also wider questions about the internal consistency of the NPM (see McLaughlin et al., 2002 for an up-to-date review). Hood (1995: 107), for instance, describes the NPM as a 'Babel of tongues', while Ferlie et al., (1996: 10–15) talk about an 'empty canvass' onto which 'you can paint whatever you like'. The thrust of this literature has been to problematise the NPM and to question the idea that it represents a unified body of ideas and policies.

For us these criticisms are important. They help draw attention to the shifting priorities in government policy over time and how demands for change may have been vague and perhaps contradictory (Lowndes, 1997, Pollitt and Boukaert, 2000). That said it is possible to identify a number of underlying themes that have characterised management reform in the UK. As Pollitt et al. (1998: 34) note, while 'the history of public management reforms...contains its fair share of twists, turns and ex-post rationalisation', there has been 'a certain consistency and continuity in the objectives'. This continuity, we suggest, is especially marked where the management restructuring of professional services is concerned. Although governments have not produced detailed blue prints for such change (Harrison and Wood, 1999) one can identify a number of recurrent themes and objectives.

In seeking to generalise about these 'objectives' we would draw attention to four main issues. First is the idea of creating strong management roles and functions within professional services. Second is the demand for better systems of cost control. Third has been the emphasis on performance management. Finally, there have been more general calls for change in organisational culture.

Empowering managers

A key aim of government policy since the early 1980s (and, it might be argued, much earlier) has been to develop strong executive management roles within professional services and promote 'more visible, active and individualistic forms of leadership' (Ferlie et al., 1996). The message has been that management, as a discrete activity, is important in determining the effectiveness of public services. More attention therefore had to be given to the creation of 'an active managerial function' specialising in 'the organisation and co-ordination of services and the consideration of efficiency in service delivery' (Ackroyd, 1992: 342). It was also considered necessary to strengthen the executive authority, or 'right to manage', of these managers. Instead of acting as the passive custodians of services controlled by front line staff, they should determine policy goals and actively seek to implement them. As Pollitt (1993: 131) suggests, 'managerialists conceive of management itself as the guardian of the overall purposes of the organisation'. As such, it is through the agency of managers rather than professionals that services needed to be delivered.

Of course, introducing this kind of management involves the development of groups of people willing and able to exercise such powers and claim legitimacy for their actions. One way of doing this is to recruit a new cadre of employees to do managerial work, and to give them the control over resources and the powers they need to displace other groups from authority or modify their existing jurisdictions. As we shall see in Chapter 4 such a strategy was adopted in health. Following the Griffiths report (1983) control over hospital administration (above all finance) was transferred from committees to general managers, a majority of whom were drawn from outside the ranks of the health professions.

By contrast, in most other areas (and to some extent in health) the emphasis has been more on strengthening management functions within the existing professional hierarchy. Here the expectation is that senior (and perhaps middle ranking) professionals will adopt a managerial outlook, focusing on the achievement of 'corporate success' rather than on the maintenance of customary modes of provision (Flynn, 1999: 25). Change in these services meant extending the 'management component' of professional jobs with more time devoted to tasks such as staff appraisal, planning and the administration of budgets (Causor and Exworthy, 1999: 98). Finally, there has been a growing emphasis on management training and development. A recurring theme in policy is that management represents 'a separate type of expertise' (Hugman, 1998: 186), one that senior professionals must acquire if they are to run their organisations effectively (also see Hanlon (1998: 50)).

Financial control

A second prominent theme in policy over the past two decades is the emphasis on financial control. As we noted earlier, this was especially the case under the 1979–97 Conservative governments. According to Pollitt (1993: 49), in the 1980s a key objective was to improve the 'productivity' of services 'so that their quality can be maintained or even increased while the total resources devoted to them is held down'. After 1997 the rhetoric of policy shifted more towards the idea of modernising public services, improving their quality and 'longer-term effectiveness' (Newman, 2000: 47). But it is clear that under New Labour, 'the momentum of restructuring, cost control and performance indicators' remains important (Webb, 1999: 751–2).

One way these objectives were pursued is through the imposition of 'cash limiting budgeting' across UK public services (Tonge and Horton, 1996). Beyond this, more radical change was sought in the way resources are managed by professionals at operational levels. According to Hood (1995: 96) a key goal has been to achieve greater 'discipline and frugality in resource use'. This, in turn, implies a wider shift in the nature of professional decision-making, with more weight given to questions of efficiency and cost effectiveness. Increasingly the demand has been for 'operational priorities' to be 're-focused around cost and performance rather than equity and social impact as in the past' (Colling, 2001: 604).

In order to achieve this transformation, policy makers advocated a number of changes in the way resources are managed and deployed in professional services. First is the focus on developing 'more elaborate cost and information systems' (Ferlie et al., 1996). Initially the purpose of these systems was simply to monitor resource use. The aim however has also been to extend 'cost categorisation into areas where costs were previously aggregated, pooled or undefined' (Hood, 1995: 93). This, it is assumed, will lead to wider shifts in practice, forcing professionals to focus more on the financial implications of their work.

A further set of changes relate to the internal organisation of professional services. A recurring theme in policy is the demand for greater decentralisation of budgets to lower-level professionals or managers of cost centres (Keen, 1996). Linked to this is the goal of reconstructing professional organisations as internal trading systems in which sub units or departments buy and sell from each other (du Gay and Salaman, 1992; Colling, 1999). Ultimately such change means replacing 'traditional fiduciary relationships' with 'contractual ones...between purchasers and providers, based on price, quality and volume' (Farnham and Horton, 1996a: 260).

Performance management

A third objective of reform has been to extend performance management (Farnham and Horton, 1996b; Hoggett, 1996; Heery, 1998; Waine, 2000). Interest in performance management emerged in the early 1980s and was central to the policy of restructuring in health (Griffiths), higher education and local government (Day and Klein, 1990). More recently, under New Labour, these ideas featured prominently in policies such as Best Value (Geddes, 2001; Martin, 2000), Comprehensive Performance Assessment and clinical governance (Dawson and Dargie, 2002). As one recent policy document states, 'Systematic performance management is the key to achievement in organisations' (DfEE, 1999, para 4).

According to Hood (1995: 107) underpinning performance management is the 'idea (or ideology) of homeostatic control'. Implied is a mode of organising in which there is a 'clarification of goals and missions in advance, and then building the accountability systems in relation to those present goals' (ibid). The logic of performance management is therefore quite different to that underpinning the custodial modes of professional organisation described in Chapter 2. The focus is on management groups at the 'strategic apex' unilaterally determining policy goals and on these being cascaded down to operational levels (Waine, 2000: 244). Rather than driven by local professional concerns professional services are to be managed according to wider corporate strategies and goals that are defined centrally.

A number of benefits are believed to follow from the application of this approach to professional services. First is the idea that performance management will lead to a pattern of provision that is less operationally driven and more focused on 'core business' (Clarke and Newman, 1997: 78). This, in turn, implies a shift in the capabilities of professional organisations. Rather than being 'administrative, implementing legally prescribed services', they would become 'governmental, combining packages of services and interventions in a strategic fashion' (Greenwood and Hinings, 1993: 1064). The focus would no longer be on maintaining customary modes of provision, but on responding to changing conditions and user needs (as defined by managers).

Second, performance management is seen to offer a framework through which the practices of front line professionals (and indeed, of their organisations more generally (Sanderson, 2001)) can be more effectively controlled and directed (Waine, 2000). According to Mabey and Salaman (1998: 149):

> performance management advocates the formation of a system for managing human resources which generates personal goals from wider strategic objectives, provides information on the extent to which contributions are being made to these objectives, and supplies a means of auditing the process links which deliver the contribution.

Implied is that professional activities become increasingly bounded and defined by targets and goals that are determined centrally. The emphasis is on 'closing off ...indeterminate and open-ended features of professional practice, in order to conform with broader corporate goals and resource constraints' (Flynn, 1999: 35). Also implied is a shift in the way this work is externally monitored and supervised (Causor and Exworthy, 1999). Managers, it is argued, should encourage a more 'judgemental' (Townley, 1997) and less collegial, or supportive approach towards performance appraisal.

Changing culture

The final theme that has recurred in policy over the past two decades is that of achieving some shift in values. According to Ferlie et al. (1996: 14) 'explicit attempts to secure cultural change' through the 'projection of a top-down vision...' were viewed as crucial to the management reform agenda, especially during the 1990s. More recently, this goal has been given added emphasis with New Labour's strategy of modernising public services (Cabinet Office, 1999; Office of Public Service Reform, 2003).

Most agree that the thrust of policy has been to achieve a long-term shift in values and identities of welfare professions (Halford and Leonard, 1999; Hanlon, 1998). This meant moving from 'traditional public service values to ones attuned to the market, business and entrepreneurial values of the "new" public service model' (Farnham and Horton, 1996a: 267). Added to this is the goal of producing stronger identifications amongst professional groups towards their own employing organisations (Foster and Wilding, 2000, Laffin, 1998). According to Keen and Scase (1998: 12), this involved limiting (if not completely eroding):

> the 'cosmopolitan' orientation of professional staff to their national/professional association ethics and values in favour of the adoption of a 'local' orientation to the particular service policies and objectives of the professional's own employing authority.

Considerable attention has therefore been paid to wider goals of culture change. Only through such change, it has been argued, will more concrete and enduring shifts in management practice and organisation be achieved.

To summarise, one can generalise about certain themes and objectives that have dominated policy making since the early 1980s. Taken together these proposals amount to a qualitatively different mode of organising provision to the custodial pattern described in Chapter 2. The thrust of change has been to move from a 'bureau professional' to a 'managerial mode of coordination' (Clarke and Newman, 1997: 6). Implied by this are new structures and systems of decision-making. But also important is the intended shift in goals and priorities. In future, public organisations are to be driven by 'sigma-type values' emphasising the need to match resources to tasks, focusing on avoiding waste and increasing efficiency (Hood, 1991).

The process of change

Now that the broad objectives of reform have been outlined, we turn to the question of *how* governments in the UK sought to implement change. In doing so we draw attention to two main points. First, a key feature of change in the UK over the past two decades is that it has been 'strongly driven from the top' (Pollitt and Boukaert, 2000: 274). By contrast with other developed countries, or even earlier waves of restructuring in the UK (Hinings and Greenwood, 1988), the role of central government has been strongly interventionist and prescriptive (Flynn, 2000). This was especially true under the Conservatives (Rhodes, 1997a). As noted earlier the tendency was for policies to be formulated and imposed with only minimal consultation. By contrast, under New Labour, there are signs of a more conciliatory approach. Politicians it seems are now more aware of the need to 'win acceptance of the "necessity", or at least the inevitability, of change' (Martin, 2002: 137). But even this shift must not be exaggerated. New Labour like its predecessor has continued to be 'highly interventionist' and keen to monitor compliance with top down policy goals (Bach, 2002: 326).

Secondly, one should note the wide variety of mechanisms through which governments in the UK sought to implement change. There have been attempts to directly impose policy through core legislation and ministerial pronouncements (Ferlie and Fitzgerald, 2000). Early examples of this include moves to insert general management within the NHS following the Griffiths report and major legislation in the late 1980s aimed at restructuring health, social care and education. More recently is the prescription of new management arrangements in the NHS (clinical governance) and the imposition of performance related pay in schools. There have therefore been legal obligations to change management practice. While government often stopped short at specifying detailed blue prints a strong element of coercion has nevertheless been present.

Added to this have been isomorphic demands for change in UK public services (DiMaggio and Powell, 1991). According to Farnham and Horton (1996a: 321), since the early 1980s 'new managerialist ideas have become common currency and practice within the public services...the staple diet provided by internal and external management training courses'. A main source of such ideas (at least initially) was guidance produced and disseminated by central government and its various agencies. A key role was played, for example, by evaluative agencies such as the Audit Commission, SSI and, more recently, Ofsted and the Commission for Health Improvement (CHI) (established in 1999) (Day and Klein, 1990; Power, 1997). Increasingly these bodies saw themselves 'not simply as advisors, auditors or monitors but also as promoters of change' (Henkel, 1991: 133). While initially this took the form of persuasion – or 'covert ideological manipulation' (Isaac-Henry and Painter, 1991: 73) – by the late 1990s a more coercive element was introduced (Sanderson, 2001). Those organisations that fail to meet national targets are now more likely to be identified and ultimately subjected to direct intervention or 'special measures' (Colling, 2001: 606).

Calls for management change did not originate exclusively from government. Professional groups were also involved not least in the process of dissemination. Examples of this date back to the mid 1980s and include initiatives such as the Jarrett report (1985) in higher education and Project 2000 in nursing (Witz, 1994). These and other initiatives represent attempts by professional groups, or elite interests within them, to engage with and promote a management agenda. As such they served to increase the legitimacy of management reform and produce normative as well as coercive isomorphic demands (Powell et al., 1999). However, one should not overstate these tendencies (Kirkpatrick and Ackroyd, 2003a). In many areas the engagement of professional groups with management concerns was pragmatic, driven more by a desire to pre-empt further government intervention than by genuine enthusiasm. It should also be noted that in many cases the role of professional associations has been to substantially negotiate or even water down proposals for management reform (see, for example, Townley, 1997).

A final source of pressure for change is that which arose from wider processes of restructuring of public services after 1990. As we shall see, the nature and pace of this restructuring varied greatly between service areas. However, two broad tendencies can be noted. First has been a process described by Hood (1991) as 'disaggregation'. This refers to the break up of large public service bureaucracies into smaller, quasi autonomous 'corporatised units' such as schools, FE colleges, trust hospitals or housing associations (Hood, 1991: 5; Kessler and Purcell, 1996: 210). As a result of this process discreet organisations were created and control was transferred from local politicians to 'non elected elites' of managers (Ferlie et al., 1996). Various responsibilities for budgets, policy implementation and employment relations were also decentralised (Kessler et al., 2000).

A second tendency has been a shift in the way resources are allocated to these devolved services. Under the Conservatives, in particular, attention focused on the creation of market like relationships, forcing provider units to compete for contracts, clients or budgets (see Hoggett (1996) for a full description).

This restructuring, it is often argued, acted as a powerful galvanising force for change. Across public services the result was to clarify the management roles of senior professionals and to implicate them more fully in the running of their organisations (Flynn, 1999). Restructuring increased the accountability of these groups, to some extent giving them little choice but to become (or at least appear to become) more overtly managerial. According to Pollitt et al. (1998: 163):

> as local service-providing units become more autonomous there seems to have been a general acceptance that they needed strong central leadership if they were to remain 'afloat' in the unchartered but potentially competitive waters of quasi markets...there was a recognition that greater external freedom implied tighter internal control.

One might say therefore that the process of restructuring created incentives, both positive and negative, for senior professional groups to embrace management reform (Laffin, 1998b). However, once again, it is important not to overstate this. As we shall see, the extent to which such pressures for change were created varied a great deal both within and between public services. One should also note that policy shifts under the current (New Labour) government may have further altered or complicated this picture. Although New Labour retained many of the devolved structures established under the Conservatives, less emphasis has subsequently been placed on the use of competitive 'markets' as a mechanism for allocating resources (Colling, 2001).

Matters arising

In much of the recent literature there is a tendency to assume that, as a consequence of these pressures, the agenda of reforming public management has been largely successful. This view is especially marked in practitioner literature (Hood, 1998) but is not exclusive to it. Even in more critical accounts, it is often argued that the forces of change now outweigh those of inertia and resistance. Looking more closely at this literature, four main changes are said to have occurred.

First, is a shift in the roles and identities of senior and middle ranking professionals. Across public services, it is argued, these groups now devote more time to tasks that are explicitly managerial, such as controlling budgets and supervising staff. Linked to this have been shifts in values and commitments. Senior professionals are said to now increasingly identify with management concerns and priorities (Hugman, 1998: 186–87). Indeed, in some cases, professionals have actively engaged with the changes, regarding them as a source of liberation and enhanced power (Pollitt, 1993: 82). Clarke (1998: 242), for example notes how: 'the appeal of the new managerialism…was that it offered both the prospect of being able to "get on with what really matters" …instead of being held back by inappropriate forms of organisation…'. More generally it is argued that professionals are now more concerned with the acquisition of 'managerial assets' to enhance their influence and career prospects (Exworthy and Halford, 1999b: 134; Hanlon, 1998).

It is often recognised that the transition to hybrid professional manager roles is a complex and unstable process (Clarke and Newman, 1997: 83; Ferlie et al., 1996: 193). Groups such as school head teachers may retain their professional and caring values but apply them to their managerial roles (Fergusson, 2000). But, while such complexity is frequently acknowledged, more often than not it is assumed that management priorities will ultimately win out. The long-term trend is said to be towards greater internal stratification within the welfare professions (Exworthy and Halford, 1999a; Freidson, 1994). It is suggested that 'schisms' have emerged 'between "old style" professionals who used the language of welfare and care, and "new style" senior managers and professionals who use the language of markets and efficiency' (Webb, 1999: 757).

A second key theme noted in much of this literature concerns the implementation of new financial control systems. It is assumed that significant progress has been made in this area, with greater monitoring and devolution of budgets. There are also said to be important changes in the way services are delivered. For example, in health and social care, some note 'an explicit retreat from universalism' (Lewis and Glennerster, 1996: 201) with formal – managerially defined – procedures used to explicitly ration services. New accounting systems, many believe, are colonising professional work, leading, over time, to new mentalities, new incentives and perceptions of significance (Power, 1997; Broadbent and Laughlin, 2002). As Hugman (1998: 187) puts it: 'professional concerns with the social dimension of health and welfare have become subordinated to a particular type of economic thought'.

Thirdly, many assume there has been a step change in the capacity of senior managers to control professional work (Cutler and Waine, 1994; Sinclair et al., 1996). Frameworks of rules, targets and procedures now shape the content of this work. Front line practitioners are also more closely supervised than was the case before. According to Causor and Exworthy (1999: 85) a 'key function' of senior professionals is now to 'monitor (overtly or discreetly) the practice of other professionals, and to institute corrective action where it is deemed necessary'. It is therefore claimed that the new managerialism resulted in marked reductions in the autonomy of professionals (Lloyd and Siefert, 1994; Grimshaw, 1999; Foster and Hoggett, 1999). Those working in public services, the story goes, 'experienced "better management" as tighter control...' (Pollitt, 1993: 86).

Finally is the argument that processes of restructuring led to broader shifts in culture and values. This issue has already been discussed in relation to the shifting identifications of senior professionals and attitudes towards managing resources. But change is also thought to have occurred in professional orientations and loyalties more generally. Many argue that the process of marketisation (breaking public organisations into smaller units) led to a weakening of 'lateral solidarities' within the professions (Exworthy and Halford, 1999b: 132). This, in turn, may have served to undermine the cosmopolitan orientations of welfare professions, perhaps weakening their commitment to broader ideals of public service. Hoggett (1996: 27), for example, suggests, that a 'casualty' of restructuring 'would appear to be some kind of ethic (sometimes refereed to as "the public service ethic") which is also able to transcend the particularism of one's own situation'.

This brief account of change is compelling and it is likely to ring true for many practitioners. But, as we suggested in Chapter 1, it is not clear how far one can or should accept this version of events. While change has indeed occurred, there is a problem of assuming too readily that professional work itself has been transformed. There is a risk of adopting a 'linear metaphor' to describe change (Hood, 1998), of conflating the 'descriptive and normative aspects' of NPM and treating the claims of it's advocates 'as though they describe new realities...' (Clarke et al., 2000: 7).

An obvious problem here is that commentators overlook or down-play the resilience of professional modes of organising and their capac-ity to mediate or deflect change (Hinings et al., 1991; Mintzberg, 1993) because this is what they expect to see. As we hinted in Chapter 1 these organisations are not passive instruments of policy. It cannot be assumed that whatever new policies were deemed necessary were simply translated into new patterns of action as was required by policy makers. The capacity of professions to negotiate or 'capture' change in ways that minimise disturbance to their day-to-day activities should not be under-estimated.

A further difficulty with the notion of transformation is that it encourages us to gloss over variations in management change across public services. One might expect there to be variation in outcomes because of the distinctive patterns of professional organisation that management reforms worked against. As we saw in Chapter 2, struc-tural differences existed between public services in the UK. In some areas – for example, in social care and housing – professional work was already subject to some degree of management (or bureaucratic) regula-tion (Webb and Wistow, 1986). Beyond this are different service char-acteristics that might be important in shaping how professional groups respond to new policy initiatives. Public housing, for example, has always been provided alongside a large and vibrant private sector hous-ing market. This is in stark contrast to health, education and social care, all of which developed largely in isolation of market and private sector disciplines.

These observations call for a more thorough and comparative assess-ment of management restructuring and its consequences. Anticipating our conclusions a little, we suggest that the process of reform has been embattled, protracted and, even after more than two decades of effort, far from complete. Be that as it may, it is with the goal of examining this processes and the response to it that we now turn. Specifically we consider developments in three key sectors: health care, social services and housing. In each area similar themes and issues will be addressed. The proceeding chapters all begin with an overview of the policy context and the main factors that drove management reform. Following this each chapter presents evidence of how far change occurred, focusing on three main dimensions: the development of management roles and functions, shifts in the nature of control over front line work and changes in values and orientations. Finally, in the concluding chapter we make a broader assessment of restructuring and its consequences.

4

The National Health Service

In the fifth decade [of the history of the NHS] the health service was redefined in terms of what would be provided and how the provision was to be organised.... Managed care was introduced. But the basic problem of rationing care persisted. Cash limits on purchasing authorities and the continual pressure of efficiency savings limited the work that providers could do. By 1997, although special programmes had reduced the numbers of patients who waited more then a year for admission, waiting lists in general were lengthening, services were being cut and operations were being postponed nationwide. Consultants warned that during the winter months the NHS might be reduced to treating emergencies only, if underfunding were not remedied. The NHS was facing its worst financial crisis for a decade and was heading for financial meltdown. The reforms had not solved the basic NHS dilemma.... (Rivett, 1997: 453–4).

The focus of this chapter is on the development of new management systems and practices and their effects on the professions within the National Health Service (NHS). In some ways this is a daunting task. The NHS has been cited as the largest employer in Europe, and, with total employees well over one million in recent decades, this is entirely plausible.[1] Furthermore, the health service is far from unitary, for much of its history being split into a number of different areas of activity and semi-autonomous services. General practitioner services have always been provided separately from hospital care, and the local authorities for a long time were responsible for some personal health services within the system. Within hospitals themselves, there have been traditional differences between the district hospitals, specialist hospitals and teaching hospitals. In addition, each individual institution within the system has enjoyed considerable clinical and operating autonomy, and has often developed a distinctive culture. Thus, although as we shall see, there have been elements of centralisation and bureaucracy within the NHS, it would be wrong to think of it as being a monolith (Klein, 1995; Rivett, 1997). This remains true despite concerted attempts at rationalising and unifying the service, especially in the last two decades.

In the following account, we will consider the scope and nature of government policies concerning (and action towards) the NHS as a whole; but it is unrealistic to analyse and account for the effects of these actions on all parts of the health care system. To give an account of effects of policy that has adequate depth, in what follows attention will be mainly focused what has happened in the hospitals in the last twenty-five years. Within this, we will mainly consider developments in hospitals providing acute services. What will be said here does relate, to some extent, to specialist hospitals and there will be some asides and comments on other areas of the NHS. But, in order to simplify the discussion, the impact of management change is considered mainly in the context of the effects of policy on acute hospitals. This still makes the total population to which this analysis relates, considerable; potentially including more than three hundred thousand nurses and some seventy thousand doctors. As will be suggested, change in the organisation of hospitals has been considerable at every level: from the typical structure of the hospital itself, to the pattern of the planning and funding of provision and the internal processes of organising for the delivery of hospital care.

In this chapter, as in the other substantive chapters, which follow, we are concerned with the question of the extent to which there has been fundamental change, and if not what the limitations on this actually are. In the case of the NHS, the efforts that have gone into inducing change in the direction of a managed service have been substantial. These efforts have now lasted more than two decades, and the human and the financial costs have been large. Even after twenty-five years of reforms, few would argue that there are no problems left, or that there is little more to be done. Change has been painfully slow and often traumatic.

To give our account of what has happened in the NHS hospitals, this chapter is divided into four main sections. First we provide background information on the formation of the NHS and the professional groups that were active within it. We argue that the doctors were in a very secure position from the inception of the NHS hospitals, and, basically, their professional judgement decided what form hospital treatments took. Aided by nurses, this group decided on and implemented clinical and much other policy within hospitals. Secondly, we turn our attention to the broad policy context, by which we mean the changing political social and economic circumstances in which government-made decisions about the need for change and the decision to introduce more managed delivery of hospital care. In the circumstances, the decision to introduce a managed mode of service delivery, made at the beginning of the 1980's, seemed to be both rational and not too difficult to achieve. The remainder of the chapter, then, focuses on the assessment of change. Here three issues are considered: new forms of operational and financial control and the response of professional groups. In fact, the plan to change from administered services to managed ones, proved much more difficult than was at first envisaged because making this transition necessarily alters the division of labour between occupations and the balance of power between them. Finally, in the concluding sections, some of the more general consequences of restructuring will be addressed.

Background

At the turn of the millenium, the NHS had been in existence for a little more than fifty years. Among the publications to celebrate its 50th anniversary in 1998, the NHS produced a short history of the service to date (Timmins, 1998; for a much longer and more adequate account of the history see Rivett, 1997). The booklet by Timmins gives an overview of the NHS and its main developments in summary form. The picture portrayed is one of a system in constant change, but in fact there was, for a long period after its inception in 1948, much continuity. If there was change for the thirty years after 1948, it was mainly towards the consolidation of the system that had been established in the Act founding the NHS in that year, when the main features of the post-war health service were put in place.

Until World War II, a system of health care provision in Britain had developed but it was based entirely on local initiatives and private provision. During the Second World War, in which there were mass civilian casualties, government took steps to rationalise and control medical services for the duration of the hostilities. Before this development, health care provision had basically two bases and points of growth: first, there were local practices developed by individual doctors (which subsequently became GP services under the NHS), and a system of local (municipal and 'voluntary') hospitals which had gradually emerged, many tracing their origins from the common workhouses originally established for the relief of poverty (Abel-Smith, 1964). An emerging network of hospital institutions was not encouraged by legislation in the nineteenth century, and rather little in the first half of the twentieth. Local authorities were not prevented from organising and providing municipal medical services in hospitals, but they mainly saw their role as organising local initiatives and providing some subsidy (Abel-Smith, 1964). However, from as early as the middle of the 1920's, medical services had been removed from the emerging national insurance system, necessitating subsidies from general public funds. This laid the foundations for the NHS which features universal health care provision, free at the point of delivery.

As has been implied, the post-war NHS involved the continuation of the wartime pattern of provision in which government had taken over general control of the existing health care system. The National Health Service Act of 1948, provided, in effect, for the existing hospitals, their premises and other assets, to be nationalised. From that point on they were to be administered by regional hospital boards under the general direction of the Minister of Health. Local political interests would be served by hospitals being constituted as boards of governors of hospitals. As is well known, perhaps the most important source of difficulty at the formation of the NHS was accommodating the interests of the doctors, many of whom saw themselves as potentially being made into salaried employees of the state. Hospital consultants were a source of particular problems, and their complicity in the new system was only achieved at considerable cost (Foot, 1975; Klein, 1989: 17–25). It is surprising to find how hostile doctors were to the idea of a national system, given how strongly they supported the NHS in later decades. The agreement of the consultants was achieved at the cost of allowing them to continue with private practice (including the use of NHS hospital beds for this) and of paying them well for the numbers of patients seen under the auspices of the NHS. In addition, there was a system of distinction awards that produced high remuneration for senior consultants and the possibility of important roles advising on the organisation of hospitals.

These points illustrate the power and independence of the hospital doctors at the inception of the NHS. It is difficult to exaggerate the extent of their influence. Hospital specialists were not responsible to hospital Management Committees, but were contracted by regional hospital boards. They were thus beyond the day to day control of hospital administrators and even of the boards of governors of the hospitals in which they worked. Despite this, and because of their undoubted importance to the hospitals, senior consultants were extensively co-opted onto hospital boards and were extremely influential in determining local policies and priorities. In addition, the practical cooperative alliance that the doctors had worked out with the nurses prior to nationalisation, allowed for a system in which professional power was strong in hospitals themselves from the outset.

The hospitals represent the strongest version of custodial model of management described in Chapter 2, in which the delivery of services is controlled by professionals and the management (which is best called administration in this context) was subordinated to professional objectives and decision-making. Indeed, the pattern of practical organisation of hospitals has been characterised by Klein as the 'workers' cooperative', implying that producers were in power (Klein, 1989). During the early period, from 1948–1974, this is an accurate description to the extent that, although there were clearly both bureaucratic elements in the administration (comprised by the ministry, the regional boards and the local administrative apparatus in hospitals themselves) and political influences (contributed by local elites being prominent in the management committees) professional power was pre-eminently strong. (For a contemporary analysis, see Davies and Francis, 1976). The clinicians were the dominant occupation, and their ideas and priorities overrode other concerns. Political influences, though present at the regional and local level, were distinctly limited, leaving the bureaucratic machine, which was largely decentralised to regions, as the most obvious restriction on professional priorities.

One indication of the limitations of custodial management in the NHS was that there were large imbalances in the state support given to different regions. This was because the proportion of funds allocated reflected the historical level of provision, which in turn reflected the existing infrastructure such as the numbers of hospitals and their capacity, rather than the needs of the population. Seeing their interests mainly in terms of the use made of the resources allocated, custodial management by the senior clinicians did not address this kind of issue. It took a long time for this kind of variability to be sorted out, and some would argue it has not yet been so, as controversy over inequalities of provision in different areas persists. Yet despite this kind of anomaly, for a long time in the post-war period, the British NHS as a whole was considered to be an outstanding success. It provided high quality and entirely free medical services to a large population, and was widely admired.

It is an interesting question as to why the system, with all its inconsistencies and lack of rationalisation, worked so well. This was not effectively analysed at the time and has not been since. A good part of the answer must be that it relied on agreement between parties to work. There was a very effective division of labour between doctors and nurses, and, at the organisational level, little controversy about the way health care should be organised. The district general hospital (DGH), in which a broad spectrum of general and specialist hospital services were provided to most localities, was widely adopted as the model for the provision of hospital services. This worked in tandem with an emerging system of increasingly national specialist and teaching hospitals, which were not under the control of regional hospital boards.

In 1974 a further attempt was made to reform this system and finally consolidate it. The Porritt report, first produced in 1962, eventually resulted in large-scale reorganisation of the administrative structure more than a decade later. The administration of the local authorities (and their responsibility for ancillary services), was absorbed into regional structures of the NHS, and these were constituted as regional health authorities (RHA's), responsible for all services, i.e. all hospital *and* community services. Below this was a new tier constituted by the area health authority (AHA). In England, 90 AHA's were formed with boundaries coterminous with local government boundaries. Below this a lowest tier of administration was added at the district level for hospital administration, in the shape of the district health authority (DHA). Community health councils (CHC's) were also introduced at this stage with responsibilities to represent the consumer. In short, the administrative system became more elaborate under the 1974 reforms and included extensive consultative mechanisms.

The developing policy context

With the benefit of hindsight, some of the assumptions that underwrote the original commissioning of the NHS were extremely naïve. It seems to have been assumed that the amount of illness in the national community was more or less finite and that, therefore, the complete health of the citizenry was achievable by the adequate provision of medical services. What this reckoned without, of course, are factors of which we are now much more aware and which have rendered the task of providing health care anything but limited.

Firstly, there is the fact that medical knowledge is constantly being improved and the range of illnesses and conditions that are susceptible of effective treatment is constantly increasing. A second and related point concerns the technologisation of health care, in which the technologies and medicines available for diagnosis and treatment have become the stock in trade of new industries driven by profit orientated business corporations. The NHS was, of course, a secure market for drugs and other medical technology, providing a steady source of profit for pharmaceutical companies. The indirect support for these markets by the NHS has been a source of hidden subsidy for such companies, and helps to explain why Britain is the home of some of the largest pharmaceutical companies in the world. Third, and in some ways most important, is the point that standards of acceptable health are not absolute but conventional. Medical conditions that would have been accepted as inevitable and in some sense acceptable are now not. The public is becoming consumerist in its attitude to health matters and the medical profession is being called on to medicalise and offer solutions to problems not considered as remotely 'medical' fifty years ago. One might instance the medicalisation of contraception and infertility and the problems associated with the over and under indulgency in food.

As earlier chapters have argued, concern about the welfare state including the NHS began to mount at the end of the nineteen seventies. By that time, the service had been in existence for thirty years. It is not as if there were no problems until this point, but it was generally thought that they were predictable and soluble by improving existing arrangements. A key problem that surfaced at this time was the spiralling costs of the health service. Custodial arrangements of course, are not effective in limiting costs, in that professional judgements about what is required to be done for each patient are pre-eminent. In these circumstances, the administration is either entirely subservient to the superior status and judgement of the professionals, as was the case in the NHS, or as former professionals themselves, were sympathetic to their concerns. Given what has been said about the increasing application of technology to, and the medicalisation of, health problems, the costs of medical provision increased greatly. In the financial year 1975/76, real expenditure on the NHS exceeded 5 per cent of GDP for the first time, a proportion that governments struggled to reduce throughout the seventies and eighties. Against a background of mounting economic unrest and political pressure, the Labour administration of 1974–79 had allowed an annual growth in expenditure on the NHS to grow in real terms by 5.3 per cent per annum. The Conservative administration of 1979 pinned this back to 2.9 per cent between 1979 and 1983, and reduced it further to an average of 2.3 per cent from 1983 to 1987. (Le Grand and Vizard, 1998: 86).

Alongside the view that expenditure on the NHS was potentially, if not actually, out of control, was an awakening of consumers' interest in the service. Public opinion was increasingly critical of the autonomy of the professionals in making decisions about health policy. This was a note that the new Conservative administration sounded, and has been a consistent theme of government since the early eighties. The new government's first consultative paper on the NHS was called 'Patients First' (HMSO, 1979). In addition, the conviction soon formed that the solution to the problems of increasing costs combined with falling satisfaction levels could be effectively met by introducing management practices from the private sector. The NHS Management Enquiry, initiated in 1982, was quite unlike any previous exercise aimed at major reforms. Under the chairmanship of Roy Griffiths, a small group of business people came to an analysis of the ills of the Service very quickly, and made some simple and explicit recommendations. This was not any protracted Royal Commission, but an investigation undertaken by a group who were not disposed to recognise the elaborate arrangements for consultation (and what we have called custodial management) as acceptable, still less as a kind of management. In Griffiths' view, the problem of the NHS was simple: there was no one in charge of it.[2]

Towards managed services

As has been suggested, the last few years of the nineteen seventies was a turning point. Along with the change of government, there was a decisive change in priorities. It was probably not simple prejudice that turned the new government towards an idea of direction through management. In a context of rising inflation and industrial strife (see Chapter 3) the idea that the effective co-ordination of anything could be contrived through consensus, seemed increasingly implausible. The NHS was seen as inefficient. It was soon considered, for a variety of reasons, among them the finding that there were marked variations in expenditure and measured effectiveness that the NHS was in urgent need of reform. As a result, consensus management was abolished and the very idea is now a historical curiosity.

It is not clear that, through the nineteen eighties, there was a dramatic decline in the trust of the public in the health professionals. If there was someone to blame, it was wasteful bureaucrats rather than doctors and nurses. Certainly, the government (and, increasingly, the public) were concerned about such things as the length of hospital waiting lists, the number of delayed discharges, ambulance response times and so on. In these failures to deliver, the lack of regulation of professionals was seen, by government as key part of the problem. However, initially at least, the policy of government was not to increase direct state control of activities, but to limit the size of budgets and increase the responsibility of decision makers, so that medical services would be more effectively self-regulating. Introducing a new model of management was increasingly seen to be the way to do this. Once started on this path, however, all the impedimenta of the new public management (NPM) were progressively applied in the NHS. Audits, benchmarking, performance measurement and performance appraisal, have been major features of the new management regime. Initially, protocols for imposing standards of practice were not envisaged, but, at a later stage, they were both envisaged and imposed.

In retrospect, the diagnosis of 'what went wrong' when it was made in the early nineteen eighties, though vociferous and concerted, was unimpressive. It identified as problems for the system many of the features – such as professional autonomy – which were clearly contributory to success. It is a paradox of public goods that the more effective they are, the more they are consumed, leading to them being overstretched. It is certainly true that, in many ways, the problems of the NHS were those induced by success rather than by failure. This is a conclusion that does not seem to have occurred at the time.

General management

Within months of taking office, the first Thatcher administration repudiated the idea of a centrally planned and administered NHS in favour of a declared policy of managed localism (Klein, 1995: 124–26; Pollitt, 1993: 68–9). The development of a new kind of approach to the management of the NHS – this time more authoritarian in character – was first proposed in the early nineteen eighties. The principal recommendation of the NHS Management Enquiry under Griffiths was that 'general management' should be introduced into the NHS in order to control it. A clear management hierarchy was to be established at the centre, and in hospitals and there was to be a 'chain of accountability' from the centre to the local institutions. Crucially, to make such a system work it was recognised that clinicians must be involved in management by being made to be financially accountable for their activities. To ensure this, as Griffiths clearly envisages, the clinicians and other NHS staff would have to be subordinated to the direction of general managers (Harrison et al., 1992).

A consequence of the Griffiths reforms was that a distinctive kind of structure and pattern of managerial activities gradually emerged within the NHS. The basic concern was (and is) for financial account-ability: budgets would have to be set within expenditure levels fixed by the central government. The management hierarchy would be ac-countable for seeing that budgets were not exceeded and that the same or an increasing amount of service should be obtained from resources.[3] This type of management would take place with a context of increas-ing surveillance of performance standards in service delivery. Manage-ment, in this definition, had political backing for its authority and financial sanctions. Initially, the main responsibility of managers was keeping more effective track of the costs of hospital care and in increas-ing the ratio of quantified benefits per unit of cost (Coombs and Cooper, 1992; Harrison and Pollitt, 1994).

Clearly this whole notion could not work unless clinicians would also take responsibility for the amount of care given within their own budgets. A crucial matter was, therefore, what motivation clinicians might find for such cooperation (Hunter, 1992). At the institutional level, in the hospital trust or fund-holding general practice, managers are responsible for the use of resources within a framework of externally set budgets and funding rules. Monitoring or regulating quality is not integral to this kind of management, but could be and was added as an additional responsibility. Essentially this is the system we now have, and it is one that is vulnerable to fluctuations in the level of funding and variations in the motivation of clinicians. Accommodating to this system has been the source of many subsequent problems.

In the 1980s, emphasis was placed firmly on the rapid development of financially responsible management. Unlike any other major public services (including housing and social care), the way chosen for deliv-ering this type of management involved recruiting a new cadre of managers, as well as attempting to develop a distinctive rhetoric and expertise. In the NHS, the new managers were not to be professionals re-badged as managers. However the NHS cadre did have a particular origin, which also shaped its identity and characteristic practices. Klein (1989) was one of the first to recognise the pattern of recruitment to the new management. He wrote: 'Everywhere at every level, new managers were appointed: some brought from industry and the armed services, but primarily they were old style administrators reborn as managers, with a sprinkling of doctors and nurses' (Klein, 1989: 67). Administrators were the natural candidates for managerial posts as they knew the NHS, but they were not likely to be automatically respected by senior doctors.

The internal market

In the late 1980s establishing a general management cadre was followed by a series of institutional developments designed to establish an internal market as an additional mechanism for limiting expenditure and combining this with some kind of quality control. The key development involved separating out agencies within the system into those buying hospital services (GP's and Health Authorities), from those supplying them hospitals which were to become increasingly autonomous as 'hospital trusts' (HTs). Thus, a new stage of managerial development was entered at the end of the eighties. The White Paper, *Working for Patients* (1989), was followed by the NHS and Community Care Act, 1990. It was these changes which brought in the internal market. This involved introduction of the purchaser/provider split with hospitals and community services able to partially opt out of DHA control and become HTs. Similarly, GP's were offered the possibility to become fund-holders, thereby controlling the budget they had to purchase elective surgery, outpatient consultations, community care and pathology. Further changes to the structure of the administration followed with the Health Authorities Act, 1995. This established a system of more centralised management through the NHS Management Executive with regional offices and one hundred new health authorities (Kitchener, 1998).

Under this arrangement, HTs became relatively independent with increased powers. The newly created bodies had considerably more freedom and power than hitherto. They were free to settle pay (mainly for non professional groups), to dispose of assets, to borrow and to take control of their affairs (Carr, 1999; Bach, 1999b). In short, these new freedoms closely mirrored those in the private sector, where the important factor determining operations is the bottom line. The fact remains, however, that the HTs did not operate with the freedoms of the private sector (Kessler et al., 2000; Pollitt et al., 1998). They remained constrained and controlled by the framework of policy and standards of performance; and furthermore, what constituted the bottom line was not always clear. Nonetheless, for those HTs able to meet performance standards and which recorded high performance against the available benchmarks, the rewards could be good, both in terms of the operating autonomy allowed to managers and the pay and conditions of senior doctors. By opening out this space for cooperation, government thought it could deal with the problem of motivating professionals. And of course this is, to a considerable extent correct. But what happens if budgets are exceeded and the expected targets are not met?

The impact of NPM on the NHS is commonly associated with developments occurring in the early 1990's and, in particular, the introduction of the internal or quasi market described above. But this is incorrect, as there is much continuity in practice from the early 1980's. Historically, any control of doctors' performance had to take the form of retrospective evaluation and accountability was highly fragmented and remote. Operational management, since the reforms of the eighties had sought, not always effectively, to impose some financial discipline whilst trying to produce more output. The development of the quasi market was just another way to attempt to apply financial discipline. What this meant, however, was that NHS managers had to become concerned with the use of contracts as an additional consideration when charged with working within cost parameters. But, it often proved difficult to agree measures of performance to be included in contracts that adequately reflected the tasks to be done and the results to be achieved. Protocols specifying the services that hospitals will provide, were difficult to formulate as what counts as a treatment has to be standardised. The purchaser was supposed to be reflecting the interests of the customer, but it was often unclear exactly whose interest the purchase was representing (Baggott, 1997; Bennett and Ferlie, 1996).

Thus, with purchaser/provider splits, those responsible for service provision gained more autonomy thus making accountability, in some ways, more difficult. Health care providers are invariably more technically competent than purchasers and purchasers can only specify the nature of their demands in general terms. Effective contracting can only proceed by allowing marginal variations in activity levels with the ex-post analysis of non-elective and other unanticipated aspects of workload. The NHS is, after all, a demand led service, and a purchaser can never control adequately when and where demand will be created. The fact of the matter is that the quasi-market is not a true market – it is a managed market and checks and balances are needed for accountability to be demonstrated (Le Grand and Bartlett, 1993). For some areas of provision, geriatric care being a good example, demand in one part of the public sector, such as the NHS, is heavily dependent on supply in another, such as social services. In short, it is highly doubtful whether the quasi market, in itself, ever imposed much in the way of effective discipline.

Developments – Post 1997

By the second half of the nineties it was clear that the NHS was in deep trouble again. As the quotation at the start of this chapter suggests, under-funding and the inability of the organisation to reduce backlogs of patients, led to widespread disquiet, and was a factor in the election victory by New Labour in 1997. Since New Labour came to power, there has been more generous and secure funding as well as other changes, but the general direction of policy has not deviated. The new government's 1997 White Paper, *The New NHS: Modern, Dependable* (HMSO, 1997) emphasised a commitment to making the existing system of provision more effective. In the new government's view there was a clear need to stabilise the basis of support for the system, and it instituted a more systematic basis for financial provision. To allow for more adequate planning, there would be three-year financial settlements, adequate ring-fenced 'modernisation' funds and guaranteed annual increases in expenditure. The internal market was seen as divisive and unhelpful and was supposedly abolished. Instead there was to be an emphasis on integrated care, accompanied by a new rhetoric of collaboration and partnership. However, the separation between demand and supply was retained in some key respects. Organisations purchasing services remain,[4] but, in place of contracts, there would be longer-term 'service agreements' between purchasers and providers. In many ways this might be regarded simply as recognition of the impracticality of contracting as a way of rationing care (Harrison, 1997).

The continuity of policy stands out even more clearly however, when we consider the enhanced functions allocated to management as a necessary accompaniment to the above changes of emphasis. In place of competition, enhanced efficiency was to be secured by management, through explicit attention to performance management. Accordingly the framework within which managers would be working was to be aligned to explicit and quantified performance indicators, within a 'performance framework'. The latter involved monitoring a set of discrete indicators that, taken together, would be used to assess the performance of a trust. In addition to this, concern for quality was made central to the management function for the first time. In a supplementary white paper (HMSO, 1998), attention to quality was to become an explicit duty of care alongside financial probity (Dawson and Dargie, 2002; Davies et al., 2001). Paralleling the performance framework, then, a quality framework was also introduced, detailing clear standards to be measured. However, quality indicators are not seen as being obligatory targets. Echoing earlier emphases, quality is seen to be more a matter of background concern than a benchmark by which performance should be tested. Quality is also regarded as primarily a matter for clinicians rather than managers. However the quality framework is seen as necessarily accompanied by making senior doctors more accountable. Accordingly the government introduced the concept and practice of 'clinical governance', which is thought of as bringing together standards of quality with performance management (Harrison, 2002).

Another emphasis of the new administration was to create or encourage larger trusts and purchasing organisations and through this to achieve economies of scale. Accompanying this has been a continued emphasis on the centralisation of the responsibilities of managers within trusts, and their overall oversight (and responsibility for) the activities of clinicians. The NHS executive, set up under the Griffiths reforms has not withered away, but the emphasis by this time was on gradual withdrawal of centralised direction where hospitals meet performance standards and efficiency benchmarks. These emphases are very explicit in the latest developments sponsored by governments: foundation hospitals and the idea of 'earned autonomy'. Those trusts that are meeting performance standards (and so attract the green light of approval) are invited to acquire yet more autonomy by becoming Foundation Hospitals, while those which do not (so attracting the red light of disapproval) are given more controls on expenditure and higher levels of surveillance concerning their performance (Bull and Hamer, 2001).

The effects of new management on professional practice

It is now time to address the question of what impact all these management reforms have had in practice. However, prior to doing so it is pertinent to make a few general observations about the 'problem' of management change in this context. The NHS has a larger number and wider range of professional staff than any other branch of public service provision, and almost all the key professions in the health service are strongly organised both formally (The BMA and various trade unions) and informally (Burrage, 1992). These facts have dictated the kinds of procedures the managerial cadre have had to use in developing their role. Not being practitioners, they do not understand very fully what the work entails and are therefore in a rather weak position when it comes to controlling work performance. There is actually little prospect, for example, that managers can adopt the policy of job re-design, or impose thoroughly rationalised work discipline on organised professional employees as is habitual in private industry. Hence, if they are to have an effective role at all, health service managers must obtain some voluntary compliance from the professional carers and redirect activities largely through consent. Here the consent of the most powerful group of professionals, the senior doctors, is absolutely key. Without this, management could make little headway, and this explains the concern of managers to get senior doctors on board and involved with management and its concerns and priorities.

The painfully slow progress in the development of effective management in the NHS, is in good part explained by the contestation over jurisdictions between the managers and the doctors: the new directors of the service and the old. This is undoubtedly the seat of a real problem in the NHS: the tension between the traditional understanding of the expertise of the senior hospital doctor, which, as we have seen, included policy making and directive activities, and the developing role of the new NHS manager. To a lesser extent this is also true of nurses, for senior nurses in the NHS also had considerable latent management and decision-making functions within the traditional hospitals. Essentially, the new management had to detach the senior doctors from their old role, which involved making decisions with cost implications as an adjunct to their clinical skills, and re-engaging them as advisors to managers on matters to do with the quantity and quality of care delivery. This means, in effect, doctors helping managers to devise new care regimes, in which the costs of procedures are minimised and what is done follows best practice as far as possible.

The need for what has been called here 're-engagement' explains the recurrent efforts to formally enlist consultants and other clinicians into management positions, either as managers themselves or as advisers. Clinicians have been encouraged to take part in the management process as clinical and medical directors, to set up clinical audit and governance mechanisms and to take note of evidence-based medicine. To put it baldly, management can prevent clinicians from providing services for which there is no percentage to be gained. But whether the mechanisms through which management has to work can be anything other than very crude, is a moot point (Pollitt, 1990).

Strengthening the management function

In the circumstances outlined, it is fairly obvious that, to be successful, much thought and time had to be devoted to strengthening the management function. Being recruited mainly from amongst the hospital administrators, the new cadre of 'managers' in the NHS took some time to throw off its identification with administration and to develop a distinctive rhetoric and expertise.[5] Certainly the numbers of managers and the inclusiveness of their activities have grown considerably. In 1985 it is estimated there were around 300 NHS personnel in England formally classified by the Department of Health as managers. Although estimates of the subsequent size of the cadre differ by 1995, an extremely conservative estimate set the number at 23,000 (Coote and Appleby, 2002). More recent estimates suggest one manager to every four or five carers. The imprecision here arises form the fact that many professional jobs have been redefined as management (for example, Ward Sister becomes Ward Manager) when they have merely been given a more explicit managerial content. All we can be sure of is that the size of the group of NHS managers is larger than any other public service, with a higher ratio of managers to professionals.

There can be little doubt that a key goal of the new management reforms was to increase the ability of managers to control and direct professional practice, but what leverage could the new cadre of managers acquire and apply to affect the efficiency of professionals in the utilisation of resources (Pollitt, 1990)? In the discussion of the development of management above, it has been emphasised that the core of the new role was financial accountability. Being able to point out the financial aspects and consequences of treatment decisions was obviously a key element of the task. But this was not likely in itself to be an effective incentive able to increase systematically the efficiency of clinicians. This is the reason why the managerial role has always been augmented by other kinds of leverage, which usually had also some kind of professional backing or authority. An example here, which was applied at the 1980s, was 'clinical audit'. Clinical audit was intended to bring about effective peer review of consultant practice, in order to increase the accountability of hospital doctors and thereby, hopefully to improve the quality of care (Exworthy, 1998).

More recently, the augmentation of the performance framework with the quality framework is another indication of a similar impulse. Thus, clinical governance bears some similarities to the clinical audit approach. However, it is designed to appeal to professionals because it appears to render the introduction of external systems of accountability unnecessary. Other recent innovations that augment managerial authority are: evidence-based practice, which involves bringing to the attention of doctors evidence concerning the effectiveness of different treatments and care regimes and the setting up of the National Institute for Clinical Excellence (NICE), which also offers evaluations based on research into the efficacy of medicines and care regimes (Harrison, 2002). These agencies are designed to put pressure on doctors to change their activities, in ways that managers themselves cannot undertake. The need to leverage managerial authority in this sort of way is an acknowledgement of the inadequacy of that authority.

It can be argued that the most effective innovations by managers have resulted from appealing to practitioners' self interest, and by using a carrot rather than a stick. Broadly, there are two ways in which this has been done. The first is to offer incentive tied to more output, a perilous course perhaps, but one that is possible given capitation payments to consultants. We shall consider how this works in a later section. The second possibility is to involve professionals themselves in management careers (Dawson et al., 1995; Ashburner and Fitzgerald, 1995). The development of the career position of clinical director is a good example of the latter strategy. Dent (1996) argues that the strategy to incorporate hospitals consultants within an integrated organisational structure can be dated from the implementation of the Hospital Plan in 1962, with its commitment to concentrating resources on developing one large district general hospital within each health district. This strategy of Incorporation into management is, however, problematic, because the pay, conditions of work and status of senior doctors are already so good. It is a recurrent finding that senior doctors are often highly equivocal about taking managerial roles, and sometimes have to be bullied into taking them (Ferlie and Fitzgerald, 2000; Llewellyn, 2001; Hoque, Davies and Humphries, 2004).

There can be no doubt that, after more than twenty years of management in the NHS, the role and the function of the manager has been firmly institutionalised. It is inconceivable, that the clock could be turned back and the hospital services be provided without them. But what do they add? Does all this management activity add up to an effective mode of provision? Before considering these points in our conclusions, we will firstly consider the extent to which managers have been successful in actually controlling and directing health service professionals.

Controlling the front line

We began this section with the observation that the ability of managers to control the work of professionals is limited. This is because the work of professionals is so heavily dependent on discretion that it is difficult to routinise. In conformity with this, it is certainly debatable what effect the new NHS managers and their activities have had on professional practice. By the middle of the 1990's it was still doubtful to many researchers whether managers could be effective. Harrison and Pollitt (1994) argue that managers had not had a systematic impact on health professionals by that date. They suggested that management ideas and systems needed either to be assimilated into the professional culture (i.e. seen to be professionally legitimate) or to be backed by stronger incentives and sanctions than had been available to that point. To quote Harrison and Pollitt: 'Health professionals constitute a potential problem for management either because (as in medicine) of their claim to non-managed status or because (as in most other professions) of their claim to be managed exclusively by members of their own profession' (p. 6). In discussing this sort of effect, we must, of course, have regard to which profession we are considering. The doctors and nurses (to take the two most conspicuous groups with the NHS hospital) have differed greatly in the effects that management has had on them.

The doctors

There is much evidence that, often, senior doctors, have been reluctant to change their practices in response to management. The repeated attempts to recruit medical staff into management roles, or, failing this, to set up machinery through which they can be involved with management on a regular basis, indicates the importance of medical cooperation in change if it is to be effective.

The need to gain assent from this key group has led to both an increase in the numbers of doctors employed and in the levels of their pay. In the ten-year period from 1986 the number of hospital consultants grew at an average annual rate of 3.3 per cent and the number of junior doctors grew by 2.6 per cent. Private earnings are still allowed. Full time consultants may engage in private practice and enhance their salaries by up to 10 per cent of their gross salary. However, many consultants remain on 'part time' contracts where they can treat patients privately without restriction. There is also a distinction award scheme for consultants, and it is estimated that about one third of consultants receive an award *each year* on top of their salary. There has been a good deal of debate about the intensity of work of junior doctors, but recent changes have resulted in a new deal for them as well. Government statistics show that doctors are the highest paid occupation in the UK, above both stockbrokers and business consultants (New Income Survey, 2002).

There have, however, been some areas of change producing more effective and complete use of doctors' time and expertise. The most obvious developments have been agreements about new regimes of care in which the numbers of patients treat per consultant session and consultations per clinic have been increased. This directly serves the managerial objective of increasing the amount of care being delivered at marginally increased costs in payments to consultants. Increased throughput of patients through the system has of course increased the amount of work doctors are being called upon to do. The reconfiguration of hospital care, so that patients are seen more quickly and the duration of their stay in hospitals, where deemed necessary, has been greatly reduced is one of the most obvious changes in hospital care in the UK. So called 'day-wards', in which patients are admitted to hospital on the day of their surgery or treatment and their discharge back to their homes or 'the community', on the same day, are an example of the kind of practice, which has been widely introduced. Such practices are behind the widespread phenomenon of ward closures, which cannot be attributed to reduced provision. Clearly this kind of development, prima facie, represents increased efficiency. But the extent to which these regimes of care are also conducive to better patient health is not obvious. There is little research yet undertaken to consider whether quicker treatment is equally effective as traditional arrangements were and whether, for example, greater throughput of patients leads to disproportionately more mistakes and higher readmissions to rectify them.

Clearly, however, the new management has not achieved complete control over the deployment of medical expertise in hospitals. The continuing existence of waiting lists is perhaps the outstanding indicator that management has not delivered in this sort way. Then there are the inequities in availability of different medical procedures, not to mention the varying standards of care that still concern government.

Further comments will be made on the tendency of management to produce and encourage differences in standards of provision in our conclusions.

Nurses

The effects of the 'management revolution' (Klein, 1995: 148) have been felt disproportionately by nurses. The experience of work for the average nurse has almost certainly deteriorated in recent years. In line with this, there is evidence for the dramatic decline in vocationalism and the rise of a more instrumental and at time militant attitude on the part of many nurses (Soothill et al., 1995; MacKay, 1989; Lloyd, 1997). In recent years there has also been a crisis of recruitment into the profession (Audit Commission, 2001).

Nurses deliver some 80 per cent of direct patient care in the NHS and, not surprisingly, they constitute the largest single professional group in the hospitals. Ten years ago Thornley and Winchester (1994) estimated the wages bill of the nurses in the NHS to total £8 billion. At the time this constituted only about 3 per cent of all public expenditure, but, in the context of the NHS hospitals, it is a big target for cost reduction. Despite their relatively low levels of pay, nurses' wages constitute a large contribution to the running costs of a hospital. Any managerial group, but especially one centrally interested in costs and efficiency, may be expected to have an interest in the costs involved in the utilisation of nurses.

Almost anything managers seek to do, to improve the number of patients seen, for example, requires the agreement and indeed active co-operation of clinicians to have any chance of success. Only by agreement, with the active help of senior doctors, can new regimes of care be devised and put in place. However, the need to bring about the agreement of nurses, at the outset in decisions, about the general features of regimes of care is much less. For this reason they have not been co-opted to the same extent as doctors (Walby and Greenwell, 1994). It is not correct to say that nurses have been systematically excluded from decision making on general policy, but their involvement is now limited by comparison with the levels attained in the epoch of 'consensus management' during the 1970s. These days, nurses are expected to follow along and do what is necessary to deal with the consequences of decisions largely taken by others.

How have managers gained control and brought about the intensification of nursing work? Some commentators have argued for what they call the 'Taylorsation' of nursing work and envisage the extension of management control over the activities of nurses (Walby and Greenwell, 1994; Lloyd and Seifert, 1995). But it is difficult to see how this can be accomplished by managers, as they do not understand nursing and do not have the technical competence to direct nursing activities in any detail. Yet it does seem clear that the intensity of the work of nursing work has increased in response to managerial changes. It seems clear that for many, perhaps the majority, of nurses in the NHS, there has been a trend towards greater working effort being required, and it is this that underlies the change in the present attitude of nurses and that has exacerbated the crisis of recruitment into nursing. Yet, the Taylorisation thesis is too crude and has to be qualified. The intensification of nursing work has not been achieved by the application of work study: the use of the stop watch to calculate bed making speeds, for example, or of Gannt charts to redesign the ward medication round (Ackroyd and Bolton, 1999).

New management has not sought to control the costs of nursing by dictating the activities of nurses. Just as the new management has not sought direct control over the activities of doctors, so a strategy of indirect control has also been adopted towards nurses (Ackroyd, 1998). Neither has management systematically sought to reduce the level of highly skilled nurses employed in the NHS. Since unskilled nursing auxiliaries and low grade nurses are less costly, an obvious expedient for managers intent on saving money would be to introduce 'grade' dilution as it is called (Grimshaw, 1999). There is no shortage of commentators who allege that this is an important strategy of cost reduction employed by contemporary managers. Lloyd and Seifert (1995), for example, suggest that NHS managers use such things as staff reductions, casualisation and what they call 'skill mix changes' as general strategies for the reduction of staff costs in NHS hospitals.

However, it is difficult to find systematic evidence that supports this sort of allegation. What data there is seems to show marginal *increases* in average grade of nurses employed. Data collected by Thornley from the 1980's for example, when nursing was facing the acute challenge posed by the reforms following the Griffiths Report, show that the ratio of qualified to unqualified helpers, auxiliaries and trainees grew steadily in favour of qualified nurses (Thornley, 1997). It would seem that even during the testing period of the 1980's the title and position of the qualified nurse had been effectively guarded. Similar trends have continued more recently.

There is more evidence to support the idea of 'casualisation', in the sense that more temporary and agency staff are being used, but this practice seems to be in response to the shortage of nurses available for full time employment. The use of temporary and part time staff does not involve grade dilution and seems to be an expedient that managers are forced into rather than being a deliberate policy. It is an effect rather than a cause of disaffection among nurses (Audit Commission, 2001).

As has been suggested above, the most significant change in British hospitals has been the introduction of new regimes of care. The widespread adoption of these is also the basic reason for the intensification of nursing work. The increasingly rapid throughput of patients through the hospital, the increasing use of day surgery and short stay wards, though obviously allowing more use of the same amount of capital equipment, also makes for more use being made of nurses. Changes in care regimes have in obvious ways greatly increased the intensity of work for nurses. These days, patients remain in hospital for short periods of time, but remain there during their periods of maximum vulnerability. To have to see and to treat more patients and more vulnerable patients involves nurses having to familiarise themselves with more case notes and more conditions. Today, of course, nurses also manage patient discharge and are responsible for the complete interface between hospital care and care in the community. The concept of the nurse being responsible for the whole period of a patient's treatment and care was recognised with the inclusion of a named nurse in the Patient's Charter (introduced in 1991).

At the same time management has increased the numbers of patients, it has also demanded changes in the ways they are treated. Management now expects a different set of standards with regard to manifest 'customer care'. Such attention to packaging and presentation is an ideological imposition in many ways. However, it is an unavoidable expectation for front line workers in the new NHS. Nurses these days have to spend a great deal of time reassuring patients and heading off and dealing with their queries and complaints. Fieldwork in hospitals suggests that the need to give attention to the voice of the patient makes a substantial contribution to the demands placed on nurses. But the basic and key point to note here is that by altering regimes of care managers also change the context within which nurses carry out their work and exercise their professional autonomy. By increasing the numbers of patients with which nurses are confronted, they, also, indirectly, reduce the time available to treat each of them and in which to look after their welfare.

In short, by changing the design of care in hospitals, management sets key conditions within which the nurses have to work. In this way, nurses are being induced to work a great deal harder. They must work harder unless they are prepared to disregard their own ideas and standards about what is appropriate to adequate hospital care. Thus, although management has also *not* taken direct control of nursing work, it has nonetheless proceeded to change key aspects of the context of nursing work indirectly, and has gradually changed key parameters nursing work. Nurses have been left with the capacity to organise themselves to a considerable extent; but they do so under conditions that are not in their control. By such means there is little doubt that the work of many nurses has been intensified by the activities of managers in the NHS. Any changes to the way in which nurses carry out their work is likely to have an enormous impact on patient care.

To be sure, all is not gloom and doom and there are some countervailing trends. As we have seen, there has been the widening of the scope of nurses' work as they are given increasing responsibility for overall patient welfare (Guest et al., 2001; Redman et al., 2000). If this came along by itself, without any increases in the numbers of patients seen, it would very likely be welcomed as job enrichment. Also, at some levels, there has been increasing involvement of patients in clinical decision at the one end and administrative work at the other. Because of shortages in the supply of doctors and the expense of their work, in some specialties in some areas, management has encouraged nurses to build on their traditional roles and explore new areas of practice (Dent, 1998). Nurses have also reacted positively to changes in doctors' hours and new technology, assuming new roles and responsibilities. There has been the introduction of nurse prescribing and nurse practitioners with nurses emerging as clinical leaders as well as general managers in some hospitals.

Some elements of reform therefore support positive changes. The interest in increasing qualifications and responsibility of senior nurses is evident, with the advent of nursing consultants and the reintroduction of the 'modern' matron. However, such changes and developments are remote form the experience of the average nurse. For them, some minor aspects of job enrichment pale into unimportance when they come along with the kind work intensification described above (Ackroyd and Bolton, 2002).

Changes in values and orientations

Finally, we turn to consider whether the management project has led to shifts in values away from professional attachments towards a more positive and businesslike orientation. It has been a persistent goal of reform to change practices and attitudes and values. The idea here is not only to break down devisive professional attachments but to create positive attachments to the work organisation and the produce a closer alignment of professional interests with management concerns.

There is some evidence for changes of this sort. Research by Kitchener (1998; 1999) suggests the emergence of new values and orientations amongst professionals. More generally, research that has focussed on professionals who occupy roles that bridge between managerial and clinical hierarchies such as the heads of clinical directorates (where strong commitment to new values might be expected) has come up with mixed results. In a interesting discussion, Lleywllyn (2001) argues that there is considerable accommodation of the management perspective by the medical managers occupying clinical director roles. By contrast, Ferlie and Fitzgerald (2000b), after reviewing the structural changes that have been introduced with the introduction of the NPM into the NHS are equivocal on the crucial question of the extent to which there has been a shift to a new cognitive framework. They write that: 'There was still uncertainty about the extent of underlying change in the cultural and ideological sphere and the possibility that "hybrid" or "sedimented" cultures could emerge' (2000b: 9). Support for this comes from a range of other studies. Looking at senior clinical managers in a weaker trust, Hoque et al. (2004) suggest that there is considerable distancing from the values of management. A UK wide survey, with over 1000 respondents, also noted considerable cynicism and disinterest in management amongst Clinical Directors (who made up half the sample) (Davies et al., 2003). Given that these studies were not undertaken at an early point in the introduction of management, it seems that strong attachment to managerial values is taking some time to develop.

Detailed studies of nurses' culture have found considerable scepticism about the values associated with management and cynical detachment (for example, Bolton, 2002). Pressure of work and the serious shortage of nurses have are clearly not conducive to the development of positive attitudes towards managers. Unlike the doctors' remuneration, pay for nurses remains low and, against a background of increasing work, nurses are increasingly dissatisfied with it. To make a reasonable living, those remaining in the profession work extra hours and shifts. The Institute of Employment Studies in 1997 maintained that a quarter of all nurses had a second job and around half work on the 'bank' in addition to their normal work, doing around an extra

11 hours per week (Buchan, Seccombe and Smith, 1997). It is not surprising therefore that they experience low morale and stress. At the 1997 Association of Healthcare Human Resource Managers conference, it was revealed that 29 per cent of nurses report work related stress (up from 17 per cent in the general population) and that nurses lead the way in psychiatric outpatient referrals compared to other health related occupations (AHHRM, 1997). The new public management is not, therefore without its costs in human terms. This is infertile ground for engendering positive attachment to managerial attitudes and values.

One of the interesting ideas in the recent literature is the possibility of persistent professional values taking over and pervading management, rather than the reverse. This possibility has been described as: 'provider capture of the management agenda' by doctors, as suggested by Hunter (1993). Other authorities have suggested comparable things (Power, 1997; Pollitt et al., 1998). Such writers argue that it is equally likely that management practices will be shaped by custodial assumptions as it is that those custodial assumptions are shaped by management ideas and values. This is also very much the conclusion reached by McNulty and Ferlie in their recent book on reengineering initiatives in health care (2002).

Conclusion

The development of management has been a consistent emphasis of the many developments of the NHS since the beginning of the 1980's reviewed in this chapter. As measured by the number of managers employed and the change in institutional structures and practices, new management has been pushed further in the NHS than in any other area of social provision. There is evidence of an increase in middle manager roles while overall numbers of 'non-productive' staff have burgeoned.

The NHS has fundamentally changed as a result of this new emphasis. The basic change in outlook, so far as the designers of the system were concerned is discernable from the phrasing of legislation. The 1946 Act, which established the NHS laid a duty on the government to 'promote the establishment...of a comprehensive health service designed to secure improvement in the physical and mental health of the people...and the prevention, diagnosis and treatment of illness'. This may be contrasted with the 1990 Act, which consolidated an institutional framework within which management roles would be indispensable. The 1990 Act refers to the obligation of every Trust 'to ensure that its revenue is not less than sufficient...to meet out-goings...[and]...to achieve such financial objectives as may from time to time be set by the Secretary of State'.

Reorganising of health care by the introduction of management has taken a great deal of time and has not been costless in itself. Introducing management into the equation has, in this example, introduced a new occupation and a new hierarchy. Many of the organisational changes associated with these developments have also been hugely costly. For example, the introduction of the split between purchasing and providing, which, as we have seen is still with us, did not create a market, and yet has greatly increased the numbers of staff required to make the system work. Also, the national managerial chain of command that for a long time merely duplicated the bureaucratic governmental structure is itself not costless. As we have seen, government has seen the need to invent a whole series of other agencies and quangos to do give leverage to management and to do things that management could not achieve for itself.

And yet, the things that management have done that have been successful are relatively simple. Reconfiguring regimes of care to produce greater patient throughput, for example, by the more efficient utilisation of operating theatres and hospital wards, has saved substantial costs by utilising hospital capital equipment and personnel more intensively. But this is not a complicated set of processes procedures and it is obviously something that might have been innovated in other circumstances. Being introduced in the way they have, such changes have had a series of very different effects on the conditions of work of the different groups of occupations within the NHS. The doctors have experienced only limited erosion of professional autonomy, and the increases in their remuneration and the provision of new career routes are at least commensurate with their increased work. Ability to resist encroachment on their autonomy is made effective by strong professional organisation which has shielded doctors from control and rendered the pace of change painfully slow. As we have seen, the nurses have fared less well under the new regimes of care, and the consequences for them have been undesirable. Furthermore it is difficult to see the contemporary hospital as the moral community it evidently was in the 1960's.

The extent to which here has actually been general improvement in the standards of patient care is by no means clear. Two of the many unexpected outcomes from the managed NHS are: firstly, that the result of decades of change is that there has not been improvement in service commensurate with the cost; and secondly, that what improvement there has been, has been patchy and uneven. It is in the nature of control systems that give incentives for good performance and punish failure that they tend to produce conformity to expectations and bring forth both excellence and its lack. The end product is more inequality in provision. It is clear that active management is not the best means for reducing differences of provision. Being traditionally based on a competitive principle, management usually leads to differences of performance emerging. Among the faults of a managed mode of delivery for public services is, then, that it leads and encourages inequalities of provision. This leads to and encourages yet more incentives and punishments.

There is evidence that *some* hospitals trusts have become smoothly functioning and self-regulating business units, responding to budget pressures and competition and able to deliver excellent services. It is also the case that many trusts do not.

5
The Personal Social Services

> The manifestations of stress and unhappiness in today's local authority social services departments were various, serious and pervasive. Social workers talked of how commonplace it was to see colleagues in tears. I heard stories of social workers throwing all their papers on the floor and walking out, of people locking themselves in rooms of just disappearing from the office for hours on end. Going sick for some time each week or month seemed routinised in many agencies and was one of the most cited examples of a stress survival strategy. A large number of the long-serving fieldworkers I met had recurring and serious health problems, which had resulted in extended periods of absence. Many spoke of being emotionally and physically exhausted by the demands of their work. Social workers talked of being completely 'wrung out' by Friday night: of how their personal and social lives had become stunted as a consequence (Jones, 2001: 551).

In this chapter we assess management change in local authority social services departments (SSDs). As in health, over the past two decades considerable effort was made to reform practice in this area. From the mid 1980s dominant modes of professional organising were strongly criticised as inefficient, self-serving and largely ineffective in terms of meeting the needs of clients. Questions were raised about the presumed failure of these systems to control the work of front line professionals and ensure accountability. Indeed, for many, the personal social services '...became a metaphor for all that was considered to be wrong with the welfare state' (Harris and McDonald, 2000: 57). Increasingly, policy makers argued that existing modes of organising were inadequate and that radical change was necessary to modernise services (Dominelli, 1996; Langan, 2000). As we shall see, these concerns led to moves first by Conservative and, more recently, New Labour, governments to restructure management. One might say that the past two decades witnessed a 'pandemic of organizational change' (Hunter, 1996). Yet, questions remain about the extent to which such pressures have led to transformations in practice. It is far from clear that SSDs have been re-cast into the kind of efficient, 'managed' professional services envisaged in policy and guidance.

To address these concerns this chapter is divided into four main sections. First we provide background information on the formation of SSDs and the nature of professional organisation within them. Following this, our attention turns to the broad policy context and to government attempts, over the past two decades, to restructure management. Section three – the main body of the chapter – then focuses on an assessment of change. Here, three issues are considered: the development of management functions in SSDs; new forms of operational and financial control; and the response of professional groups. Finally, in the concluding section, some of the more general consequences of restructuring will be addressed. Our analysis suggests that in this sector, even more than in health, governments faced an uphill battle in their attempts to re-shape professional work and organisation. Although SSDs were restructured, new management practices were slow to develop and were often ineffective. Overall our conclusion is that it is in this sector where the professions have been least prone to support or engage with the management reform agenda.

Background

The main focus of this chapter is on local authority Social Services Departments (SSDs).[1] These were first established in England and Wales after 1971 following the recommendations of the Seebohm report (Webb and Wistow, 1987). The function of these departments was and remains, to assess social care needs and provide (or, increasingly, commission) services for different client groups (adults, children, and families) within a given geographical area. In 2002 there were 149 local authority SSDs in England, employing 277,200 staff. Approximately 44,000 of this workforce are social work qualified (SCHWG, 2003).[2]

It has often been noted how the Seebohm report represented the 'high tide' of social work in UK (Langan, 1993: 48). As we saw in Chapter 2, it led to the rapid consolidation of the profession based on the idea of generic knowledge and nationally accredited training. Within the new SSDs social workers represented the 'dominant occupational voice' (Lymbery, 2001: 371) and were able to successfully monopolise senior management positions. One survey found that 89 per cent of managers had been involved in 'social services work' over the previous ten years (Lawler and Hearn, 1997: 209). More generally Seebohm articulated what seems, in retrospect, a very optimistic vision for social work. The new SSDs, it was assumed, would ensure universal entitlements to welfare provision based on citizenship rather than targeting the most needy and underprivileged. Emphasis was on the wider rehabilitative purpose of social work, breaking into cycles of deprivation and fostering community care (Evandrou and Falkingham, 1998). To be sure these policy developments were not entirely unopposed. As we shall see there was growing concern over the policing and social control aspects of social work role that became more pronounced in the 1970s (Howe, 1986). But the Seebohm report did represent a major boost to the profession and, more generally, to the idea of greater state funding for and involvement in the provision of the personal social services.[3]

In organisational terms, the new SSDs were markedly more bureaucratic than the acute hospitals described in Chapter 4. Bills et al. (1980: 63), for example, note how in this context:

> the professional practitioner is employed to act as an agent of the employing authority, to carry out its specific policies and programmes as these develop. Managerial relationships are constructed to ensure that work is carried out accordingly.

The bureaucratic nature of SSDs was evident in the detailed rules governing decision making (derived from legislation) and in structures of control based on hierarchical chains of command. SSDs were characterised by high levels of specialisation and a rigid division of labour. There was (and remains) a deep divide between the functions of generic, or client-based, field social work teams and in house resources (such as residential and day-care services) (Challis, 1990).[4]

For many social workers these structures represented a 'perverse imposition' on their professional autonomy. This, in turn, resulted in considerable tension between senior administrators and front line staff within SSDs (Howe, 1986: 1; Jones, 1983). However, one should not exaggerate this. In most departments a pattern of custodial administration similar to that described in Chapter 2 emerged. In this context 'management' (even if recognised as such) tended to be weak, unobtrusive and ineffectual as a mechanism for controlling and directing services (DHSS,1986: 15; Parsloe, 1981; Satyamurti, 1981: 36–37). At local levels, professional groups, either in area teams or residential establishments, were able to exercise a degree of *de facto* control over the way services were provided and organised (Clare, 1988: 497; Lymbery, 1998; Kitchener et al., 2000). This also fostered a strong sense of professional identity and a commitment to local clients and existing patterns and levels of service (Clarke, 1995). A degree of slack in the system (relative to today) meant a greater possibility for front line staffs to shape their interactions with clients and in some cases develop a role of 'advocacy' on their behalf (Jones, 2001: 549). It might be argued therefore that the 'bureau-professional hierarchies' of UK SSDs 'were as much a basis for the power exercised *by* social workers as the basis for the exercise of power *over* social workers' (Harris, 1998: 844).

The changing policy context

Since the mid 1970s there has been a marked shift in policy towards the personal social services the main thrust of which is away from the vision articulated by Seebohm. Such change began soon after the formation of SSDs, with a 'chaotic retreat from growth' in the mid 1970s (Webb, 1980). From that point on, public expenditure changed from being viewed as part of the solution – a benign instrument to achieve social progress – to part of the problem. In the context of a more general fiscal crisis (see Chapter 3), real expenditure on the UK personal social services fell between 1976 and 1981 and remained at a low level of growth through most of the 1980s (Evandrou and Falkingham, 1998).

With the advent of the Conservatives after 1979, pressures on expenditure were intensified and linked to more general shifts in policy. From the early 1980s, political demands for change mounted in a climate of growing concern over spiralling budgets (for example, for residential care) (Lawson, 1995: 71) and a succession of highly publicised inquiries questioning social work judgment (Parton, 1991; Stevenson, 1994). As we saw in Chapter 3, in this period the New Right played an important role in highlighting the so-called failings of social work. Professional social workers, in particular, were castigated for encouraging dependency culture and promoting the interests of producers over consumers (Cochrane, 1993).

These developments led to moves by the then Conservative government in the late 1980s to seek radical reform. A key vehicle for change was the NHS and Community Care Act (1990) (see Kirkpatrick (2004) for a more detailed discussion). This legislation aimed at achieving a transformation from institutional to community based services (or from residential to domiciliary care) and encouraged 'needs' rather than supply led approaches to service organisation. SSDs, it was argued, should focus on identifying need and the strategic commissioning of services rather than on their provision. Considerable emphasis was also placed on developing a mixed economy of care, with local authorities acting as purchasers of services from the independent sector. To facilitate this goal overall responsibility for coordinating and funding community care was transferred from the NHS to local authorities.

A further piece of legislation, the Children Act 1989, also heralded important new directions in policy. The main aim of this Act was to create a unified and coherent framework for public and private child welfare law, altering the grounds upon which the state (represented by the social work profession) could intervene to protect children (Parton, 1991). One consequence of this has been a shift towards more tightly regulated and, in some cases, risk-averse approaches towards decision-making (Bilton, 1998).

The 1990s therefore represented a period of radical transition in the field of the personal social services. While SSDs were to continue to play a 'lead agency' role in coordinating care, they would be far less involved in providing it (Means and Smith, 1998; Clarke, 1995). There was a substantial transfer of local authority owned provision (especially of residential care) to the private sector. Increasingly the focus was on a more 'restrictive vision of social work' one that was focused on the provision (or commissioning) of services that were targeted and cost limited (Lymbery, 2001: 374).

Importantly, all these demands for change were introduced in a 'climate of financial retrenchment' (Lewis and Glennerster, 1996: 70). Unlike the previous decade the 1990s did see a real term increase in public expenditure (Evandrou and Falkingham, 1998). But his was not sufficient to keep pace with unit costs or the necessity to respond to other demands (such as for improved monitoring and new management systems) (Means and Smith, 1998). Consequently, most SSDs were forced to make cuts in the overall levels of services they provided (or purchased) – especially in areas such as residential care (Evandrou and Falkingham, 1998: 254). Financial constraint led to the introduction of policies of charging for services not previously charged for (Means and Langan, 1996) and the use of explicit rationing and means testing (Challis et al., 2001). Finally, budgetary pressures were associated with a rise in the caseloads of many front line professionals and growing demands on them to speed up the pace of work (Rushton and Nathan, 1996; McGrath et al., 1996; Postle, 2002). As Jones (2001: 553) suggests, many social workers were 'pressed to be speedy in their assessments, limit the contact with the potential client and get in and out quickly'.

In many key respects these broad trends in policy and funding continued after 1997 (Orme, 2001). New Labour did not reverse earlier policy goals (relating to the mixed economy) and continued to highlight the so-called failures of the social services (Langan, 2000; Jones, 2001: 560). Indeed, under the banner of 'modernization' central government has become even more prone to intervene to change practice. To this end, detailed national performance targets have been established, with SSDs facing growing pressure to involve their users (SSI, 2002). New regulatory agencies have also been created to promote modernisation goals, such as the National Care Standards Commission and a Social Care Institute for Excellence. Finally, there have been moves towards the greater central direction of professional training and education, most notably with the formation of the employer-based agency, Training Organisation in the Personal Social Services (TOPSS) and General Social Care Councils (Orme, 2001).

Towards managed services

Interest in reforming the management arrangements of SSDs dates back almost to the time of their formation with numerous initiatives aimed at re-training senior professionals (Younghusband, 1978: 313; LGMB, 1988). By the 1980s, pressure for such change grew in the context of financial constraint. SSDs (and other local authority departments) were urged to devolve budgets to cost centres and invest in systems for financial monitoring and control (Challis, 1990; Flynn, 1987). An important role was played here by the Audit Commission (founded in 1984) and the Social Services Inspectorate (SSI). These bodies actively promoted ideas about management within the sector (Henkel, 1991). They also produced a succession of reports highlighting weaknesses (such as inadequate planning and control) and the necessity for investment in 'management structures and systems' (Day and Klein, 1990: 28; Audit Commission, 1985; DHSS, 1985; SSI, 1986).

After 1990 calls for management were further intensified in the wake of major new legislation (described above) (Langan and Clarke, 1994).

It was argued that radical change was needed to achieve the shifts in policy heralded by the NHS and Community Care Act and Children Act 1989. The expectation was that SSDs would be transformed into 'managed services', focused on meeting needs, targeting resources and effectively regulating the practice of front line professionals. To this end considerable emphasis was placed on developing systems for strategic planning, financial control and the management of contracts and human resources (Harris, 1998; Wistow et al., 1996). There were also calls for a major rethink of the way professional work itself was organised. SSDs were obliged to implement purchaser-provider splits (DH and PW, 1991; Lewis et al., 1996) and systems of 'care management'. The latter sought to formally separate professional tasks associated with assessing needs and the formulation of care packages from those of actually providing services (Huxley, 1993; Lewis et al., 1997).[5] Finally were calls for the development of performance management regimes and more 'inquisitorial' approaches towards staff supervision and appraisal (Rushton and Nathan, 1996: 359).

In some respects the pressure to implement management change was less intense in SSDs than in health (see Chapter 4). No attempt was made to re-organise the sector as a whole or create new management boards that were independent of local political control (Clarke, 1995). However, while all this ensured some continuity with older ways of working in SSDs, the pressure on senior professionals to change was nevertheless considerable and hard to ignore. Most SSDs did undergo some process of formal restructuring during the 1990s. While the effectiveness of new management practices may be questioned most departments did establish formal systems for financial control, implementing purchaser provider splits and care management systems (Lewis et al., 1996; Walsh et al., 1997; Challis et al., 2001).

The advent of a New Labour administration did not see a major reversal of policy with regard to developing management (Inman, 1999). If anything the desire for change in this area become even more pronounced and urgent as government sought to modernise provision. One indicator of this is policy initiatives such as Best Value (Orme, 201: 619). By early 2001, 315 Best Value reviews had been conducted in the social services, most calling for changes in management systems (SSI, 2001: 22). Under Labour more emphasis has also been placed on the use of coercive methods to achieve reform (Langan, 2000). This can be seen in the enhanced regulatory role of the Audit Commission and SSI and in the policy of subjecting local authorities that fail to change to a variety of 'special measures' (SSI, 2001: 25).

Assessing the impact of the new management

In this section we turn to the question of what impact, if any, these demands for management reform had within UK social services. In particular, we ask to what extent older, custodial patterns of professional organisation were displaced or eroded? To address this issue we focus on an assessment of the evidence for change in three key areas. First is with regard to the development of the management function in SSDs. Second is the extent to which new forms of financial and operational control have been established. Finally are questions about how far broader shifts in culture and orientations occurred.

Strengthening the management function

In the previous chapter we saw how a key mechanism of change in health was the restructuring of services – to create single purpose organisations – and establishment of a new cadre of general managers. By contrast, in social services no such cadre was put in place. Here the focus was (and remains) on developing strong management functions within existing professional hierarchies and the framework of local authority control. As such one might raise questions about just how much has changed behind the façade of major new policy announcements and formal programmes of restructuring.

Evidence for change

Focusing on the evidence for change, the first observation to make is that senior and middle ranking professionals in SSDs are now clearly more involved in management than before. In most departments, 'budget management and control' has taken on far greater importance (Jones, 2001: 552; Means and Smith, 1998). According to one report there has been 'an impressive investment in staff time and technology' in this area (SSI, 1999a: 21). Added to this is evidence to suggest that senior professionals are spending more time on activities such as contract management (Wistow et al., 1996; Johnson et al., 1998; Kirkpatrick et al., 2001) and strategic planning. This later activity has been given particular emphasis as SSDs are now required to produce detailed 'children's services plans' and 'community care plans' that state how resources are to be deployed. Finally, there has been an expansion in management responsibilities for personnel administration (Keen and Scase, 1998; Whipp et al., 1998). Even by 1990, 63 per cent of local authorities in England had delegated these tasks to SSDs or were in the process of doing so. Increasingly this has meant that: 'Issues such as the administration of agreements, selection of staff, staffing levels, deployment of labour, overtime, grading variations and staff appraisal are now much more likely to be done by line managers than in the past' (White and Hutchinson, 1996: 195). The trend in many local authorities is for central personnel functions to be broken up and for local managers to be more involved in decision-making about staff training, recruitment and selection.

The upshot of these changes, many argue, is that SSDs have become less collegial and more centralised in their mode of decision-making (Means and Smith, 1998; Balloch et al., 1998). Lymbery (2001: 377–378) refers to a 'shift in power from social work practitioners to a managerial elite'. Elsewhere it has been noted how senior professionals are now more likely to impose change and adopt confrontational, or 'macho', styles of management towards their junior colleagues (Jones, 2001). While it is obviously hard to generalise, the trend does seem to be towards an approach to decision-making that is more top-down and which involves minimal or 'spurious' consultation with lower level staffs (Syrett et al., 1997: 162).

A further indicator of a shift towards 'managed' services is the delegation of responsibility for budgets and other administrative functions. This has especially been the case in adult services, following the implementation of care management. One recent survey, found that 82 per cent of SSDs in England had devolved some budgetary authority to purchase community based care packages to 'first tier management or below' (Challis et al., 2001: 679). In children's services a similar trend is apparent. For example, in children's residential care one study noted a 'general trend was towards greater decentralization' of budgets to unit managers of homes (Kitchener et al., 2000). Quite often these budgets were not fully devolved and local management discretion over resources was extremely limited (Wistow et al., 1996; Keen and Scase, 1998). But even accepting this, it is clear that the overall trend has been away from centralised administration. The once rigid divide between professional and managerial domains of work at lower levels has slowly been eroded.

Finally there are signs that senior professional staffs at all levels within SSDs are receiving more management training than before. Balloch et al. (1995: 40) note 'a renewed emphasis on the importance of management training' following the NHS and Community Care Act. Similarly Rai (1994) found that most SSDs did provide some kind of training and that 60 per cent were planning to expand provision, while

Lawler and Hearn, (1997), in a survey of over 100 third tier managers, found that 44 per cent of the sample were in the process of receiving some kind of management qualification. More recently this trend has continued with a majority of middle and senior ranking professionals acquiring a management qualification (SCHWG, 2003). Of course, questions might be raised about the quality of this training and the extent to which it is based on systematic human resource planning (AC/SSI, 2001). Nevertheless, the fact that many SSDs are investing in this area is significant. Management assets and skills, it seems, have now become as important, if not more so, than professional competencies and credentials (Hugman, 1998; Lymbery, 2001: 375).

Some limits of change

The above observations point to a shift towards stronger and more centralised management functions within SSDs. However, while this change is significant, it should not be exaggerated. Despite rising investment, in most cases, management systems and capabilities remain weak and underdeveloped (Whipp et al., 1998; AC/SSI, 1999a; AC/SSI, 1999b; SSI, 2002). Even in the area of financial management it has been noted: 'most councils do not fully understand costs and struggle to forecast future activity and expenditure' (SSI, 1998). Many SSDs have been unable to devolve budgets completely or establish internal trading systems (between purchasers and provider functions) (Wistow et al., 1996: 75; SSI, 1999). Few it seems have adopted the kind of systematic approach to financial accounting envisaged in policy and guidance. In children's services, especially, the focus remains on monitoring expenditure levels and short term 'crisis measures' to bring budgets under control (AC/SSI: 2001: 15; AC/SSI, 1999a).

Management weaknesses in SSDs are even more profound when one turns to the activity of planning and the development of services. In most cases, the approach remains 'ad hoc or opportunistic' (SSI, 1999: 77), with Community Care Plans often representing little more than 'public relations exercises'. Indeed, the general conclusion of a number of investigations is that UK social services have yet to achieve the kind of 'whole systems' approach to strategic planning envisaged by the NHS and Community Care Act (Audit Commission/SSI, 1999a: 32). The vast majority of departments, it would seem, remain essentially operational-led rather than needs driven in focus. There has been no dramatic change in the capabilities of these organisations or movement away from the older pattern of provision whereby services tended to be allocated along customary lines.

A number of explanations can be given for this rather limited and slow change. First is the weak tradition of managing in social services and, until recently, a lack of core skills – or 'mental furniture' (SSI, 1999) – to deal with the complex work of strategic planning and setting up information systems. Beyond this is the fact that SSDs remain incorporated within the framework of local government. The political nature of decision-making coupled with the continued use of incremental budgeting has made it especially difficult to engage in long term strategic planning (SSI, 2002). As one report (SSI, 1999: 73) noted:

> Commissioning and planning are often incremental and cautious activities, where the key aim is not to disturb the status quo...SSDs can't plan each year as if everything is up for grabs and can be rationally determined.

SSDs even more so than health trusts and housing associations discussed elsewhere in this book must operate within a context of considerable uncertainty over resources. While it may be possible to formulate plans for the development of services it is often hard to see these through to completion as local political priorities change (for an example of this see Kirkpatrick (2003) on the restructuring of children's residential care).

Finally, growing resource constraints have been important in limiting change (Langan and Clarke, 1994; Huntington, 1999: 242). In the 1990s, when the pressure to reform management was greatest, the number of senior posts in the sector as a whole fell by 9.7 per cent (LGMB/CCETSW, 1997: 45–46). This trend has continued subsequently with a decline in the number of central and strategic staff in SSDs (SCHWG, 2003). Under such conditions it has been extremely hard to implement new management systems. Even the SSI now acknowledges: 'The impact of budgetary pressures slowed down the pace of modernisation and deflected senior managers away from more strategic shifts in changing the way they arranged and provided services' (SSI, 2002: 22).

Controlling the front line

As suggested earlier a key feature of policy since the late 1980s is the attempt to achieve greater standardisation and control over social work practice. In services for children and adults attention focused on reducing the autonomy of front line staff in terms of how they define client needs, provide services and allocate resources. In the former, the objective has been tighter managerial control 'through procedures intended to regulate decision-making in high risk areas such as child protection' (Rushton and Nathan, 1996: 372; Howe, 1992; Bilton, 1998). Linked to this was considerable interest in promoting standardised approaches to assessment and care planning, for example, with initiatives such as *Looking After Children*, adopted in the mid 1990s (Ward, 1997) and, more recently, the *Framework for the Assessment of Children in need and their families* (SSI, 2001: 31–32; Webb, 2001).

In adult services one can note a similar drive towards standardisation (Lewis and Glennerster, 1996; Lymbery, 1998). Here, as we noted earlier, SSDs were obliged to implement systems of care management. This meant a narrowing of professional activity to focus only on the commissioning of services. It also implied the use of 'core assessment schedules' and 'structured forms, involving ticking boxes, which direct the practitioner to areas of assessment and supplies them with the alternative responses they may make' (Sheppard, 1995: 74).

Finally, in all services, government has called for greater controls to be established over the way in which resources are allocated (Challis et al., 2001). From the early 1990s local authorities were encouraged to develop eligibility criteria and access thresholds to ration services and to ensure consistency in allocation. After 1997 this objective was given added emphasis with Labour's *Fair Access to Care Initiative* (DH, 2002).

There has therefore been a strong policy drive to regulate the decisions of front line staff. Such change was deemed necessary to make providers more accountable and to ensure consistency of access to services (AC/SSI, 1999b). Yet, it is far from clear just how far these broad goals were achieved. Whether or not managers in SSDs (and ultimately policy makers) are now better able to control and direct operational decision-making is open to question.

Evidence for change

From the available research it is evident that there has been some movement towards proceduralism and management control. A majority of local authorities implemented procedures for assessment and care planning, both in services for children and adults. In the former, even by the late 1990s, approximately 90 per cent of local authorities in England and Wales implemented the new *Looking After Children* guidelines (Ward, 1997). Linked to this were changes in the way social work professionals make decisions (Garrett, 1999). Smith (1997), for example, notes a 'growing concentration on the externally measurable element of practice (performativity) rather than the internal and relatively intangible, quality of relationships (caring)'. Similarly, Postle (2002: 343) reports how care managers in two SSDs were adopting more 'reductionist' or 'tick box' approaches to assessing need.

The demand on staff to conform to procedures, it seems, also led to changes in the pattern of work. Numerous studies reveal how social workers now devote an increasing proportion to their time to administrative tasks associated with completing forms and recording information (Hoyes et al., 1994: 14; Challis et al., 2001: 675). Jones (2001: 552) suggests that some community care social workers now spend up to 90 per cent of their time on 'paperwork' or administration, compared with 30 per cent previously. This fact, combined with growing pressures to speed up the pace of work, led to 'more mechanistic, time limited and regulatory contacts with clients' (556). Carey (2003) also found that care managers were devoting a greater proportion of their time on routine paperwork, with up to 25 hours (out of a total of 35 each week) spent confined to the local authority department office.

A second key change in management practice concerns new rules designed to target and explicitly ration resources. This has been most apparent in adult services. Here the trend has clearly been towards the adoption of strict cash limits for care packages and the widespread use of formal eligibility criteria to target services according to levels of risk or dependency (SSI, 1999; Challis et al., 2001: SSI, 2002). Although less pronounced in children's services, there has also been a move towards gate keeping panels and 'access thresholds' (SSI, 2002; Whipp et al., 1998). Taken together these developments suggest a greater level of management direction over the way resources are allocated by front line staffs. A core part of social work decision-making, it seems, is now concerned with 'scrupulous gate-keeping and strict rationing of scarce resources' (Harris, 1998). For many professionals (especially those in adult services) practice is now unquestionably budget-led such that almost everything they do is defined by the availability of finances (Carey, 2003).

Finally, there are signs in many SSDs that greater emphasis is now being given to the monitoring and evaluation of the 'performance' of front line staffs. This can be seen with policies relating to staff supervision and the establishment of systems for formal appraisal (in some cases linked to wider initiatives such as *Investors in People*). Whipp et al. (1998) for example found that a majority of SSDs had adopted policies aimed at regulating both the frequency and content of supervision – the latter focused on making supervision more 'judgmental' or inquisitorial. More generally, it has been noted how, in most SSDs 'the development of better performance management is a priority' (SSI, 2001: 8).

How much control?

The changes described above are clearly significant (Sheppard, 1995; Ironside and Siefert, 1998; Braithwaite, 1999; Lymbery, 2001). Harris (1998: 858) suggests that the 'emergent trend' is now quite unambiguously towards 'proceduralisation and commodification of the social work labour process'. Lymbery (1998: 875) also argues that restructuring led to 'a form of practice dominated by unimaginative, routinised, bureaucratic approaches: in fact, precisely the form of practice that should no longer be considered as social work'. Management restructuring many believe has had a profound impact, undermining the autonomy and, ultimately the skill base of social work. Increasingly, social work is being redefined as a 'case-accountable, managerially controlled and procedurally regulated activity' (Bilton, 1998: 201).

However some caution is required when drawing this conclusion. While there can be no doubt that the overall level of bureaucratic oversight has increased, these changes have been more variable and often much less effective than many assume. There is evidence to suggest that front line staffs do not always follow or conform to procedures for care planning and means-testing. For example, with regard to the use of standard assessment forms, one national inspection (SSI, 1994: 20) found that 'staff who were unhappy with the documentation were either not using it, completing it on return to office, or adapting it as they saw fit'. Similar conclusions were drawn from studies looking at the implementation of the *Looking After Children* procedures for care planning (Ward, 1997; SSI, 1997; Grimshaw and Sinclair, 1997). According to Ward (1997: 126), in many SSDs there existed 'an almost wilful refusal to regard the materials as more than additional paperwork'. More recently, it has been noted how considerable variation exists in the nature of procedures adopted, such that 'between SSDs, and sometimes within them, there are different definitions of what constitutes an assessment' (SSI, 1999: 40). In many cases, assessment forms provided only general or loose guidelines for decision-making, with front line staff continuing to rely heavily on 'personal preferences combined with local working practices' (ibid, 15).

A similar picture emerges when we look at the practice of explicit rationing in SSDs. A recurring theme in a number of SSI and Audit

Commission reports is the variable quality and effectives of procedures designed to regulate this activity (AC/SSI, 1999b; AC/SSI, 1999a; SSI 2002). In some departments, rules for determining eligibility are tightly drawn and offer little scope for the exercise of professional judgment. Yet, many other examples can be given of where this is not the case and where decision-making is more likely to follow older, custodial, patterns (Means and Langan, 1996; Bradley and Manthorpe, 1997). One report found that in some SSDs eligibility criteria were 'easily fudged' and that quite often staff 'applied their own judgments' (SSI, 1999: 46). Decision making about resources tended to be either 'idio-syncratic or based on logics other than those stated in the eligibility criteria' (ibid). It has also been noted that the lack of clarity in proce-dures is a key factor leading to 'inconsistency of access to services both within and between councils' (AC/SSI, 1999b: 3).

A further reason for not exaggerating change is the limited effective-ness of performance management systems in many SSDs. While this issue has been given a higher priority in recent years it would be a mistake to assume that – with the possible exception of child protec-tion teams – practice itself is always more closely monitored than before. Many studies draw attention to the way front line supervision continues to be dominated by operational concerns and the mainte-nance of collegial relationships (Shaw, 1995; Heyes, 1996; Berridge and Brodie, 1997; Kitchener et al., 2000). According to one report (AC/SSI, 1999a: 31) 'Too much emphasis is placed on workload management and not enough on skill development and staff performance'. Beyond this are signs that, paradoxically, front line staffs now receive less formal supervision than was the case before (Lewis and Glennerster, 1996: 143; Thompson et al., 1996: 656; Rushton and Nathan, 1996: 363). In one national survey Balloch et al. (1995) conclude, 'Super-vision and support from experienced staff for those starting their current job was patchy'. Across the sample 'cutbacks' meant that only 43 per cent of managers and 66 per cent of front line staffs received anything like regular supervision. More recently, Postle (2002: 344) observed how: 'Few opportunities existed for care managers to reflect on their complex work in supervision because an increasing amount of managers' time was taken up with meetings'.

It would appear therefore that the practice of supervision in SSDs has not been substantially reformed. If anything supervision may be less frequent and effective than in the past. One consequence of this is that many areas professional work continue to be 'invisible' to higher-level managers and local politicians (Kitchener et al., 2000). Also implied is that front line staffs now receive less support from their senior colleagues than before. Increasingly these professionals are left to make complex and time limited decisions on their own. As one social worker interviewed by Jones (2001: 559) put it: 'There is a kind of macho sense around that you don't look for help in your work'.

Finally one might point to the limited use made of information systems to monitor staff 'performance'. In the literature it is frequently argued that these systems greatly enhance management control 'through on-line recording, bypassing the need for retrospective accounts in parochial professional supervision sessions' (Harris, 1998: 857). Implied is a kind of remote control, allowing managers to measure task completion from a distance. However while there is evidence of this kind of practice – for example, in some care management teams (Carey, 2003) – it is far from universal. As one SSI report (SSI, 1999: 16) concludes, 'Line managers seldom endorse case records', while 'routine auditing of samples of case files only occurred in two of the seven SSDs'. Similarly a joint study conducted by the Audit Commission and SSI that same year (AC/SSI, 1999b: 28) noted how managers were 'not using the information that is available to assist them in monitoring activity or performance'. From these and other studies the impression gained is that senior professionals in SSDs are either unwilling or (more likely) too busy to make more systematic use of management information systems (AC/SSI, 1999a).

To summarise, over the past decade there has been an extension of management control over the work of front line professionals in SSDs. Decisions regarding how needs are assessed and the allocation of resources are more regulated and directed than before. Yet one cannot say that older custodial patterns of administration have been fully displaced. In many areas professionals are not closely supervised and continue to exercise discretion over the way services are provided. Quite often there has been a growing demand for this kind of local discretion as senior professionals themselves face rising workloads and get bogged down in fire-fighting. This is not to deny that the pattern of work in SSDs has changed with more time spent on administration and form filling. But the extent to which this activity is always more closely managed than before remains open to question. Senior professionals have often lacked the skill, time or inclination to implement the kind of systematic control regimes envisaged by policy makers and management consultants.

Change in values and orientations

In this final section we now turn to the question of how far restructuring led to changes in values and orientations. A goal of government policy has been (and remains) to achieve an enduring 'cultural revolution' within social services (Audit Commission, 1992a). The focus has been on 'changing the whole nature of the work of SSDs in order to introduce market principles', to ensure professionals 'learn new ways of thinking and behaving' (Lewis and Glennerster, 1996: 72). Implied is that staff must develop a stronger loyalty to their employing agency and accept the new realities of managing finite resources. The more recent drive for 'modernization' also requires 'confident staff supported by confident organisations and a change in social work culture...' (SSI, 2001: 7). Hence, the achievement of some kind of culture change is a high priority. But how likely is it that such a change has occurred? To what extent have social work professionals supported reform and actively engaged with management ideas and goals?

It is undoubtedly the case that restructuring and moves towards a mixed economy of care had an impact on values and priorities. Numerous studies highlight changes in the language of social work teams – especially those involved in care management – and the growing emphasis on budgets, consumers and formal targets (May, 1997; Kelly, 1998; Carey, 2003). Discourses associated with the commercialisation of care and means testing did, to some extent, colonise professional decision-making.

That said, it is questionable how far professionals have accepted or fully come to terms with the wider agenda of management reform. Most studies reveal a marked difference in response to change between senior professionals and rank and file staff. With the latter, commitment to management ideas and goals is either very weak or non-existent (Phal, 1994; Syrett et al., 1997; May, 1997; Jones, 2001; Postle, 2002). Typical are the findings from a study conducted by Syrett et al. (1997) based on interviews with 80 staff in one SSD. This found 'little evidence of any existing or developing congruence between the "new" managerial culture and the "old" culture of social work'. More likely was 'overt antagonism' to use of new management labels and titles and a 'deep rooted hostility to the central tenants of managerialism' (160). A similar picture emerges from SSI annual reports (SSI, 1997; 1998). Quite often these lament the persistence of strong professional sub cultures that promote 'unhelpful attitudes, malaise or resistance to change' (SSI, 1995).

This tendency may be explained in various ways. First, are genuine concerns amongst front line professionals about the appropriateness and desirability of management reforms. Many staff held (and still hold) strong ethical reservations about the shift to what they see as 'cheque book social work' (Lewis et al., 1997) and the practice of charging and explicit rationing of services (Hoyes et al., 1994; Bradley and Manthorpe, 1997). According to Carey (2003: 133):

> New idioms such as those of efficiency and economy, which have now possessed social care...appear insensitive, inappropriate and vulgar – especially when they nearly always imply an encouraged drive for cost cutting and a quest for 'cheap' and often poor, services.

Linked to this are more general concerns about the bureaucratisation of work, declining professional autonomy and the future ability of social workers to meet or respond to client needs. Such change was often seen as encouraging superficial relationships with clients, increasing the risk of poor assessments and the possibility of ineffective forms of intervention (Jones, 2001).

There has also been considerable staff resentment over the way change has been imposed. According to Phal (1994: 206), social workers often seemed to experience the changes as 'something done to them as opposed to with them'. Balloch et al. (1998: 334) note how a key source of dissatisfaction stemmed from 'the way the department is managed' and the lack of 'attention paid to suggestions'. Under these conditions it is hardly surprising that many staff did not develop a stronger sense of ownership or commitment to reform.

Finally, one might point to how growing work pressures and the need to respond to competing demands have undermined enthusiasm and support for change (Balloch et al., 1999). As we saw, there is evidence of growing work intensification in SSDs with rising case loads and demands to speed up the pace of work. Front line professionals are increasingly forced to reconcile contradictory demands in their work. Care managers, for example must now respond to the policy goal of assessing and meeting client need while, at the same time, operating within ever more strict budgetary constraints (Langan, 2000: 157). These conditions, one might argue, are hardly conductive to rising staff support for management objectives. Instead, the trend seems to be towards a 'generally demoralised and dissatisfied workforce at practitioner level, with few indications of optimism about their work' (Postle, 2002: 336).

As one might expect, amongst senior professionals there has been stronger support for management ideas and goals (Langan and Clarke, 1994: 89; Nixon, 1993). This is manifest in the 'business orientation' that has emerged in many SSDs (Harris, 1998: 856–8) and the growing number of 'market enthusiasts' (Wistow et al., 1996: 30–32). Lewis et al. (1997: 23) talk about how many professionals now 'relish the changed environment in which they may exercise their entrepreneurial skills'. Across UK social services, there has been a general 'readiness... to endorse a comprehensively critical judgment of previous standards of social care' (Langan, 2000: 158). Senior professionals, it would seem, have been particularly compliant in accommodating the management change agenda.

For many observers this support for change is indicative of a more general process of fracturing within social work, between rank and file staff and a 'separate and freestanding class of managers' (Hugman, 1998: 187; Lymbery, 2001: 377). The latter, it is claimed, have now completely 'lost touch with the welfare ideals of social work' (Jones, 2001: 559). However, while there are signs of such change one should not overstate those tendencies. To do so is to ignore the persistence of older custodial orientations amongst social care managers. We may also fail to account for those factors that are working to undermine the commitment of senior professionals to the reform process.

A recurrent theme in many studies – including some reported above – is the complex and uneven response of social work professionals to recent changes (Thomas et al., 2000: 23; Whipp et al., 1998). While some have actively supported reform, many others (perhaps the majority) experienced 'divided loyalties' (Postle, 2002; Lewis and Glennerster, 1996: 72; Lawler and Hearn, 1997: 207; May, 1997). As such, one cannot assume that the shift in orientations noted earlier has been universal or complete. In many cases senior professionals adopted a pragmatic stance towards change. This in turn had implications for the nature of restructuring, leading this group to seek to interpret demands in ways that partially accommodate social work values and minimise disruption to existing practice (Heyes, 1996; Froggett, 1998: 39).

A prime example of this attempt to 'minimise disruption' is the way policies of care management were implemented. During the early 1990s there had been considerable 'agreement with the problems care management was intended to address...' (Petch et al., 1996: 7). However, at the same time, few senior professionals were prepared to support the narrow, 'administrative' version of care management that was advocated by government policy and guidance (Huxley, 1993;

Lewis et al., 1997). In most cases it was assumed that this would lead to an overly narrow division between the tasks of assessing needs and providing care and that a broader definition – one that incorporated 'traditional social work skills' – was preferable (Lewis and Glennerster, 1996; McGrath et al., 1996). Consequently, in a majority of departments, the trend has been towards considerable surface compliance with policy (Challis et al., 2001: 673). Instead of reorganising professional work, most, it seems, 'have simply redefined the role of social workers...to approximate to care management roles or have simply relabelled existing posts' (Cambridge, 1999: 397).

A further problem with exaggerating change is that we might fail to account for the fact that, where senior professionals are concerned, management restructuring has involved costs as well as benefits. With regard to costs a number of points can be made. First is evidence of growing levels of stress amongst this group (Balloch et al., 1995; Thompson et al., 1996). This has been attributed to the increasing difficulty and complexity of management work in SSDs and a growing sense of confusion resulting from the need to respond to often ambiguous and conflicting policy demands (Balloch et al., 1998). Huntington (1999: 241), for example, suggests that, senior professionals have been 'caught in a web of contradictory injunctions and uncertain role definitions'. Thomas et al. (2000: 23) also note a growing gulf existed between 'preferred managerial styles and those dominant in the organisation'. Beyond this, it appears that work intensification has contributed to rising stress levels. One national survey conducted in 1995 reported that a majority of managers were 'unable to reach planned work-load targets' and had 'too much administration and paper work' (Balloch et al., 1998: 337). More recently, SSD managers have been 'overwhelmed' by new demands created by local government re-organisation (Craig and Manthorpe, 1998) and policy changes associated with modernisation and Best Value (Orme, 2001: 619; Geddes, 2001).

Second are signs that the job position of senior professionals in UK SSDs has become more tenuous and insecure. Until recently (with the rapid expansion in agency working) this group were most likely to be employed on temporary (or fixed-term) contracts (Andrew and McLean, 1995). There is also a greater chance that the pay and remuneration of senior professionals will be variable or linked to some kind of performance related pay system (LGMB, 1994). Finally, one might question the assumption that during the 1990s, entry into management equated with improved career prospects. As we saw earlier, in this

period the number of management posts in the sector as a whole actually fell (LGMB/CCETSW, 1997: 45–46). Linked to this has been a
process of de-layering in many SSDs, especially following local government re-organisation. According to Craig and Manthorpe (1998: 198):
'Internally, many local authorities had "stripped out" layers of middle
management to save costs (beyond the levels required simply by
"downsizing")'.

Managerial work in SSDs has also been made harder by growing
conflict with junior staffs (Phal, 1994; Syrett et al., 1997). According
to Jones (2001: 552) older collegial and support relationships 'had
largely disappeared' such that 'the divisions with management were
more stark'. The job of the manager, it seems has become increasingly difficult and unrewarding in the face of staff hostility and resistance to change. Social care managers may become isolated
from their junior colleagues, either blamed directly for the decline
in services or criticised as 'reactive incompetents' (Huntington,
1999: 25).

These observations lead one to question the idea that a powerful and
self-confident new cadre of professional managers has emerged in UK
social services. In many areas custodial orientations persist and continue to shape practice. More importantly are forces working to undermine the enthusiasm and commitment of senior professionals. This is
not to deny that some did actively support and engage with the new
management. Rather the point is that this tendency was not universal.
Often support for change was half hearted or pragmatic at best. In
many cases the impact of reform was to create what Thomas and
Dunkerley (1999: 28) aptly describe as a 'disillusioned and demoralised
middle management stratum'.

Conclusion

The evidence presented in this chapter is testimony to the dramatic
changes that took place in the world of the personal social services.
There has been a marked retreat from the ideal of universal provision
based on citizenship rights, towards services that are increasingly targeted and means tested. Similar to housing (discussed in the next
chapter) the focus of attention is now on the most deprived and least
privileged groups within society. As we saw, all this did not lead to the
abolition of social services departments. These grew in size during the
1990s and took on a key 'lead agency' role in the coordination of community care. But importantly, SSDs are no longer substantial providers

of care in their own right. Even by 1997 the independent sector share of the community care budget for adults had risen to 52 per cent of the total (Edward and Kenny, 1997). SSDs have been effectively transformed into enablers of services that are delivered by a large and growing private and voluntary sector.

The impact on professionals has been mixed. During the 1990s the number of social workers employed in UK local government grew, and the more recent introduction of state registration will further consolidate this process. However, this 'success' has been achieved at the expense of the (already limited) institutional autonomy of this profession. As we saw, central government and employers are now more willing and able to prescribe the process and content of social work education and training (Orme, 2001). Tightly drawn legislation and guidance was also introduced, notably in the area of children's services. As a result, over the past decade social work did become a more case-accountable and procedurally regulated activity.

There have also been some important shifts in management practice within SSDs. Substantially more time is now devoted to core management tasks associated with financial management, purchasing and strategy. In line with policy guidance and the demands of regulatory bodies most SSDs established systems for cost control and performance management. These systems had some impact on the work of front line practitioners, reducing their room for maneuvre in decisions concerning how services were allocated and, arguably, making this process more transparent. Finally there has been a substantial increase in management training in this sector and some evidence of shifting identifications and support for change amongst a cadre of senior professionals.

Notwithstanding these developments, on the basis of the evidence reviewed above, our conclusion is that management practice in SSDs has not been transformed. As we saw there remains a significant gap between the theory and practice of strategic planning in SSDs. Services often continue to be allocated along customary lines as opposed to strategic assessments of local needs. It was also noted that while front line practice is probably more tightly regulated than before, management surveillance is neither as universal nor as effective as many assume. Finally and perhaps most importantly, is the very limited evidence of change in orientations and values within this sector. For most professionals engagement with management ideas and priorities is at best pragmatic. Across the sector there are signs of a deep-rooted cynicism about change and little sense of optimism amongst staff about the future.

In some respects these outcomes are not surprising. The history of SSDs is one of ongoing struggles between the interests of professionals and administrators. Recent developments, one might argue, have only exaggerated this trend. Professionals in this sector traditionally eschewed managerial concerns and priorities, especially those linked to monitoring practice and controlling resources. Added to this is the fact that many staff, even at senior levels, lacked the necessary skills or training necessary to implement complex policy requirements. Unlike the new health trusts and housing associations, SSDs remained within the orbit of local government and under the supervision of local politicians. This fact, one might argue, further problematised change. Shifting political priorities at the local level represented an added source of uncertainty for managers (especially where resources were concerned) and made it hard, if not impossible, to engage in serious long term planning.

Under these conditions the task of reforming management practice in SSDs was never going to be easy. But, making it even less straight forward was the way policy was introduced. As we saw there had been little consultation prior to restructuring. At local levels the top down nature of change created a strong sense that the new management was something being 'done to staff rather than with them'. Also problematic was the sheer pace and quantity of new policy initiatives. One report notes how managers in London 'are being tied up in restructuring or making new organisations work' and urges 'an end to the constant reorganisation' facing local authorities (Downey, 2002). Even the main regulatory bodies in the sector now acknowledge this problem. A joint review by the Audit Commission and SSI (2001: 2), for example, remarks on how 'councils can be excused for feeling bombarded by policy initiatives' and admits 'some councils get submerged and overwhelmed'.

Finally, one might point to the way in which competing demands and expectations held back change. This has been most apparent where resources are concerned. Cuts in middle management and problems of staff retention limited the time available for senior professionals to plan services or engage in effective supervision. It has also been hard to generate enthusiasm for change as services are steadily being downsized (and agencies forced to concentrate on an ever narrower spectrum of need). These conditions it would seem were not very favourable to root and branch management reform. As one SSI report noted: 'Councils increasingly identify budget pressures, lack of resources, the impact of increasing demand and overspends as risks and barriers to progress' (SSI, 2002: 63).

To be sure it has not all been bad news. Some might argue that a greater focus on the costs of different types of provision was long overdue in SSDs. For certain users the shift to care management was also positive, ensuring a greater fit between their assessed needs and preferences and the kind of services received. New systems of monitoring helped to increase the transparency of front line decision making, arguably reducing the risk of malpractice (Whipp et al., 2004). But these gains came at a very high price. There is now mounting evidence of rising levels of stress and demoralisation in the social care workforce and record levels of sickness and absenteeism (Penna et al., 1995; Thompson et al., 1996; Collings and Murray, 1996; Balloch et al., 1998). While these outcomes are not entirely the result of management restructuring (social workers now operate in a context of rising social inequality and deprivation) few would deny that it has been a key factor. Over the past decade there has been a trend towards work intensification and deteriorating relationships between junior and senior professionals. Excessive bureaucracy and the shift towards more narrowly defined and financially driven approaches towards providing care also undermined morale. As Carey (2003: 126) puts it: 'For many social workers the "creative" and "rewarding" elements of social work have now been removed from the occupation...encouraging a sense of alienation and despondency for employees...'.

In the long term this state of affairs may have a damaging impact on the nature and quality of services provided by SSDs. Historically these services were dependent on a sense of professional vocation and a willingness to work beyond contract. The risk today, however, is that management reforms will undermine this ethos and 'weaken still further the local and moral economy that still prevails and, arguably, still sustains the best social work practice' (Langan, 2000: 167). Added to this is a growing trend for experienced social workers to leave the profession or seek alternative ways of working, such as though temporary employment agencies. In London turnover rates have reached alarming proportions – over 40 per cent in some local authorities (Lymbery, 2001). Fortunately these problems have been recognised and measures to improve staff retention and recruitment introduced. But whether this will be sufficient to re-build the morale of social work is questionable. New Labour, as we saw, has no intention of reversing the reforms initiated under the Conservatives. If anything the pressure on SSDs to modernise while operating under conditions of increased financial stringency and growing need will only intensify.

6
Social Housing

The *housing profession*, if indeed such a collective body can be said to exist, has also experienced a rude awakening. Having entered the 1980s as a disparate, insular and rather reactionary collection of individuals, the 1990s have seen a more concerted attempt to establish a credible image for housing management. As the representative body for housing professionals, the CIH has raised the profile of the housing profession, establishing itself as a recognised source of expert advice and knowledge. Such a role has been largely supported by the government through the DoE and Audit Commission, recognised as contributing to the better management of public housing (Pearl, 1997: 207–208).

The provision of housing by public sector officials differs from our other two illustrative examples of public service professions in three important ways. First, there have been two distinct providers of public, or what is now referred to as social housing: local authorities and housing associations.[1] While local authorities have dominated provision numerically, the profession emerged from the voluntary housing association sector and today that sector is expanding at the expense of local government provision. The second major difference identified is the uncertain nature of the housing management task and its domination by other professional groups, including: architects, engineers, planners and surveyors. While membership of the Chartered Institute of Housing (CIH) has continued to grow in recent years, the professional basis of housing management is frail and so too is the ability of this group to exert de facto control over provision (Franklin and Clapham, 1997; Walker, 2000). Finally, in contrast to the NHS and social services, which are primarily grant funded and allocate services to users bureaucratically, in housing there has always been a direct economic relationship between producers and users. Though the rents charged may be subsidised, there is a transaction backed up by a contractual landlord tenant relationship, which specifies the expected standards and behaviour of both parties.

Notwithstanding these differences, reform to the social housing sector over the last two decades has been substantial. Change has been driven by privatisation, competition, performance assessment and measurement, choice, decentralisation and the introduction of private sector management practices (Walker, 2001). The Conservative administration clearly sought to reduce the size of the sector, giving sitting tenants the choice of owner occupation, promoted quasi-autonomous housing associations, shifted the balance of funding from supply to demand-side and constrained the role of local authorities, promoting them as strategic enablers. As with the other services considered in this book, this policy legacy has been perpetuated by the post-1997 New Labour administration, although here as elsewhere there have been shifts in emphasis. Most notably is the new regime of Best Value, the growing focus on regulation, the development of complex local, regional and national planning frameworks and the role of housing in social exclusion.

It is important to note, that in focusing upon the housing management profession, or members of the CIH, a wide range of others public sector workers and professionals who are involved in the provision and delivery of housing services are overlooked. Professions excluded from the housing production process include: architects, engineers, planners and surveyors. In the ongoing management of homes, built environment professionals will play a role in the maintenance of the stock, while social housing tenants may be in contact with community development, local economic development, social work and regulatory and law enforcement professionals. These professions may work for other public agencies, tenant-led organisations, voluntary organisations or the private sector. As we shall see it is, in part, this complex setting that has facilitated a more complete adoption of management practices in this sector than elsewhere.

To address these concerns this chapter is divided into four main sections. First we provide background information on the formation of local authorities and housing associations and the nature of professional organisation within them. We then turn our attention to the broad policy context and to government attempts, over the past two decades, to restructure management. The balance of the chapter then focuses on an assessment of change. Here, three issues are considered: the development of management functions; new forms of operational and financial control; and the response of professional groups. We show that attempts to reform professional work have been more successful in housing than elsewhere. The goal of creating the kind of efficient, 'managed' professional services envisaged in policy has, to some extent, been achieved. Finally, in the concluding section, some of the more general consequences of restructuring are addressed.

Background

As noted earlier, the work of housing professionals has historically been dispersed between the local government and voluntary sector. In UK the emergence of a local government housing dates back to late nineteenth century, to the failure of the private sector to provide housing of adequate standards for working class households and the difficulties experienced by early housing associations to provide low rent housing and deliver management and maintenance services of an appropriate standard (Daunton, 1987; Merrett, 1979; Swenarton, 1981). Cole and Furbey (1994) suggest that by the time of the First World War, council housing was increasingly seen as the solution to these problems. Two factors are highlighted by commentators: the introduction of rent control and the statutory responsibility for local authorities to survey needs and make plans for the necessary extra buildings. Both requirements were contained in the Housing and Town Planning (Addison) Act, 1919. From this period council housing, supported by additional legislation, grew into the dominant rented tenure in England and Wales.

Like the SSDs that came into their own in the early 1970s, following local government reorganisation, separate housing departments were also a product of this era. The Cullingworth Report (CHAC, 1969) argued for the establishment of comprehensive housing departments to co-ordinate and plan services and to implement a social housing management role to act as a counterweight to the technical professions' domination of council housing that was argued to be resulting in management problems (Laffin, 1986). Prior to the 1970s housing functions within a local authority were often still a product of the role and involvement of other professional groups. For example rent collection was managed and controlled by the treasury as a financial enterprise, repairs and maintenance was associated with engineers and new building with architecture.

Although the Cullingworth Report led to some changes, even two decades later, responsibility for all housing functions was still unlikely to be in a separate housing department (Davies and Niner, 1987). Research by Maclennan et al. (1989) in the late 1980s demonstrated that allocation was the only function guaranteed to be located in a housing department. Over 25 per cent of authorities reported that functions including housing welfare advice, rent collection, capital programmes or housing related benefits were not provided within their housing department. By the mid 1990s this position had not changed markedly (Bines et al., 1993) and, indeed, deteriorated following the reform of local government in England and Wales during this period (Walker and Williams, 1995). A stand alone housing department was, crudely, a product of stock size and thus an urban phenomena. The majority of local authority housing departments were located in small district councils. The small scale of these authorities meant that housing was most likely to be under the roof of a joint department, the twinning being normally with environmental health. Consequently, decision-making about housing management and its delivery could be under-taken alongside, if not led by, environmental health professionals (Thomas, 1998). Given these circumstances it is not surprising that housing management functions remained, as in the past, dispersed across the local authority (Walker and Williams, 1995).

By contrast housing associations developed in a different era; thus the sector is characterised as diverse and complex. The common denominator is that rather than being politically controlled organisations they are managed by a voluntary board elected from a membership base (Kearns, 1994). Malpass (2000) identifies four waves of formation, noting that they all produced very different types of organisation. The first wave captures the diverse range of voluntary, philanthropic and model housing companies developed prior to 1914. The 1920s and 1930s saw a range of worker, employer and improvement organisations – a number of these small societies bought all their management services from independent providers. It was during this period that the phrase housing association was first coined. The 1960s and 1970s saw a new wave of associations and marked the beginning of an era of state sponsorship and their expanding public policy role. Cost rent and co-ownership associations were established in the early 1960s by the Conservative government to fill gaps in the private rented and home ownership sectors. They had a strong technical focus, reflecting the priorities of professions of the built environment. There were also a number of charitable ventures during this period often linked to existing organisations, including churches or charities such as Shelter. These initially operated on a voluntary basis providing homes to those in greatest need or who were excluded from council housing provision. It was during this period that as the sector began to expand and to recruit paid staff.

Associations grew rapidly following the 1974 Housing Act, which established a grant funded regime and a policy focus on regeneration. The Housing Corporation, initially established to fund associations under the legislation of the 1960s, administered these funds and was given a formal oversight role. Much later housing associations were promoted as the main providers of social housing, following the development of quasi-markets in the late 1980s (Le Grand and Bartlett, 1993). This was one of the main drivers of growth in the sector during the 1990s. Finally a fourth wave of development followed the large scale voluntary transfers (LSVT) of local authority stock into the sector, which commenced in the late 1980s. This movement initially reflected the privatisation aspirations of Conservative local authorities, but is now more typically associated with resource constraints in local government as a whole.

All this points to considerable diversity within the housing association sector. But while diverse, the concentration of ownership in a relatively small number of organisations is beginning to result in growing similarities and convergence in objectives, management and organisation.

In numerical terms local authorities have dominated the sector, managing a substantially higher number of homes and employing more staff: around 55,000 at the end of the 1980s (Cole and Furbey, 1994). Table 6.1 shows that, in terms of stock holdings, the voluntary sector was almost insignificant in 1971 and even in 1981 accounted for only 2.3 per cent of the total, compared to 28.1 per cent for local authorities. However the table also reveals the changing pattern of social housing provision. There has been an absolute reduction by around 2.2 million homes in the local authority sector from 1981 to 2000 and the growth by around 1.4 million in the housing association homes. More will be said about the nature and consequences of this shift later.

The characteristics of management and organisation

The traditional purpose of both local authorities and housing associations has been to provide and manage and maintain housing for those on lower incomes. While the balance of production and management has waxed and waned and the client groups housed changed, focus on

Table 6.1   Local Authority and Housing Association Stock Holdings in England 1971–2000

	1971		1981		1991		2000	
	n	*%*	*n*	*%*	*n*	*%*	*n*	*%*
Local authorities	4,593	28.3	5,061	28.1	3,858	19.5	2,862	13.6
Housing associations	8	–	422	2.3	627	3.2	1,387	6.6
Total	4,601	28.3	5,483	30.3	4,485	22.7	4,249	20.2

Note: Percentages are the national percentage of each kind of tenure. The 1971 housing associations data refers to 1970
Source: CHAC (1971) and Wilcox (1999)

these activities remains the primary objective of stock holding organisations. Legislation and guidance has been developed to meet this need, and targets policy arenas such as homelessness, allocations, and needs assessment. The primary role of a housing professional is to manage and maintain social housing.

But despite these broad similarities in function differences in ownership resulted in very different forms of organisation. Local authorities, by their very nature, are geographically focused upon one area. They have statutory responsibilities, notably for assessing housing needs, maintaining a housing register and towards homeless households. They are politically controlled organisations, with decision-making powers resting with locally elected politicians and directors of housing sitting in the top two or three tiers of the organisation. Council housing is provided by lower tier district and unitary authorities. The smallest provide only a few thousand homes and the largest urban authorities, at their height, could manage in excess of 100,000 homes.

Housing associations also vary in forms of ownership, management and organisation. While they are all non-profit they may adopt different rules, for example, charitable or industrial and provident. They range from highly localised (e.g. co-operatives, alms houses and community based housing associations) to regional and national organisations. They have no statutory responsibilities and are managed by a non-political voluntary board. In contrast to a local authority, their structures are very flat with the chief executive reporting directory to the board of management. The smallest associations (typically almshouses and co-operatives) provide only a limited number of homes and the largest now manage around 60,000. Amongst the

2,000 housing associations registered in England the means size is 750, although this disguises the skewed distribution of property ownership. For example, 81 per cent of all associations own less than 250 units. The eight per cent of associations owning over 1,000 homes own 92 per cent of the stock, which is concentrated in 412 organisations.

By comparison with the other sectors considered in the book housing professions have had only limited success in controlling their employing organisations. Professionals from other services could be directors of joint housing departments (a theme perpetuated during the 1990s when a number of authorities merged their housing and social service departments) or long standing housing officers who were not members of the professional institute. The institute was also seen as the professional body of local government, and relatively few association staff joined this or any other professional body. Partly this was due to the weakness of the profession and limited success in achieving closure (Ackroyd, 1995a; Cole and Furbey, 1994; Franklin, 2000). According to Stewart (1988: 39):

> Housing management may not constitute a profession in the sense of the established by the older professions. The very use of the word 'management' to describe the profession suggests not a profession, but a particular management role requiring specialist skills or knowledge.

In essence, housing management is a technobureucratic profession (Larson, 1977) – the primary claim of expertise being administrative skill or the ability to 'run things'. This is reflected in the CIH's emphasis upon the tasks and skills of housing management work (for example, rent collection, maintenance, allocations and more recently anti-social behaviour) rather than seeking to establish a wider knowledge base or an underlying philosophy for the profession (Cole and Furbey, 1994; Clapham, 1997).

Recently, as we saw in Chapter 2, the housing profession has been successful in consolidating its position and extending membership beyond the local authority sector. While the absolute number of local authorities with professional members has remained relatively static between 1985 and 2002 the number of housing associations has increased dramatically, as have voluntary and representative and private sector organisations. These changes reflect the broad restructuring in the sector. The number of organisations with professional members now stands at 1,888, a 164 per cent increase between

1985 and 2002 (Institute of Housing, 1985; CIH, 2002). But while numbers have risen and professional organisation improved, housing managers fail to dominate the sector as a whole. Only 10 per cent of housing workers were members of the CIH by the late 1990s. The upshot of this is that the sector is not easily characterised (in the same way as health and social care) as being professionally managed.

Turning to the question of the management of social housing, local authorities have historically been highly bureaucratic and hierarchical forms of organisation. Control was exercised from the centre by mechanistic and standardised co-ordination with formal procedures or rules of behaviour typifying a process of administration with limited professional discretion. Paid officers were recruited by local authorities soon after they commenced building houses. By and large officers had some freedom in decision-making. But often needed to refer problems up the hierarchy to senior officers and often to local politicians. Examples of councillors making detailed decisions, particularly in relation to the allocation of council housing, persisted until the mid-1990s when legislation was introduced to restrict such practice.

This bureaucratic context clearly limited the development of a custodial management approach, although it did not exclude it altogether. Managers were able to oversee local forms of organisation and service delivery and develop minimum standards while government oversight focused upon design, output of new dwellings and capital costs. But others could influence what was considered to be appropriate practice. The most notable area where discretion has been exercised is in the allocation of public housing and the management of tenancies. While local authorities must house those in greatest need there has been an ongoing debate about the deserving and undeserving poor. Housing workers were able to exercise choice over who gained access to the waiting list and thus social housing. This was often exercised when potential applicants were given a 'home visit' to assess their suitability for housing or by building in restrictions to access to the waiting list. Henderson and Karn (1987) show how these criteria were used to restrict access by ethnic minority groups to council housing in Birmingham. During the periods of expansion for local authorities, during the 1950s and 1960s and for housing associations during the 1970s, resources were by and large plentiful, therefore allowing staff substantial freedom and discretion. Front line decision-making was largely built upon prior experience and reflected a tendency for provision to follow a customary pattern.

The diversity of the housing association movement resulted in a wider range of organisational forms and management approaches.

However, this diversity together with the limited size of the sector meant that the internal management characteristics of housing associations are harder to define. All associations had, and continue to have, a management committee of typically unpaid volunteers. Historically board members of charitable trusts would work to ensure that the founders' wishes were complied with, while housing societies shareholders' primary purpose would be to raise resources (Malpass, 2000). Early voluntary housing associations had no paid staff and very small ones continue with this pattern of management. In the early 1970s questions were posed about the management capacity of associations. The CHAC (1971: 26–27) reported that only a fifth of 'traditional associations had a relevantly qualified person working full time, and at least two fifths were without and qualified help, even on a part-time basis'. However, in most cases (85 per cent) at least one of the relevant professions was represented on the Committee. Where housing associations did have staff these were able to exercise freedom within the constraints of the objectives of the organisation (Malpass, 2000).

Our conclusion at this stage is that the model of custodial management practised by housing mangers is weaker than in both health and social services. Housing managers may conform to the notion of being difficult to control because of decentralised decision-making. However, local politicians exercised substantial control over the housing process. While housing managers, or ex-practitioners, may have overseen the service, the fragmented nature of decision-making, together with the uncertainty of the task, resulted in a position where other professionals were just as likely to exercise control over the housing service. Indeed, as late as 1986 the Audit Commission (1986a) was recommending that councils should have a chief housing officer to overlook and better co-ordinate all housing management activities. In short, a weak profession resulted in a diluted model of custodial management in the housing sector.

The changing policy context of social housing

The fiscal crises of the mid-1970s had a marked impact on housing provision. Resources fell spectacularly, with a 71.5 per cent drop in public capital between 1980 and 1999 (Wilcox, 1999). It is from this time that the decline of council housing begins. Attitudes towards public housing shifted following construction failures (for example Ronan Point), the emergence of 'difficult to let' estates (Cole and Furbey, 1994; Power, 1987) and, above all, the ongoing political support for and subsequent growth in owner occupation (Saunders, 1990). The Labour government's policy review in 1977 produced the first clear policy statements that placed owner occupation as the preferred tenure that households were expected to aspire to. This resulted in the introduction of planning and rationing mechanisms for the allocation of resources to and by local housing authorities.

After this major changes were associated with two periods of externalisation of services (Kirkpatrick et al., 1996). The first, from 1979 to the mid-1980s, under the Conservative's, was concerned with privatisation. This was manifest in housing with the 'Right to Buy' policy (with over 2 million homes sold) and tight controls over public expenditure which led to severe conflicts between central and local government. It also included the compulsory competitive tendering (CCT) of a number of manual local government services, such as council housing repair and maintenance services.

The second phase, from the late-1980s onwards, involved restructuring along market lines, those services that could not be fully privatised. This involved the fundamental restructuring of social housing provision and management and the further extension of CCT (Barker et al., 1992). Though the powers of local authorities had been eroded, the late-1980s saw a new role as they were promoted as strategic enablers who co-ordinated the action of agencies to provide new homes and housing services. The other side of the coin, however, saw their provision role externalised to housing associations in the Housing Act, 1988. From this point on the voluntary sector became a mainstream 'instrument of housing policy' (Malpass, 2000, p. 155) which, as we have seen, changed associations as organisations. By 1999, local authorities completed only 79 new homes, in comparison to just of 67,000 in 1980 (reflected in the changing tenure patterns shown in Table 6.1). Market mechanisms were also introduced to housing associations through competition for fixed grants for new builds. Furthermore housing associations had to raise private finance to fund the balance of the fixed grant – around 50 per cent of the capital costs of new build.

In this period the regulation of housing associations was enhanced to ensure accountability for public funds and also to give confidence to private finance institutions. The 1988 Housing Act saw the break up of the Housing Corporation from a Great Britain wide organisation to one located in England. Other bodies, Tai Cymru and Scottish Homes, took on similar functions in Wales and Scotland respectively (Walker and Smith, 1999). A notable impact of these changes was the strengthening of the regulatory role of the Housing Corporation. This role allowed the corporation to withdraw development funds from poorly performing associations.

While the state supported the growth of housing associations, the externalisation of council housing was led by local government itself. Large scale voluntary transfer – introduced through the Housing Act of 1989 – resulted in local authority housing departments transferring much of their stock to the housing association sector. Some early transfer authorities did this for ideological reasons, to support the Conservative privatisation agenda. But, during the 1990s the main driver for such change was the desire to escape an increasingly stringent financial regime that threatened to increase rents by over 100 per cent. There was also a desire to address stock maintenance issues and meet housing needs. Since 1989 over one million units have been transferred, predominately in South East England where the capital value of stock is high and transfers are on-going business concerns.

The policy of transferring stock away from the local authority continued under the New Labour government. They have supported a larger programme of transfer than the prior Conservative regimes and devised a number of new internal decentralisation routes, notably ALMOs (arms length management organisations). Here the local authority retains ownership of the stock but manages it through a semi-autonomous independent organisation with its own board. The rationale for this remains financial, although issues of management have become more important in the decision making process to establish an ALMO. While local authorities have begun to provide new homes again, the main providers remain housing associations.

In addition to these exit routes from the public sector a variety of tenant-controlled opt out schemes have been developed. For example, one London borough transferred all its housing activities to a tenant-managed organisation (Darke and Rowland, 1997). Here management and decision-making is externalised whilst ownership remains with the local authority. Other schemes have sought to increase tenant control and choice, and the history of tenant involvement in social housing is long (Caincross et al., 1996; Ward, 1974). During the 1980s a number of models were experimented with, ranging from the right to information and to be consulted, through to support for ownership co-operatives (Boyne and Walker, 1999). The Labour government have continued to support these initiatives and have promoted Tenant Compacts that seek to increase the level of tenant participation by specifying service standards (Albourne Associates, 2003). Although the adoption of various forms of tenant control is limited as a total of the social housing stock, the range of voice mechanisms has extended tenant voice and tenants' rights affecting the management and culture of social housing providers.

Broader changes to the management of local authorities under the Local Government Modernisation Agenda and the new Best Value regime have seen the promotion of continuous improvement. In the association sector similar processes of rational planning and organisational review are also required (Walker, 2003). Furthermore, the introduction of inspection under the Best Value regime initially placed local authorities and housing associations on very similar footings. As of April 2003 the Audit Commission inspects both housing associations and local authorities and is putting in place a common inspection framework (Audit Commission, 2003).

These policy changes have resulted in a number of outcomes (Boyne and Walker, 1999). The most notable ones affecting the nature of housing work are the process of residualisation of stock and people and financial pressures. Local authorities now hold poorer quality stock and house the poorer sections of society who cannot afford to purchase their home. This has increased the proportion of tenants who are welfare dependent and who, in turn, are more likely to need welfare and personal intensive housing management services (Walker, 2000). A residualisation process of the population, rather than the stock, has been seen in the housing association sector, which increasingly houses only those in greatest need. Overall, social housing in Britain is perceived of as a stigmatised tenure of last resort.

Towards a managed service

Advice has been provided to housing authorities on their management arrangements for service delivery for nearly a century (CHAC, 1938). However, the major forays to reform the management arrangements of local authority housing departments commenced during the 1960s and 1970s. An early example was the Cullingworth report and the corporate management fad that swept through local government at this time. Substantial pressure on management arrangements also emerged in the mid 1980s with the publication of a number of critical Audit Commission reports (Audit Commission, 1986a, 1986b). Pressure from such sources has not abated over the following two decades and this has encouraged housing providers to improve their management structures and systems (Audit Commission, 1992b, 2000; Audit Commission/ Housing Corporation, 1997).

Demands for management in the sector are typically associated with the major programme of welfare reform that commenced in the late 1970s. Resources were reduced and planning mechanisms put in place by the Labour administration. By the 1980s, commentators from the left and right accepted that change was necessary. Writers on the left identified public housing as paternalistic, bureaucratic and distant, as witnessed by a group of authors who, from the 1970s, argued for 'tenant control' and decentralisation to small scale and responsive organisations (Walker, 1991). However, the main drive for change came from '… successive Thatcherite governments [that] perceived public housing as inefficient, monopolistic, dependency-forming and mollycoddling' (Pearl, 1997: 3). The Conservative party's underlying belief in free markets resulted in explicit policies to 'role-back the state'. In the public housing sector this was expressed in terms of large cuts to budgets, reductions in the provision of public housing through sales to sitting tenants, attempts to re-balance the producer consumer relationship towards tenants and the introduction of a range of market mechanisms (Boyne and Walker, 1999).

The main villains in this story were local authorities. Council housing, in particular, was pinpointed as being in 'crisis' by the Audit Commission (1986a). Although the Commission's evidence has been refuted they cited a list of deficiencies in the management of council housing that fuelled the perception of an incompetent and paternalistic bureaucracy. Faults included poor design, poor maintenance, lack of choice in the rented sector, high levels of homelessness and weak financial and management control. This was seen as leading to 'difficult to let' estates, ghettos of social disadvantage and high levels of customer dissatisfaction.

The proposed solutions to these problems focused on enhanced management practices: clear lines of management accountability throughout a local authority housing department, banishing red tape through the removal of unnecessary administration, increasing financial control over capital and revenue and attracting private sector funds to finance much needed capital expenditure. The more robust research of Maclennan et al. (1989) questioned the extent to which there was a crisis in council housing, highlighting examples of good management. But even this study alluded to problems associated with the virtual absence of performance monitoring, weak customer feedback and involvement mechanisms, not to mention substantial variations in cost between local authorities and housing associations. A strong belief in management as the main solution to these problems was firmly established during this period. For example, a direct outcome of the *Nature and Effectiveness of Housing Management in England* study (Maclennan et al., 1989) was the introduction of the Report to Tenants regime in council housing (Symon and Walker, 1995). This required every housing authority to report on the performance of their authority annually. These performance measures formed part of a wider approach to information availability witnessed through the 'Tenants Charter' in 1980, the 'Tenants Guarantee' in 1988 and the Social Housing Standard and Citizen's Charter in the early 1990s.

The process of externalisation in the local authority sector (described in the previous section) further intensified the shift towards management. The Right to Buy represents the single largest privatisation programme in Britain. In England alone it had raised £27.56 billion by 2002/03 and lead to the disposal of over 1.5 million dwellings into the owner occupied sector. This had a major impact on management in the sector and the profession. Firstly, the best stock has been sold leaving local authority managers with the task of maintaining and repairing poor quality dwellings. This required a greater emphasis on management and financial monitoring. Second, the poorer sections of society now lived in council housing and therefore required more welfare intensive housing management services.

The introduction of CCT into housing management services in England in 1992, not surprisingly, led to further attention being focused on management. The presumption behind the introduction of CCT was that it would place pressure on costs while increasing quality by giving tenants greater choice. Given the difficulties in defining the nature of housing management, much of the debate was about what constituted 'defined activities' and was therefore subject to contracting. Nonetheless, the focus of CCT was upon the managerial aspects of management services and, in particular, the technical parts that could more easily be specified.

Stock transfer is the third area of externalisation to have management implications. As local authority housing departments have transferred into the housing association sector so they have be subject to pressures, from government, funding bodies and regulators to enhance management arrangements. These have emerged from the mixed funding regime introduced in the late 1980s that established a business culture in social housing (Walker, 1999, 2000). By introducing private finance into the day-to-day management of social housing organisations the dominant pressure has been to maintain financially viable entities. The Housing Corporation, as regulator, also played a key role in this. Its regulatory regime demands regular and sophisticated accounting data and promotes sound organisational management. The introduction of private finance into housing associations is, therefore, a major driver of the shift towards 'managed' services.

Under New Labour the focus on enhancing management capabilities has continued. There are now common performance measures for the local authority and housing association sectors. Under the Conservatives local authorities were not subjected to new oversight arrangements. New Labour, however, brought local authorities onto a similar footing as housing associations that were heavily regulated following the quasi-market reforms of the late 1980s. Local authorities and housing associations are now subject to inspection through the Audit Commission Inspectorate, which is exerting convergence pressures between the two sectors through its expectations of what good management is (Grant, 2003). Guidance on management is also ongoing. The Housing Corporation continues to support management training (underwriting part of the fees for a Housing MBA run at the University of Birmingham's School for Policy Studies).

In short, over the past two decades there has been substantial and intense pressure for reform to produce services that are managed.

Assessing the impact of the new management

As with our prior two case study chapters we turn our attention to the impact, if any, of the demands for management change on housing services. The major variance from the two preceding chapters is that in housing custodial patterns of professional organisation were far weaker and decision making roles more fractured between providers. Processes of displacement and erosion are therefore played out in different ways. In questioning the development of the management function, examining the extent to which new forms of financial and operational control have been established and in exploring shifts in culture and orientation it becomes clear that significant change has occurred both in the local authority and voluntary sectors.

Strengthening the management function

If the reform mechanism in health was service restructuring and the insertion of a cadre of general managers and in social services, enhancing management functions within the existing professional hierarchies, in housing the story has been one of extending managerialisation through the development of non-political forms of quasi-organisation and financial regulation (Pollitt et al., 1998; Walker, 2001).

The scope of local authorities' and housing associations' strategic role was interpreted narrowly as their role as agents of state policy implementation during the early 1980s. The introduction of Housing

Investment Plans (HIP) for local authorities in the late 1970s was initially a tool of national expenditure controls. But in recent years individual housing organisations have developed their own strategic awareness and practices (Greer and Hoggett, 1999). Strategy is a tool used to co-ordinate the mixed economy of provision, partnerships and alliances and resources (Audit Commission, 1992b, Reid, 1995). It is also a method of assessing organisational performance by both sectors (Audit Commission, 2003).

The growing emphasis on strategy and planning has clearly altered the role of senior and middle managers in local authorities and housing associations. Indeed, their involvement in management surpasses the expectations of the corporate planners of the 1970s. For housing associations the growth of planning developed in the early 1990s when private finance institutions required detailed cash flows, financial forecasts and business and operational plans prior to lending for new developments. These plans are now part of the routine management procedures of all major housing associations (Walker and Smith, 1999). For example, English housing associations have to submit, online, their accounts on a quarterly basis to the regulator, the Housing Corporation. The stress placed on financial management is seen across the housing association sector. Most associations produce corporate and business plans for funding bodies and regulators. Detailed operational plans resulting in individual targets for members of staff often sit behind these plans.

Whereas the above pressures were experienced by all developing housing associations, local authorities were able to self-select to have their management function enhanced. If an authority sought transfer or had groups of tenants seeking to establish tenant-managed organisations then there were strategy requirements. Authorities seeking transfer must undertake detailed stock condition surveys (valuations) and produce detailed business and operational plans to satisfy government, the regulator and finance houses that they are capable managers. Housing departments that remain in local authority control do not, however, completely escape the emphasis upon rational planning. The role of the HIP has changed from a expenditure control tool alone to one that strengthens processes of management and government control. For example, in Wales the Housing Strategy and Operational Plan required, during the 1990s, authorities to submit annual plans on their broad strategy. Authorities had to conform to detailed guidance together with a range of oversight mechanisms to ensure their proposed strategy was implemented. In practice, authorities often resisted such top-down approaches and refused to specify policy in some areas, such as option appraisal of future forms of ownership of the stock. However, this was often politically motivated rather than officer-led.

In local authorities the strengthening of the management function has trailed the housing association sector. Skills had been partly developed through the introduction of new accounting procedures, the requirement to appraise options to achieve decent homes standards by 2010 and through the Best Value regime. But it was not until 2001 that authorities were expected to produce business plans (DETR, 1999). Government recommendations on the content of these plans reads like an MBA strategy course: mission statements and objectives and a timetable for achieving them, reviews of prior targets, analysis of the internal and external environment, option appraisal, financial forecasts, sensitivity analysis and success criteria. The modernisation agenda of the New Labour government has perpetuated and deepened these planning requirements. Housing strategies are now required from authorities to demonstrate how they will meet national quality standards, how they will implement the strategies specified by the regional housing forums and to specify how they will raise standards set down by the regulator. If they do not comply with all the above intervention may occur.

Budgeting and financial control has also moved from a backroom activity to the corporate centre of housing associations and local authorities. While cost parameters are still controlled by government the change over the last two decades has been quite remarkable. Prior to 1988, finance was an administrative function for housing associations reflecting the grant led regime that covered association development and operating costs (Walker and Smith, 1999). The introduction of private finance in the 1988 Housing Act propelled the role of director of finance onto an equal par with that of chief executive. As associations borrowed increasingly large amounts of private finance management functions were strengthened to focus upon 'core business' (Walker, 2000).

The impact of budgeting and finance is experienced differently across the sector, being more acute in LSVT associations (National Audit Office, 2003). In the early years after transfer these associations are highly indebted and must work to an agreed business plan that typically includes pledges to tenants to repair homes and limit rent increases. This led Pawson and Fancy (2003) to observe that while most LSVTs will be financially viable in the longer term, in the short term the need to adjust to change creates many difficulties.

The nature of housing association boards has also changed since the late 1980s. The introduction of private finance saw a reduction in the voluntary nature of the board and its replacement with 'professional boards'. This, as we hinted earlier, has been at the expense of the housing profession. Most professionals recruited to boards have been accountants or lawyers, able to understand and interpret the complexities of private finance and other general managers with relevant experience. Such skills may be a necessary requirement given changes in the nature of the business. In 2004 an association with around 4,000 homes is likely to have a turnover of around £20 million. Indeed, Malpass argues that 'the genuine voluntarism of the past has become (since 1974) a form of managed voluntarism, and this is now being joined by what might be depicted as the bogus voluntarism of the LSVT associations and companies' (2000: 259). He also speculates that the loss of independence is a price worth paying for the increased levels of output achieved across the sector and the improvements in organisational practices.

Extensive change has been witnessed in the local authority sector as well. The 1989 Local Government and Housing Act achieved what governments had been seeking to do for a number of decades, the successful ring-fencing of the housing revenue account. This Act required local housing authorities to balance their revenue account at the end of the year based only upon housing resources. No longer was it possible for authorities to subsidise council housing from the general fund. The level of control that central government could exercise was considerable and extended to rent setting for each authority. This in turn reduced the flexibility authorities and housing managers had in the management and maintenance of council housing. As in the housing association sector, these reforms have affected the day-to-day work of housing officers and reinforced the notion that managing housing is first and foremost a business where the books have to be balanced. Only when this has been achieved can wider and more social objectives be pursued.

There has been tendency within housing organisations to seek to centralise control through tighter co-ordinating mechanisms tied into governance structures. Even organisations that place a strong emphasis on accountability and community involvement have tended to centralise key decision-making roles. Executive powers of managers increased following a number of structural changes, such as the establishment of executive-controlled subsidiaries within housing associations (Audit Commission, 2001; Mullins and Riseborough, 2000), the transfer of local authority housing departments into the housing association sector (releasing them from political control) (Pollitt et al., 1998) and, more recently, the establishment of ALMOs. A further indicator of centralisation is the growing importance of management functions associated with information and communication technology and financial control (Mullins, 1999; Pollitt et al., 1998).

Competition has affected housing services in a number of ways. Evaluation of LSVTS suggests that levels of outsourcing have increased markedly (Pawson and Fancy, 2003; MORI et al., 2003). Areas contracted out included: repairs and maintenance, legal services, ground maintenance and IT services. Generally speaking contracting was more likely amongst smaller LSVT associations. These experiences amongst LSVT are likely to be similar to the ways in which CCT impacted on housing management in the 1990s. It led to more emphasis on the management component of professional work, focusing on contract specification, staff awareness of customer needs and customer care and more financial awareness (Pearl, 1997).

The limits of change

The evidence presented above indicates that management has been enhanced in both sectors, though experienced initially and more deeply in the housing association sector (also see Boyne and Walker, 1999; Walker, 2001). But having said this, measuring the extent to which these reforms have become embedded in housing services is a complex task. This complexity arises from the extent of change that has taken place and the focus of academics and regulators. Public management scholars and housing academics have not turned their attentions to issues of managerialism within the housing sector. Consequently the only assessments of devolved budgeting are promotional (Holder, 1994) and no attention has been given to issues such as human resource management. Regulators have predominately focused on policy issues until recently. Nonetheless, there are indications that some changes have penetrated to a greater depth than others.

Competition has clearly extended across the two sectors, but more so in the housing association than the local authority sector. Any developing association is subject to competitive pressures and both sectors in some areas compete for tenants. However, the extent of CCT in the local authority sector was limited to around a four year period, in effect coming to an end in 1997. Of the 113 unitary, London boroughs and Metropolitan districts 65 have housing management contracts but only 7 use external contractors (Davis-Coleman, 2003).

Transfer organisations clearly signify a radical form of external decentralisation. However, many early transfers were undertaken with no competition because the new housing associations were established for the explicit purposes of taking on the local authority stock. As a result of this, where transfers took place they were often initially 'business as normal' (Pollitt et al., 1998, p. 154). However, in the longer term exposure to the housing association sector may lead to gradual changes in the style and nature of management (Walker et al., 2001). Measures to increase competition have also been subsequently introduced in some local authorities (for example, Liverpool city council).

Many housing organisations are adopting a tight/loose configuration (Ferlie et al., 1996). The 'core' controls the budget, overall strategy and business plan, but retains only a general oversight of operational decisions (Mullins, Reid and Walker, 2001). This has led some commentators to question the extent to which the corporate core of the organisation always retains control over operational matters. Mullins (1997) argues that performance measures used by many associations are driven by external benchmarks set by the regulators which, in turn, are complied with only ritualistically within the organisation. If control is not emphasised through this process it can permit the reestablishment or continuation of custodial forms of management.

In the housing association sector systemic performance management regimes have been promoted since the mid 1980s (NFHA, 1987). However, evidence suggests more of a culture of statistics than performance in the local government sector (Boyne et al., 2000).

For a local authority to receive ALMO status it has to receive positive judgements from the housing inspectorate. However, the Audit Commission (2002c) points to a number of ongoing weaknesses in ALMOs. These include: gaps in information to residents, limited complaints procedures, poor planning and monitoring of repairs, inconsistent application of policies and the lack of competition in procurement.

Controlling the front line

Attempts have been made to increase control over front-line decision-making. Guidance on the nature of conduct of work has increased over the last decade. This guidance, in the form of government prescriptions or best practice promoted by the profession, regulator or trade bodies is now extensive (e.g. CIH, 1993; Audit Commission/Housing Corporation, 1997). Guidance is increasingly addressed at both housing associations and local authorities. In what follows we explore the extent to which these broad goals have been achieved and whether managers are really in control of the decision-making process.

The thrust of policy advice to housing services is to further reduce the autonomy of front line staff. Notable examples include the 1996 legislation on homelessness which sought to restrict the discretion of housing officers in the assessment of a homeless determination (DoE/Welsh Office, 1995) and the development of common housing registers, some of which seek to impose common methods of needs assessment. Standardised practices have also been promoted by the CIH since the early 1990s (CIH, 1993). The CIH and the Housing Corporation, frequently working in conjunction with the Audit Commission, produces regular good practice guides and advice. The level of data available on the practice of other social housing providers is extensive. Not only is the good practice available electronically, national databases are available through subscription to benchmarking clubs. These provided social housing organisations with rapid information on management practices used elsewhere across the sector. All this marks a shift away from locally determined housing practice and has extensive effects on service delivery and the day-to-day work of housing officers.

Producer control over the process of allocation has been further eroded over recent years as social housing landlords have adopted a 'choice-based lettings' scheme. This scheme shifts the balance of power towards applicants. In the past applicants were required to meet specific criteria and could reject only a limited number of housing choices presented to them by the landlord. By contrast, the choice based scheme uses limited waiting access criteria rather than an individual property being offered to one applicant. Properties for let are advertised in the manner of an estate agency and applicants who are interested in the property register their interest. The applicant with the highest need as assessed by the limited criteria is then offered the property. Once an applicant is on a list housing officers have reduced discretion over who may be allocated a tenancy.

The variety of tenant voice mechanisms discussed above has also limited professional discretion. There is substantial variation in the extent of tenant decision making between and within social housing organisations, ranging from fully tenant managed organisations, in the case of Kensington and Chelsea, to consultation. However, what is clear is the ongoing growth of tenant involvement (Bines et al., 1993; Albourne Associates, 2003). For example, over 80 per cent of social housing landlords had consulted their tenants on at least one or more issue in

1990/1991; 35 per cent of housing association had tenants on their board, as against 16 per cent of local authorities. While the promotion of participation and the existence of tenants groups was more of an urban phenomena in the 1980s and 1990s (Bines et al., 1993), the requirement under the Labour administration for of all social landlords to have a Tenants Compact in place has ensured that participation structures and process are now in place in every authority in England and Wales. These structures are seen to be leading to change in working practices. Tenants' representatives surveyed in recent research identified reduced paternalism from members and housing officers and felt that they were becoming equal partners with their landlord (Albourne Associates, 2003).

The policy processes of externalisation and managerialisation discussed above have resulted in a focus upon 'core business'. This centres on efficient financial management, on the collection of rents (to ensure that loans can be repaid), the allocation of homes (to ensure rent is not lost) and the maintenance of the stock (to ensure its credit worthiness). These changes impact on management arrangements and are witnessed in organisational targets (required by the regulatory and finance houses) that are translated into individual performance indicators for front-line housing workers. Within housing associations the scope of many housing officers has been reduced as cost pressures and associated management practices have been brought into their day-to-day work.

Enhanced management control may also have resulted from changes in the regime of inspection and audit. The Housing Inspectorate, like the Best Value inspectorate, works to a model of corporate management (Andrews et al., 2000) and promotes integration, common mission and standardised practices. Local authority housing departments that fail to conform to the model receive low scores. The model used in the housing association sector, while different, also promotes a common form of management behaviour. The results of these inspections have to be taken seriously because they matter for ALMO status (which brings new resources), in the Comprehensive Performance Appraisal scores and for access to development programmes for associations. If an association receives a low score it is deemed 'in supervision' and placed under detailed scrutiny. Increased control over service delivery and the actions of front line staff is also being achieved by the detailed scoring systems used by the Audit Commission Inspectors. In particular, the shift away from a producer focus is maintained as the Commission seeks to ensure that services are accountable to users and rewards are put in place that emphasise management goals.

Not all change to front-line work is externally imposed. Many organisations have introduced change to the nature of housing management work and the ways it is experienced by workers. Notable here has been the widespread introduction of call centres (Walker et al., 2001). The intention of call centres is to make changes in the skill mix and to alter professional demarcations. General administration, routine and 'low grade' work, is focused in the call centre, allowing housing officers to concentrate on more complex issues (Walker, 2001). Call centres further specify the nature of the business to be conducted and identify what is and what is not acceptable for an organisation to do, notably altering the nature of the personal contact between officer and customer.

Some barriers to control

As with our prior discussion of evidence on the limits of change the authors are again faced with incomplete information. Virtually no work has been undertaken on the use of performance related pay or the growth of performance appraisal. From the discussion above one might assume that management controls have been further strengthened. However, while this is likely to be the case, there are also indications that such controls are neither complete nor universal.

One of the central areas of debate to emerge over the shifting balance of producer control over services relates to the area of participation. Although a large number of participation schemes have been promoted, questions can be raised about the extent to which customers views are taken seriously. Research findings have long demonstrated that many social housing organisations and their workers pay lip service to goals of enhanced customer involvement (Albourne Associates, 2003). However the increasingly positive assessments of the success of tenant participation schemes (Oxford Brookes University, 2002) would suggest these are having an impact – only the degree remains unclear.

Guidance on performance has been provided in the housing association sector since the late 1980s (NFHA, 1987) and the capacity for performance measurement has been noted (Maclennan et al., 1989). By contrast the evidence from local government is of a culture of statistics, reflected in a tendency for staff and managers only to pay lip service to performance targets and assessments (Walker, 2001). This is somewhat surprising given that a proportion of government resources are allocated on the basis of these performance measures, in order to encourage particular forms of behaviour.

Changing the culture of housing organisations

The argument presented in this section is that custodial management has been further reduced in the two housing sectors and that senior, and many rank-and-file, professionals now support and engage with management practices. Cultural change was promoted by the Conservative and New Labour administrations. The Conservative's desire was to create more customer focused and performance management orientated organisations with a competitive outlook and a focus on value for money. While some facets of this agenda have been diluted in recent years the theme of culture change remains central, alongside other messages about continuous improvement, devolution to the front-line staff, innovation and partnership (Office for Public Services Reform, 2003).

There is clear evidence that values and orientations are now more closely aligned with business practice. This has especially been the case in the housing association sector (Walker, 2001). Pollitt et al. (1998) argues that the managerial notion of quality has been more widely accepted in the LSVT sector than elsewhere across public service provision. Survey and case study evidence presented by Mullins (2000), Pollitt et al. (1998) and Walker (1998; Walker and Jeanes, 2001) also indicates the growing voluntary adoption of private sector management practices in the housing association sub-sector. There has been a great deal of experimentation with practices such as business process re-engineering, total quality management and customer care. All this reinforces our position that housing association managers and staff are more comfortable with the discourse of managerialism and consumerism than is the case with social workers and doctors.

Cultural change can also be noted in the local authority sector. Survey data collected in 2001 reveals that informants from 70 housing authorities express positive attitudes towards the New Labour governments modernisation agenda in relation to competition, continuous improvement, customer focus, devolution to the front line, innovation, partnership and performance measurement (Walker and Enticott, 2004). Responses by housing officers, collected two years later in 2003, indicated a similar level of support for management change (expect in relation to devolution to the front-line). This suggests that the cultural values associated with management reform are becoming more deeply rooted in local authority housing departments.

Unlike social services, and to some degree the NHS, the customers of public housing may have choices that they can exercise. The introduction of the quasi-market reforms in the late 1980s, which offered tenants the possibility of choice, led to a debate about the nomenclature of public housing users (Symon and Walker, 1995). No longer is the term client judged appropriate, as it has connotations of patronage and professional power. Many organisations now actively refer to their tenants as 'customers', to imply that they are valued and their views will be taken on board. These changes in language are reflected by the extent of tenant participation, discussed above.

There is also evidence of changing staff loyalties and identifications. Recent work published by government on staff attitudes in transfer organisations supports the contention that housing associations have been deeply affected by the programme of reform over the last two decades. For example, 'performance management' is seen as a key organisational culture characteristic of transfer organisations. Nearly all have performance appraisal systems compared to around half of all housing authorities. The majority of staff were found to have a very high understanding of their employer's objectives (considerably above levels found in the public sector as a whole) and they were more likely to be able to let their employer know about how they feel about things at work, to be kept informed by their employer, to trust their employer and work as a team (MORI/IRIS consulting/Aldbourne Associates, 2003). Pawson and Fancy (2003), drawing upon evidence from LSVTs that transferred prior to 1999, report the views of senior managers who see the new organisations as egalitarian, inclusive and encouraging of initiative. This is in stark contrast with the old bureaucratic and hierarchical work environment of local authorities. Many of these characteristics suggest that managerial attitudes are very strong in the social housing sector.

But despite all this one cannot say that the shift to management values and orientations has been entirely unproblematic. Commentators note (Clapham and Franklin, 1997; Franklin, 2000; Walker, 2000) that the diametrically opposed forces of residualisation (housing the poorest) and managerialisation (focusing upon core business) have re-opened the debate over the nature of housing work by challenging the capacity of social housing organisation to provide a welfare based service when it is most needed. Professionals have responded to these tensions by reintroducing welfare housing management, re-titled 'community development', embracing youth, care and support, transport and furniture projects (Clapham and Evans, 1998). More recently these types of initiatives have been transferred to the national policy level and housing organisations, since 1997, have been given a central role in regeneration (Social Exclusion Unit, 2000). These practices and the cultures associated with their provision are very different from those promoted by the new managerialism and may in future be a source of growing tension.

In summary we argue that in housing notions of quality, customer focus, performance and managerialism have taken root. For many these ideas are not seen as a threat to professional identities, but as a potential way of furthering professional goals and influence. All this suggests that housing professionals have engaged pragmatically with the new managerialism, certainly when compared to their counter-parts in health and social care.

Conclusions

The analysis presented in this chapter leads to a stark conclusion: Housing is being slowly transformed into a managed service. The origins of the profession encapsulate diverse approaches and organisations. Unlike health or social services they have not been predominately located within one state organisation, but rather across two jurisdictions. This has resulted in different conceptions about the nature and form of housing work and different professional bodies reflecting these approaches. The provision of housing is also somewhat different from health and social work. Social housing has never been the main provider of housing, as the NHS has of health for example. Because it did not have a near monopoly position it has been an easy target of reform. The rapid reduction in the size of the sector though sales to sitting tenants and the alternative choices and aspirations of most households for owner occupation has made the sector susceptible to change. Furthermore, general resource constraints have led to firstly the housing association sector in the late 1980s and then the local authority sector in the late 1990s accepting strong oversight and the imposition of management in return for increases in resources, some of which were relatively modest. However, it is important to note that while sector wide change can be imposed on unwilling organisations, many local authority housing departments voluntarily sought a more managerial context in which to work.

If the two sectors explored in this chapter started with different outlooks, beliefs and approaches to the management task, in the early years of the twenty first Century the evidence is now of convergence. Managerialism developed more quickly in the housing association sector, predominately in response to private finance. However, local authorities are playing a game of rapid catch-up. They are experiment-ing with arm-length forms of organisation that require enhancements in management or alternative funding opportunities that are pushing them further down the managed service road. Those remaining in the local authority sector do not escape these pressures as the Audit Commission with its corporate model of management imposes its view upon local government.

Many housing professionals engaged with management reform and regarded it as having to positive outcomes. The customer culture pro-moted by government and regulators has been variously assessed to have improved responsiveness to users needs (Boyne and Walker, 1999). Tenant satisfaction in LSVT associations is generally acknowl-edged to be higher than in the former local authorities and sets high standards for other housing associations. However, there is still little systematic evaluation of the effects of the reforms on economy, effi-ciency and effectiveness. Also, in one critical area for public services, Boyne and Walker (1999) argue that changes associated with competi-tion, performance indicators and organisational size have resulted in a decline in equity. Services may therefore be better managed and organ-isational arrangements more appropriate, but a price may have been paid to achieve this outcome.

7
Conclusion: Taking Stock of the New Public Management

> The fact is that complex work cannot be effectively performed unless it comes under the control of the operator who does it. Society may have to control the overall expenditures of its Professional Bureaucracies – to keep the lid on them – and to legislate against the most callous kinds of professional behaviour. But too much external control of the professional work itself leads...to centralisation and formalisation of the structure...The effect is to throw the baby out with the bathwater. Technocratic controls do not improve professional-type work, nor can they distinguish between responsible and irresponsible behaviour – they constrain both equally. That may, of course, be appropriate for organisations in which responsible behaviour is rare. But where it is not – presumably the majority of cases – technocratic controls only serve to dampen professional conscientiousness (Mintzberg, 1993: 212).

From the preceding chapters it is clear that, over the past two decades, public services in Britain were subjected to some unprecedented demands for change. Conservative governments initially sought to control the costs of welfare provision, but subsequently turned to the reorganisation of services by introducing more management to augment their cost cutting agendas. They did this on the assumption (which was not seriously disputed) that doing so would increase efficiency. Broadly speaking, the goal was to substitute a model of managed provision for the existing 'custodial' producer driven approaches to organising work. This turned out to be a project involving fundamental reform, which, as time went on, drew intellectual credibility from private sector management ideas to which successive governments were increasingly and overtly committed.

More recently, under New Labour since 1997, the emphasis of reform shifted to an agenda of 'modernisation'. This has been apparently less doctrinaire and more pragmatic, as in the suggestion 'what's best is what works' (Cabinet Office, 1999). But the use of management as a means of transforming the way services are organised and delivered remains central. Today, perhaps even more so than a decade ago, the dominant image projected by politicians and the media is of a public sector crying out for change. This message is reinforced by a constant barrage of critical reports highlighting performance failure, the limited availability and uneven quality of services.

This book has been specifically concerned with the way these policies worked themselves out. Our starting point was the perception that there have been some persistent threads in managerial reforms. We noted how these were brought to bear in different ways in different sectors of the welfare state, and that such differences might be systematically compared for their effectiveness. Thus, our analysis departs from the emphases found in other studies, which either analyse public services as separate cases – usually in order to consider particular problems – or emphasise the same general trends in them all. Our goal was to be more focused and to come up with a more subtle and directly comparative account of the reform process. Hence this book has sought to calibrate, more precisely than is commonly attempted, the variable degrees of new management developed in chosen areas of public services – health, social care and housing.

In the previous three chapters a substantial body of evidence was presented focusing on developments in three services. The purpose of this final chapter is now to stand back from this and draw some broad conclusions. Anticipating those conclusions a little, comparative analysis of health, social services and housing suggests that effective reform has been inversely proportional to the efforts expended on it. The most sustained efforts to introduce management have been undertaken in the NHS, although this has not yielded proportionate results. There have been changes and improvements, yes, but nobody would pretend that the vastly increased expenditure on administration and the decades of change in the organisation and delivery of care, eliminated the problems governments set out to address. By contrast, the shift in housing toward a more managed system has been more effective (at least in administrative terms). The new housing associations were a success despite the much lower level of attention and resource being devoted to this sector by government.

A further objective of the chapter is to consider some of wider consequences of public management reform. From the outset we thought that reforms were likely, other things equal, to have somewhat different efficacy to what they aimed to replace. Whatever particular direction reforms took, they were imposed on something quite specific that, whatever its efficiency, was already functioning. Before there was 'new management', management functions were undertaken by other agencies – largely by the professionals themselves – supported by a relatively passive administration. At the very least, the introduction of new management is likely to disturb these traditional patterns of working. At worst, it may provoke resentment and lack of co-operation, where they did not exist before, without achieving anything more efficient. We find that these outcomes have occurred, affecting the effectiveness of management reforms very profoundly. However, what we were not prepared for was the extent of the ability of existing relationships to impede change and the ineffectiveness of the new arrangements.

In order to develop the argument of this chapter, we will make systematic comparisons between the three sectors under consideration. In the first main section, we spell out more fully some key differences in government policies. Although the content of policy has not varied, we argue that there are important ways in which it's application differed and in the extent to which new management structures and practices were implemented. We will then turn to consider what these reforming efforts came up against, and look at two types of obstacle. Firstly, the way reforms were introduced caused problems and impeded progress. Such things as the lack of consultation, the speed and scope of reforms, acted to undermine the ability and willingness of professions to change. Secondly, we will argue that an even more significant barrier to change has been the organisation of the professions working in the different public services. Here we suggest that the strength of professional attachment to the public sector ethos is the key to understanding their response. It is also argued that professional modes of organising were crucial in understanding how change unfolded.

Finally we will consider what the overall consequences of this restructuring effort have been and whether the benefits outweigh the costs, or vice versa. Our analysis suggests that a very high price has been paid in the UK for what stand as only minimal improvements in the quality and efficiency of public services. This, in turn, raises a number of fundamental questions about the purpose and desirability of ongoing administrative reforms.

Comparing management reform in three sectors

This section highlights some of the main points of comparison between health, social care and housing. To do so we focus both on similarities and differences in terms of broad goals (what change was attempted?), the process of restructuring (how was change attempted?) and the shifts in practice that were accomplished.

Policy goals

The first point to make is that plans to restructure provision in all three sectors were informed by similar objectives and assumptions. Central was a belief in the transformative potential of management ideas based on a 'favourable analysis of the achievements of the corporate sector...' (Pollitt, 1993: 7). This, in turn, was rooted in the dominance of new and different ideas about public service, what Hood has labelled 'sigma type justifications' (Hood, 1991). These values emphasised the need to match resources to tasks and the importance of efficiency. Success would be assessed in terms of outputs and, in particular, tangible results. In all three sectors we consider, the broad thrust of change was to establish entirely new forms of managed provision with qualitatively different competencies and capabilities.

One can therefore generalise about a similar model or template of managed provision that was intended. However this is not to suggest that this 'model' was applied in the same way everywhere. Although the same ideas were in use, in some sectors certain aspects of the new management were given more emphasis or weight than others. For example, the need to develop strong management functions was emphasised everywhere, but different routes to this goal were chosen in different places. The rhetoric of consumer choice was also emphasised, but the examples of actually introducing it, in a serious way, are few. We saw in Chapter 6 considerable importance was attached in housing to the goal of extending direct user involvement in the running of services. By contrast, in health and social care, despite much talk of empowering users and moves to establish systems for quality assurance, there were no comparable moves to extend client participation.

Process or reform

Turning to the process of reform what stands out is the top down nature of change. In all three sectors extensive use was made of core legislation and executive powers to drive through the new policy agenda. An important role was played by regulatory agencies such as the SSI (now superseded) and Audit Commission in promoting management ideas. Most recently these bodies have started to monitor progress against national performance targets, seeking to identify both high performing and supposedly 'failing' services.

Generally speaking professional associations were not involved in the formulation of policy and, in some instances, hardly consulted at all. In health and social care major new legislation (the NHS and Community Care Act 1990) heralding the internal market was effectively presented to the professions as a fait accompli. Only in housing was the professional community more involved in shaping policy in relation to the voluntary transfer of housing stock from local authorities. But even here some question how far professional involvement was essentially reactive, a pragmatic move to pre-empt a less desirable intervention by central government (Pollitt et al., 1998).

There were also some important differences between health, social care and housing in the timing of reform. Although government thinking made the same transition, from an initial focus on economy to the development of management, it did so over different time periods. In the NHS, government moved swiftly to implement general management structures – following the Griffiths report (1983). This indicates that health – as the most costly of public services and also the one towards which there was the most widespread public commitment – was seen to be the most urgent case for reform. By contrast, government was slower to move towards managed provision in social care and housing. In social services it was not until the early 1990s, following major legislation, that pressure to adopt management practices intensified. In housing, new policy dealing with the management of services was also slow to materialise, despite major cuts in provision that had caused some difficult problems that were clearly in need of attention.

Added to this were some marked differences in the methods used by central government to drive through policy change. Here it is useful to focus on two issues, both of which were alluded to in Chapter 3. The first concerns the agents that successive governments relied upon to implement change. Second is the variable extent to which services were re-organised.

Chosen agents of change

One of the decisive limitations facing any government keen to induce changes in administration is that of finding a cadre within services willing and able to take over or to develop the executive powers required. Full implementation of a private sector model would suggest that managers have generic skills not particular ones, and that managers need not share the skill and abilities of the people they manage. This generic model of management works well in many contexts, but it runs into problems when the skills involved are both scarce and esoteric. Managing people whose skill you do not understand is also likely to be problematic, especially in highly professionalised settings. For these reasons it may be easier to adopt an alternative strategy of recruiting managers from amongst practitioner groups. Here the emphasis is on persuading professionals to devote more time to management and for those in charge of institutions (and their support staff) to devote all of their time to these activities. Usually, it was anticipated that professionals would undergo training and take on new management responsibilities, such as staff supervision and the administration of budgets, even at lower levels.

In all three services under consideration there have been clear moves to develop management by creating strong executive leadership roles. However the focus has differed. In the NHS, government policy translated into both kinds of strategy in an attempt to develop a strong management function and ethos within hospitals. On the one hand, a new cadre of managers was recruited and given new executive powers. On the other hand, because it was recognised that the new managers could not control the work of clinicians, concerted attempts were also made to draw senior clinicians into management activities as well, training them and familiarising them with management concerns and priorities. Thus, uniquely in the NHS, there is both a generic class of managers and increased management training for professionals. Greater managerial responsibilities are passed down even to quite junior professionals by such expedients as giving them responsibility for their own budgets. Whether the preservation of distinct hierarchies allows for professionals not to identify with management entirely, is obviously an arguable point. But the fact remains that very concerted attempts have been made to develop management practices in the NHS from a very early point.

If we compare this with the situation in social services and housing, in both cases attempts to develop management practices came at a later stage. Moreover, the primary source of management for these services was the professional groups themselves. In social services, the social workers, as the dominant professional group, maintained a monopoly on recruitment to senior managerial roles. The cost of this however, was the need to take on the management agenda to some extent and accommodate it. This, as we saw, became a source of considerable internal tension and conflict within SSDs that is still ongoing.

Finally, in the case of housing, a quite different dynamic was played out. Here there never was a secure professional monopoly of senior positions to start with. A relatively weak profession viewed change as an opportunity to advance its interests and actively (if not always successfully) tried to colonise new management roles and functions. Housing professionals, as we shall see, were also more favourably disposed to the values of consumerism and cost control and were less prone to question the logic of such change.

The reorganisation of services

A further way in which reform was pursued was through the wholesale re-organisation of different public services. The evidence collected in this book is testimony to the numerous changes in the formal organisations for service delivery legislated for or voluntarily adopted. All three services underwent major re-structuring. An important dimension of this was the creation of new single purpose authorities with general management boards. This represented a significant development in formal organisation, involving the removal of general authority (weakening accountability to local politicians) in favour of the focused exercise of power by managers. Emerging from this were entirely new, self-regulating, provider organisations with distinct legal identities and varying amounts of autonomy to deploy resources and staff (Hoggett, 1996; Kessler et al., 2000).

This type of restructuring was especially marked in housing and health. In the NHS not only was each trust hospital allowed to develop a new cadre of professional managers, management power was given a new context in which to operate. In this case, the traditional independence of different hospitals made possible a relatively smooth transition to the provision of services through hospital trusts. In housing, the transition was less dramatic and some professional functions remained within local government. However, from the early 1990s there has also been a strong move to create self-managing housing trusts and associations.

Only in the personal social services was restructuring of this kind less dramatic. While certain responsibilities were devolved to departmental level, there were no real moves to create single purpose structures. The day-to-day administration of services remained firmly within the ambit of local government. As a result in social services managers faced greater uncertainty over funding and, arguably, were less able than their counterparts in the NHS and housing to exercise discretion. In this sector the gap between a policy rhetoric of empowering managers and the realities of the institutional context seemed especially wide (Keen and Scase, 1998).

Outcomes

Our review of the literature suggests that in all three sectors under consideration, management reforms did have a considerable impact, most notably in terms of the new declared priorities of service provision. Public services became more financially driven, transparent and, arguably, more accountable. As we shall see, there is also evidence of work intensification and rising levels of user throughput.

Added to this are a host of changes in the formal organisation of services and management systems. Everywhere more time and resources are now devoted to backroom tasks associated with planning, strategic management, contract negotiation and financial monitoring. Professionals at all levels are now more likely to undergo management training and take on management responsibilities. Examples of this include moves to devolve budgets to clinical directorates within hospital trusts and to care management teams in social services. Connected to this is the development of new systems of financial and operational control. In all three sectors greater emphasis is placed on assessing the costs of services and their explicit rationing based on recognition of cost implications. As we have seen, systems of performance appraisal, performance review and clinical audit were also established. Although not always effective, these did increase the ability of managers and policy makers to control and monitor the work of front line staff. In this respect one might say the reforms were partially successful in terms of 'closing off...indeterminate and open-ended features of professional practice' (Flynn, 1999: 35).

Notwithstanding these developments, it is clear that change has not been as radical as many assume. As we shall see in the next section, there is little evidence of the fundamental shifts in practice. One should also note the variable nature of the effects of policy across the three sectors in question. Our analysis of the evidence indicates that the most obvious effects of the new policies are in housing. Here the shift towards 'managed provision' has been most pronounced. In this sector, new structures and decision-making systems were implemented with some success – especially in the context of housing associations. There has also been a greater acceptance of and engagement with management ideas and priorities on the part of senior and front line professionals. This is especially true with regard to notions of quality improvement and customer empowerment. By contrast, in health and social care, the shift to managed provision has been less complete and significantly more contested. It is therefore necessary to recognise the fact that changes have been variable and essentially path dependent. In some contexts management ideas and practices were implemented more fully and received greater support than in others.

A rough attempt to summarise these findings can be found in Table 7.1. The first eight rows indicate that it is the NHS where the greatest effort was made to drive reform, in terms of timing and the

Table 7.1   Comparative Analysis of Policy in Three Sectors

	NHS Hospitals	*Social Services Departments*	*Housing Services*
1. Top-down Implementation	+ + +	+ + +	+ + +
2. Early implementation	+ + +	+	+
3. Pressure for change from regulatory agencies	+ + +	+ + +	+ +
4. New cadre of managers	+ + +		
5. Management roles and training for senior professionals	+ +	+ + +	+ + +
6. Management responsibilities for all junior practitioners	+ +	+ +	+ +
8. Single purpose structures	+ + +	+	+++
9. Actual development of management structures and systems	++	++	+++

Note: The weightings allocated are as follows: high (+++); medium (++); low (+)

range of mechanisms used. However, interestingly, this effort did not translate into a high level of implementation (see row 9). By our, admittedly rather crude, calculations, it is in housing where change was most durable and effective. This was also the sector where, arguably, the least amount of effort was expended by governments on the pursuit of reform.

The 'problem' of reform in UK public services

So far we have focused on comparing the impact of policy and the variable development of new management. But what also demands explanation is the question why, across all three services, was the change not more dramatic? Our analysis reveals that older ways of working and professional assumptions continue to be important, even in housing. For example, despite considerable investment in strategic planning there remains a tendency for services to be allocated along customary lines. This was especially apparent in health and social care. In the latter we saw how many local authorities lacked information about user needs and how in some cases strategic plans represented little more than 'public relations exercises'.

There is also evidence to suggest that front line practitioners continue to exercise a high degree of tacit control over the process of service delivery. While there has been a marked proliferation in the quantity of rules and procedures, these have not always been implemented. This is especially true in health where the ability of doctors to control service provision remains considerable. Even in social services and housing front line practitioners continue to interpret rules governing how services are rationed or needs assessed. Added to this is the piecemeal development and coverage of new systems of performance management. In all three services we saw how 'performance' information was often not collected and rarely used systematically to monitor practice. Indeed there are signs that, as management workloads increase, many front line staff now receive less formal supervision and support than before (for a similar account in the civil service see Foster and Hogget (1999)).

These observations therefore question the effectiveness of the new management in public services. It seems that older custodial approaches to service provision retain much of their potency and influence. For some this may come as no surprise. But for us it is important to explain why it is that more substantial progress was not made. This is especially given the time resources devoted to the task of developing a system of managed provision.

In what remains of this section our goal is to address these questions. We argue that attempts to transform management practice encountered two kinds of obstacle. Firstly and somewhat paradoxically, is the reform process itself. Our analysis suggests that the way the reforms have been introduced was a key factor undermining the willingness and ability of the professional groups to change. Second, and for us more important, is the nature of professional values and modes of organising against which policy was directed. These institutions, we suggest, have been surprisingly resilient and effective in terms of mediating and resisting change.

The reform process and its unintended consequences

One might identify a number of characteristics of reform that worked against change. First and most obvious is the fact that policy makers sought to impose restructuring with minimal consultation. As we noted earlier, the professions were viewed as 'part of the problem rather than the solution' and were largely excluded from the policy loop (Laffin and Entwistle, 2000: 211). At local levels, the demand for a rapid cascade of change gave managers little time or scope to consult with staff or unions, even if they had been inclined to do so (Fairbrother and Poyner, 2001). After 1997, this basic approach to implementation did not alter significantly (Bach, 2002). The thrust of policy continues to be on the need for rapid change, stressing the 'failure' of existing public services and professionals to deliver improved services.

The impact of this top down style of change is hard to gauge, although one might reasonably assume that it was negative. According to Hinings and Greenwood (1988: 112), radical change in professional contexts is far 'less likely to follow an imposed alteration of prescribed frameworks...'. Denis et al. (1996) also note how, in health organisations, only collaborative approaches are likely to succeed. More generally it is argued that professional associations play a key, perhaps decisive role, in the dissemination and legitimation of new management ideas (Powell et al., 1999; Greenwood et al., 2002). Where these groups are excluded or only partially involved the result may be heightened resistance, cynicism or only surface compliance with policy demands (Oliver, 1991: 168). Hence, it might be argued that attempts to impose change were detrimental. Even the Audit Commission (2002d: 28) now admits that many front line staff viewed change as an 'external imposition...rather than a locally owned priority'.

A second feature of reform, preventing it from being as effective as it might have been, relates to the speed and pace of new policy. All three sectors discussed in this book experienced a continual process of restructuring, downsizings and new policy initiatives. The 1990s were characterised by a 'helter-skelter succession of different organisational formats, a new one seemingly being invented long before any rational assessment of its predecessor' (Pollitt et al., 1998: 178). If anything, from 1997, these tendencies become more pronounced. One recent survey found that 54 per cent of those working in local government and 51 per cent in health services reported a major organisational change in their workplace in the previous year (UNISON, 2001). A study of social services in London also noted how a majority of managers were 'tied up in restructuring or making new organisations work' (Downey, 2002).

Again, while difficult to assess the full impact of this aspect of reform it was likely to have been detrimental. An obvious problem is that in many public services professionals and administrators simply lacked the management skills and capabilities to implement change, let alone in the timescales demanded. It is also possible that the 'unrelenting stream of initiatives and short-term service targets' disorientated managers at local levels, distracting them from the pursuit of longer-term policies and goals (Bach and Winchester, 2003: 31). No sooner had one set of organisational arrangements and procedures been put in place when a torrent of new policy demands emerged. The cumulative effect has been a growing sense of 'initiative fatigue' amongst front line staff and their managers (Buchanan, et al., 1999; Guest and Conway, 2001). A recent survey by the Chartered Institute of Personnel Development (CIPD) (2003) found that the pace of restructuring was placing 'significant strain on line managers who may not have the resources or support to deal with...change'.

Finally one might point to the way public service organisations in the UK have been forced to respond to a range of, sometimes, competing policy requirements. Looking at the broad sweep of management restructuring it is easy to assume that successive governments had a clear and well-defined project in mind. But as we have seen this was patently not the case. Policy developed in a piecemeal and sometimes ad hoc fashion with objectives shifting over time (Harrison and Wood, 1999). The reforms were characterised by a multiplicity of objectives and demands and quite often these were in competition with each other (Pollitt, 1993; Lowndes, 1997). One example of this is the tension between moves to devolve authority, 'empowering' managers, and efforts to centralise control over resources and other key policy decisions (Hoggett, 1996; Kessler and Purcell, 1996). A further example is the tension between the goals of improved economy and the requirement that public organisations manage services more effectively. Pollitt and Boukaert (2000: 159–61) characterise this as a conflict between two sets of ideas that were influential in the UK and elsewhere. On the one hand are micro economic ideas that tend to 'prioritise efficiency and savings' and on the other is management thinking, focusing on 'improving performance in a broader sense'. In practice these ideas were (and remain) hard if not impossible to reconcile. In all three sectors considered here, attempts to enhance management practice were directly undercut by moves to contain or reduce costs.

These and other competing policy demands made the shift to managed provision more difficult to accomplish. Local managers and professionals were often unable to implement change under such conditions. It is hard, for example, to develop more effective strategic planning when the resources and staff available for such back room tasks are steadily cut back. Harrison et al. (1992) note how mixed policy objectives also produce a deep sense of confusion, 'puzzlement' and cynicism at local levels. This might increase the likelihood of what Greenwood and Hinings (1996: 1029) describe as 'idiosyncratic interpretations' of policy goals and 'either deliberate or unwitting variation in practices'. Across all three sectors local actors were forced into positions of having to accommodate and balance out different requirements. This led many to implement structures that only partly reflected the original intentions of policy makers (Foster and Hoggett, 1999). Often, what emerged were organisational arrangements that may have satisfied external stakeholders but which were largely incoherent and ineffective (for an account of this in social services see Challis et al. (2001) and Kirkpatrick (2003)).

In combination these aspects of the reform process made the task of implementing policy harder and more fraught than might otherwise have been the case. Yet while this is important for our understanding, it is not sufficient to explain why so little progress was made. At the end of the day, had there not been more fundamental opposition, many of the problems listed above would probably have been overcome. It is to that 'opposition' and the sources of it that we must now turn.

A more fundamental problem: the institutions of welfare professionalism

We contend that the main obstacle to reform in the UK has been the institutions of welfare professionalism against which it has been directed. One aspect of this are deeply embedded values that shape and provide justification for professional action. Professional groups operate with very different definitions of their cultural resources (Savage et al., 1992) or 'cultural capital' (Hanlon, 1998: 48–50). On the one hand, there are professional claims that are based on a 'commercialized' version of professionalism, which frequently combines technical ability, managerial skill and economic rewards. This can be contrasted with a different image of professionalism based on a public service ethos, which puts technical skill together with the provision of services on the basis of need rather than on the basis of ability to pay. It is a continuing allegiance to this kind of ethos, we suggest, that is central to understanding why changes have often been slow and contested.

Also important here are aspects of professional organisation itself. As we saw in Chapter 2, these organisations were the product of regulative bargains between the state and professional groups seeking occupational closure. This process helped to reinforce existing jurisdictions and guaranteed the professions varying degrees of control over the means and ends of service delivery. It is therefore for this reason, as well as the attachment to certain values, that some professional groups have actively sought to defend the status quo. Under these conditions particular modes of organising become extremely hard, if not impossible, to disassemble or redirect.

In what remains of this section we now consider these issues in more detail, starting first with the question of values and second the nature of professional organisation.

A continued attachment to public service values

It is highly likely that the current attachment of many social workers and doctors to public sector values was forged in the era of custodial management in the first three decades of the existence of the welfare state. In this connection, it is interesting to contrast with the dominant views at the inception of the NHS, in which quite different values were exhibited such as a strong attachment to market and resistance to the state (especially by consultants). One might argue (and many do) that current developments are leading us back to this situation (Hanlon, 1998). If this is so, we might expect attachment to the old values of public service would gradually wane under the constant pressure for change. However, what is compelling is not that there is no evidence for such change, but that the trend is weak and consistently found only among particular subgroups within the professions as a whole.

Our analysis shows that many social workers and doctors were entering management and working according to different goals and priorities. This was especially true amongst senior professionals, many of whom actively engaged with new management ideas. For some change presented an opportunity to improve services and perhaps enhance their own influence and career prospects. We therefore reach similar conclusions to those outlined elsewhere in the literature. Restructuring, as Exworthy and Halford (1999: 13) suggest, may 'herald new patterns of compromise and collaboration between managerialism and professionalism'. One might also see the emergence of new constituencies and interests within the professions and, over time, a fracturing of older collegial relationships (Leicht and Fennel, 2001; Webb, 1999).

Connected to this were some important variations in response between sectors. Amongst housing officers, unlike social work and medical professionals, there was more acceptance of commercial values and of management. This is in good part because the link between professionalism and public service was less secure within this occupation. Housing officials are representative of a 'technobureucratic' or organisational profession (Larson, 1977; Fincham, 1996). From an early stage these services were more tightly managed themselves and were closer to what Webb and Wistow (1987) describe as a 'discretionary' rather than a 'pure professional' model of organisation. Given this, it is perhaps not surprising that certain features of the new management were adopted here much more readily than elsewhere. Senior administrators faced less well-grounded commitment to alternative values from front line practitioners amongst this group and were more able to drive through change.

But despite these trends, one is hard pressed to argue that the shift towards management values is universal. Many, even in management positions, were divided over the merits of reform, their support for management being pragmatic or lukewarm. Often, limited acceptance of new values resulted in what is called strategic compliance (Gleeson and Shain, 1999). Our consideration of the literature also reveals that, for many front line practitioners, public service values retain much of their potency. In this way our conclusions reflect a growing body of research and opinion (Guest and Conway, 2002; Bryson, 2004). Pratchett and Wingfield (1996), for example, note how a majority of local government officers continue to positively identify with the notion of a public sector ethos. Morgan et al. (2000: 105) also find that the commitment of public service workers has proven 'surprisingly robust' in the face of management restructuring.

These professional values do not exist in and for themselves, but are connected with, support and reinforce key aspects of practice. It is this difficulty of breaking down such values that helps to explain the slow, contested and piecemeal nature of change. Overall it seems that only limited progress has been made in terms of 'constructing articulations between professional concerns and languages and those of management' (Clarke and Newman, 1997: 76). This is not to say that all professionals in the social services we have been examining did not (and do not) accept the legitimacy of the new management. Rather, it is to argue that professional orientations and values remain the basis of day to day practice. The primacy of professionalism as a principle for the organisation of work has not yet been consistently overridden by management, still less superseded by managerially driven ways of organising work. As Clarke (1998: 242) suggests, older values 'linger on not just out of nostalgia, but because the *specific* practices of welfare provision continue to require particular combinations of…competencies and orientations'.

Professional organisation

Turning now to professional organisation, there are several aspects to be examined. The most obvious connection is between values and everyday practices. As we saw there is much evidence that front line professionals continue to exercise a high degree of control over the process of service delivery. This is an aspect of what has been called 'internal closure' by some analysts of the professions (Ackroyd, 1996; also see Chapter 2). By this is meant that a professional group preserves the exclusive right to undertake their work without interference or encroachment from other occupations in the workplace.

Professional work is organised by the maintenance of internal closure in such a way that it protects the ability of professionals to exercise discretion. This remains true even though many of the services under consideration in this book (including some of those delivered by the NHS) are relatively standardised and their accomplishment is routinised. Partly because of this and changes in technology, it has been possible for managers to impose stricter control on operational decision making. But, at the same time, there are obvious limits to this process. A great many activities and operations remain indeterminate and incapable of being formally programmed. There remains what Flynn (1999: 34) describes as an '*irreducible* core of autonomy'. While the desire and intention to increase supervision has undoubtedly become stronger, in most areas an effective defence of discretion has been mounted through closure.

It is also true that the perceived interests of the professions are linked to the ability to sustain the exercise of discretion, and this runs counter to the expectations of management reform. In all three sectors one might argue that the reforms constituted both a threat and an opportunity (especially where senior professionals were concerned). But change was persistently understood as more of the former than the latter. As Kessler and Purcell (1996: 216) suggest 'the presence of professional groups, reinforced institutionally through their associations...helped preserve a set of values and principles potentially in tension with the newer managerial practices'.

This response is understandable given the historical experience of professional groups. The medical profession has, over many years established exclusive control over the licensing and discipline of practitioners. Theorists of the professions call this external or labour market closure. Social workers have also sought to develop something similar by insisting on social work qualifications and graduate entry to the profession. In both cases, a degree of success in terms of securing a monopoly for services in the labour market, translated into the ability to exert control over service provision itself. One might argue therefore that in both areas there existed a strong incentive to defend the status quo.

By contrast, housing was (and remains) a weak profession based on flimsy claims to special expertise. Housing administrators compete for influence with other more established groups, including surveyors, architects and civil engineers. To use the technical term, their external closure was far from complete. These conditions suggest that there was more of an incentive for housing professionals to engage with the new managerialism. By doing so, they might further strengthen professional claims and increase their independence vis-à-vis other more powerful occupations.

Hence, in housing the new managerialism seemed to offer the occupation some opportunity for the advancement if the professional values could be redefined. We saw in Chapter 6 how there had been strong support amongst the practitioner community for transferring housing administration to the voluntary sector. While this was partly pragmatic, it also served to advance professional interests (Flynn, 1999: 31–32). Through restructuring, 'housing managers were able to some extent retrieve former freedoms and to build upon them further' (Pollitt et al., 1998: 179). However, it is difficult to identify a comparable benefit that might accrue to the social workers of the doctors and nurses. For these professions, redefining the values of the profession would seem to risk weakening their structural advantages in internal and external closure.

Thus, aspects of professional organisation, such as the perceived value of external and internal closure worked against the new management. A key feature of custodial administration was a tendency to resist or seek to mediate top down policies, and this has simply continued. To be sure this did not prevent restructuring or changes in practice (especially with regard to the management of budgets). But it did create strong pressures for 'convergent' change focused primarily on maintaining the status quo (Greenwood and Hinings, 1996: 1024). Across public services, the new management was either partially or entirely 'captured' by provider interests and concerns (Denis et al., 1999). Even when there is a substantial body of support amongst professionals for change – what Greenwood and Hinings (1996) describe as 'reformative commitment' – the dynamics of professional organisation were such as to help reinforce older ways of working (for a recent example of this see McNulty and Ferlie's (2002) account of business process reengineering in the NHS).

Professional power and the negotiation of policy

There is an understandable tendency of observers to confuse the prescriptions made by the advocates of the new public management with changes that have actually occurred. What our analysis shows however is that this kind of thinking is highly problematic. In the UK a number of factors worked to hold back the progress of public management reforms. The willingness and ability of professions to implement new policy was undermined by the way reforms were introduced. But more important than that has been the resilience of the professional institutions against which new policy was directed. Where these institutions are very strong, not even concerted managerialism can override them, or at least not very quickly. It is not the pressure to induce change that will ensure its effectiveness so much as the acceptability of change given the established character of professional projects.

Table 7.2 represents a crude attempt to gauge the relative strength of these professional institutions. While it would be perilous to attempt to draw any hard and fast conclusions from such data, a number of points can be made. First concerns the different capabilities of the professions in health social services to successfully resist or mediate change. Perhaps not surprisingly we see that it is in the NHS, especially amongst doctors, where this capacity is strongest. In social services one also finds an albeit less well entrenched professionalism able to mediate reform. Finally, in housing, the professions have lacked both the ability and, one might argue, the inclination to strongly oppose change.

Table 7.2   Comparative Analysis of Professional Organisation

	NHS Hospital Doctors (Nurses)	Local Authority Social Workers	Housing Managers
1. Strength of attachment to professional culture and values	+ + + (+ + +)	+ + +	+ +
2. de facto professional control of day to day work practices	+ + + (+ +)	+ +	+
Professional Closure			
4. Internal	+ + + (+ +)	+ +	+
5. External	+ + + (+ +)	+ +	+
Overall measure of capacity to resist or mediate reform	**HIGH (MEDIUM)**	**MEDIUM**	**LOW**

Note: The weightings allocated are as follows: high (+++); medium (++); low (+)

This analysis is especially interesting when looked at alongside Table 7.1. Doing so reveals that it is health where professional organisation is strongest and where there have been more concerted efforts to impose the new management. In this case the strength of professional organisation is only marginally exceeded by the policy levelled at it, which could well account for the marginal and faltering amount of change. Looking at the scoring for social work, on this reckoning, it seems that the professional organisation of social workers was stronger than the policies brought to bear. This too may help explain certain outcomes, such as the highly embattled situation in this service. Finally, although less weight of policy has been brought to bear on housing professionals, it is interesting to note that it is in this sector where professional organisation was weakest. Again, we express some diffidence about reading too much into this sort of data. But it is undoubtedly interesting that it is where the institutions of professional control were weak and where the least effort was made to induce new management that most progress was actually made.

To conclude, what we are suggesting is that the pressure of reforms must be weighed against the organisation of key professional groups and the extent to which these groups locked themselves into strategies of resistance. If professional values and institutionalisation are robust, they will continue to be operative and affect behaviour, despite the extent of the restructuring ranged against them.

Assessing the costs and benefits of reform – was it worth it?

In this final section we focus on the wider consequences and outcomes of the new public management in the UK. Throughout this book we have seen how a major justification for change was that existing modes of professional service organisation were failing or had become redundant. The modernisation of public services, adopting ideas and practices from the private sector, was viewed as an absolute necessity. Reform, according to Tony Blair, 'is not the enemy of public service in Britain; the status quo is' (Quoted in Bach (2002: 328)). But as time and resources continue to be poured into this reform effort one might reasonably ask: what has been achieved? What have been the benefits of restructuring and how do these stack up against the very real costs?

Any attempt to evaluate public management reforms in the UK or elsewhere is likely to be fraught with difficulty. The very concept of 'results' or 'outcomes' is ambiguous depending on the context and on the perspective of those making the evaluation (Pollitt, 2000). A full assessment of the new public management is therefore beyond the scope of this chapter. Instead what will be attempted is a more general review of the main outcomes of government policy. This will firstly consider how far management restructuring did achieve certain objectives intended by policy makers. Second, the wider costs and unintended consequences of change on professional services are described.

What has been achieved?

The first point to make here concerns what Pollitt and Boukaert (2000) describe as operational results and in particular those associated with cost control and efficiency. Here it would seem that the public management reforms did have a marked impact. As we saw in Chapter 3, during the 1990s, although public expenditure rose in real terms, as a proportion of GDP it remained relatively stable. There is also much evidence to suggest that in this period, rates of activity and work intensity increased (Guest and Conway, 2001; Cully et al., 1999; Audit Commission, 2002d). Case study research from individual services points to rising levels of user throughput and turnover (Ackroyd and Bolton, 1999; Foster and Hoggett, 1999). More generally Green (2001) finds that, between 1992 and 1997, 49 per cent of public services managers (57.4 per cent in education) perceived that work had intensified compared with 32.5 per cent in the private sector. To be sure, these outcomes cannot be attributed directly to changes in management

(Pollitt, 2000). Nor should we assume that rising levels of efficiency and throughput necessarily meant improvements in the overall efficiency of services (Osborne and McLaughlin, 2002). But what seems undeniable is that, through management reform, government was more able to control expenditure and find ways of squeezing greater physical productivity from the workforce (Colling, 2001: 618).

It is argued that public management reforms led to changes in the process of decision-making, or the way services are provided (Pollitt and Boukaert, 2000: 115). Important here is the claim that managed provision resulted in a more accountable mode of professionalism (Day and Klein, 1990). There is said to be greater transparency in the system as a result of increased monitoring, supervision and the publication comparative performance indicators. Such information means that managers have a better idea of what is wrong with the services they direct and, arguably, are more able to deal with malpractice and poor standards (Sanderson, 2001; Bach and Winchester, 2003: 310). More transparency may also help managers achieve consistency in the level and standard of provision across areas and groups of professionals (Foster and Wilding, 2000).

Thirdly, management reform is said too have resulted in a more user-oriented mode of professional practice. To some extent this amounts only to changes in language and to the prominence of discourses of quality and consumer empowerment (Martinez-Lucio and McKenzie, 1999). As the Guardian recently observed, 'there is now a more consumer-oriented feel to government services' (Guardian, 2003a). But it is also argued that management restructuring did help make services more focused on the needs of individual clients. In some areas, users now have a degree of choice in service provision, while in others (such as housing and education) there have been clear improvements in user participation and voice (Bach and Winchester, 2003: 310). Of course, none of this necessarily means that clients are more satisfied than before with the services they receive. Nevertheless it does seem clear that the balance of power between professionals and users has shifted. As Foster and Wilding (2000: 155) argue: 'service users have emerged from a state of virtual social exclusion to a place at least on the edge of the stage'.

Finally it is claimed that restructuring led to a stronger performance orientation in public services (Webb, 1999). During the 1990s many public organisations invested heavily in strategic planning, seeking to allocate resources and services according to defined goals and priorities. More emphasis was placed on performance measurement and the adoption of systems of variable pay – most recently for schoolteachers (Waine, 2000). As such one might argue that professional services did become more focused on results. However, as we have seen, the extent to which this led to more fundamental shifts in practice is questionable. In the context of local government, especially, there continued to be a strong tendency for services to be allocated along customary lines. Here, and perhaps elsewhere cultures of professionalism still '...act to limit rather than excite innovation' (Greenwood and Stewart, 1986: 48).

At what cost?

So far we have suggested that management restructuring produced certain outcomes that were intended and valued by policy makers. However, after over two decades of almost uninterrupted change one could be forgiven for thinking that what has been achieved is really quite modest and unimpressive. Despite considerable resources expended on modernising services, with massive disruption to staff and users, one is hard pressed to find evidence of real improvements in client satisfaction or quality (Pollitt, 2000). Indeed there is little to suggest that public organisations today are substantially more effective or responsive than those existing twenty years ago.

Added to this is a need to recognise some of the wider costs and unintended consequences of restructuring. Firstly, is the growing burden of red tape and administration in public services. In some areas, notably the NHS, the 1990s witnessed a considerable expansion in non-productive management roles and functions. Recent labour force statistics indicate that the number of managers employed has risen by 60 per cent over the past seven years, from 22,000 in 1997 to 35,321 in 2004. The overall number of 'backroom' administrative staff had also increased, now exceeding the number of hospital beds in the service (Hope, 2004). Beyond this are also costs associated with performance monitoring and the time spent in preparation for audits and inspections (Bach, 2002; Geddes, 2001: 503). A recent study conducted by the Audit Commission (2002d) found that front line staff and managers were 'overwhelmed by bureaucracy, paperwork and targets' (22–23). Many staff, it argued, viewed paperwork as 'unnecessary' and complained how 'the content of their work was increasingly driven not by what matters but by what could be measured' (23). Similar findings come from studies dealing with specific groups of professionals such as the police (Home Office, 2001), General practitioners (Regulatory Impact Unit, 2001), social workers (SSI, 2002) and teachers (Regulatory

Impact Unit, 2000). Overall, the picture is of a public sector workforce bogged down by demands to respond to performance targets and account in detail for their actions.

A further cost associated with management reform is the rising level of stress and demoralisation amongst the public service workforce. Data from the 1998 Workplace Employee Relations Survey shows public sector workers are more likely than their private sector counterparts to experience stress and be absent through illness (Cully et al., 1999). Similarly, a national survey conducted by the CIPD found that 38 per cent of NHS staff and 30 per cent of those in local government were stressed, compared with and average of 25 per cent for all workers (CIPD Press release, 2003). These, and countless other studies, reveal a workforce that is also increasingly demoralised (Audit Commission, 2002d; UNISON, 2000). According to Guest and Conway (2002) 'levels of satisfaction, trust and commitment are all lower in the public sector'. Clearly a number of factors are contributing to this situation. However, in most accounts the process of management restructuring is placed high on the list. The imposed nature of change, deteriorating relationships with line managers and growing work pressures, it would seem, have all taken their toll (Bach and Winchester, 2003: 296).

Some observers predict that these trends will have a damaging effect on service delivery in the longer term. It is noted that rising levels of stress and demoralisation are a key factor behind the current recruitment and retention crisis facing the public sector (Audit Commission, 2002d). Over the past five years a growing number of qualified professionals – including nurses, teachers, social workers and police officers – have left public sector employment and are increasingly hard to replace. In secondary education 32,000 teacher vacancies were reported in 2001 alongside a 15.8 per cent annual resignation rate (Conley, 2002). Some local authorities, especially in London, also report shortages of up to 46 per cent for social care staffs (LGEO, 2001). Various explanations are given for these trends, including low levels of pay relative to the private sector (Elliott and Duffus, 1996). But once again, what is emphasised in almost every study is the link between rising staff turnover and deteriorating conditions of employment (Audit Commission, 2002d; Bach and Winchester, 2003). As Conley (2002: 728) puts it: 'one result of continued pressure is that public sector workers are "voting with their feet"'.

In many areas this trend exaggerated the problems of managing service delivery. Front line professionals faced rising workloads as they were asked to cover for absent colleagues (Audit Commission, 2001).

One report on social services in London found shortages had led to gaps in middle management and to 'Personal care jobs which should take 30 minutes' being 'crammed into 15 or 20' (Douglas, 2002). Responding to these difficulties, many public organisations started to rely on agency workers (Kirkpatrick and Hoque, 2004). Between 1999 and 2000 the NHS spent £810 million on temporary nursing cover, up by 20 per cent on the previous year (Audit Commission, 2001) and similar trends have been noted in social services and secondary education (SCHWG, 2003; Grimshaw et al., 2003). However, even this 'solution' carries many risks. First is the very high cost of agency workers compared with permanent staff. One recent investigation estimated that these costs might be anything up to 30 per cent extra for groups such as social workers (Community Care, 2003). Beyond this are problems of declining client satisfaction with the lack of continuity in care, not to mention costs associated with monitoring and training agency staff (IDS, 2003; Laurence, 2001).

There is reason for thinking that some of these effects are concentrated in particular institutions within the system that covers the country, and their emergence is not unrelated to the process of management development itself. It seems to be almost completely overlooked that the development of management, in the manner pursued by government policy, may contribute to both the development of good institutions and also at the same time the dynamic decline of the less good. The constant measurement of performance, which attracts rewards, is likely to incline mobile staff, particularly those who can show a track record of successful performance themselves, to move to stronger institutions within the system of provision. Similarly, relative failure, which attracts at best intensifying surveillance and control, is also very likely to drive out staff that are capable of movement. Thus management development itself is having some dynamic effects that produce success, but at the some time are likely to create failure out of mediocrity. By this accounting the policy of management is an important factor in the reproduction of management failure. It is depressing to think that this unintended, but real, consequence of the managerialisation of public services has been overlooked by all, including those most enthusiastic about change.

Related to this are longer-term negative consequences of management restructuring for the nature of relationships at work (Foster and Wilding, 2000). As we saw in Chapter 2, professional services in the UK were sustained in part by a strong sense of vocation and a pool of goodwill trust. This manifested itself in terms of a willingness to work beyond contract. It also fostered informal, collegial, relationships between groups, minimising conflict and (in most instances) facilitating the effective coordination of services. So far, the evidence is that this mode of working has not been completely undermined in the UK. However, there are signs that it is under considerable strain. In housing, social care and health we found evidence of growing conflict between front line staff and managers and reduced levels of collegial support. A study focusing on local government also found that a majority of employees had experienced a breach in their psychological contract, leading to reductions in 'organizational citizenship behaviour' (Coyle-Shapiro and Kessler, 2000: 903). There is therefore a real risk that current changes may result in a workforce that is more instrumental in its orientations to work. A sense of vocation, that once sustained the delivery of good quality public services at relatively low cost, is slowly being eroded.

The longer term implications of all this can only be guessed at. One possibility is that services become harder to organise as professionals 'forsake the communal and collegiate principle that is distinctive of the professional mode of organising work' (Friedson, 1994: 215 – in Foster and Wilding, 2000: 155–56). More instrumental relationships could mean that greater emphasis will need to be placed on (costly) formal systems of line management and performance monitoring as a way of coordinating services. Added to this is the risk that the quality of services to the client will be undermined. According to Mintzberg (1993: 211), in the long term, rising levels of bureaucracy serve only to 'dampen professional conscientiousness' and impede the ability of front line staffs to respond to users.

To summarise, it does appear that management reforms produced some outcomes that were desired and intended. However, these 'achievements' came at a very high price. After two decades of change, it remains unclear how far public services are actually more effective than before. Many front line staff operate within a regime of stifling bureaucracy and paperwork while, across public services, the ratio of productive to unproductive workers has deteriorated. The formerly highly functional informal organisation of many public organisations is under threat if not already destroyed and there is a widespread loss of vocationalism and cooperation amongst key professionals. In sum, a costly but effective bureaucratic mode of public service organisation has been replaced by a costly but doubtfully effective managed system.

Future directions

In many ways the findings reported in this book, concerning the disruptive and uneven process of reform, are not surprising. In the UK perhaps more so than any other developed country, politicians sought radical and far-reaching change (Pollitt and Boukaert, 2000; Bach et al., 1999). The imperative was to restructure public services quickly and dismantle the old post war organisational settlement. Little attempt was made to evaluate whether management reforms would actually work (Pollitt, 1995) or build upon the strengths of what had existed before. Indeed the breakdown in trust was so great that virtually no attempt was made to consult the professions. As a consequence of this politicians: 'neglected either to cherish or to build on is the potentially positive elements in traditional professionalism: the service ethic, the principle of colleague control, and the commitment to high quality work' (Foster and Wilding, 2000: 157). These aspects of professional self-regulation were either ignored or simply brushed aside. So too was the idea that change is most effective when it 'seeps in by the slow process of changing the professionals' (Mintzberg, 1993: 213). In the UK, management reform was introduced in a way that was almost guaranteed to maximise disruption and opposition. This meant that a very high price was paid for what, as we have seen, have been only modest gains in terms of improved efficiency and service quality.

In recent years there has been a growing recognition of these problems amongst some policy makers. This is reflected in the emphasis now placed on working in partnership with the professions to modernise services. In stark contrast to the public choice rhetoric of the early 1990s there is now a more positive message about the value of professionalism. According to Tony Blair, 'this is a decade when we will look to public service professionals as the new byword for can-do innovation and dynamism. For shaking things up and getting things done' (Guardian, 2002). The talk is of building on and extending notions of a public service ethic. Linked to this are moves to strengthen professionalism in some areas, such as social work, with the introduction of registration and more resources for training. In return the professions are being asked to modernise their own internal structures, for example, by removing outmoded job demarcations. This can be seen with initiatives across the public sector to enhance the role of non professional assistants in service delivery (Bach, 2002: 334). There has also been growing interest in reengineering, focusing on ways in which service provision might be organised around core processes or client groups rather than professional specialisms (McNulty, 2003).

These and some other developments suggest that, in future, it may be possible to develop a more cooperative working relationship between government and professions. However, one might question how far this will lead to outcomes that are substantially different. Public spending has increased overall since 2001, but the pressure to control resources at operational levels remains as intense as ever. Also, central government shows no sign of slowing down the pace of restructuring and policy change. According to Bach and Winchester (2003: 309), a majority of employees and managers 'would have welcomed a period of organisational stability and more generous funding so that they might recover from "reform fatigue"'. But for this current administration, 'organisational stability' is neither desirable nor possible. The emphasis continues to be on highlighting performance failure and the pressing need to reform and modernise at all costs. As such one might question the idea that, in future, the progress of reform will be any smoother or less problematic. Front line practitioners will continue to face the same pressure on resources and the same mix of competing policy demands as they did before. How far, under these conditions, it will be possible to re-build professional commitment and genuinely improve service provision remains open to question.

Notes

Chapter 1

1. In 1995/6, for example, health accounted for 22.3 per cent of total UK welfare expenditure, the personal social services, 4.8 per cent and Housing, 2.1 per cent (Glennerster and Hills, 1998: 332–333).
2. In terms of the distribution of expenditure by country, England, not surprisingly, takes up the largest share. In 1999/2000, England accounted for 81 per cent of Health and Personal Social Services spending and 69 per cent of housing (Stationery Office, 2001).

Chapter 3

1. Pollitt and Boukaert (2000: 28) note how forces of globalisation represent a 'vital background factor in prompting consideration of administrative reform', but do not determine the timing, degree or nature of such change. Other 'intervening variables' are important, they argue, such as 'socio-democratic change' (29), shifts in ideas and dynamics of the political system.
2. One of the major consequences of this process has been a marked decline in the size of the public sector workforce in the UK, from 7,185 million in 1981 to 5,093 million in 2000 (Geddes, 2001: 499).
3. In 1970 total general government expenditure in UK stood at 38.8 per cent of GDP, highest in the (then) OECD seven group. In 1998, this figure had risen to 40.1 per cent, but was then third lowest – after USA and Japan (Shaoul, 1999: 31).
4. Between 1997 and 2001, public expenditure in the UK as proportion of GDP stood at 40 per cent, compared with average of 44 per cent between 1979–97. However, in their second term New Labour pledged to increase spending by an estimated 4 per cent per annum in real terms (Bach, 2002: 324).

Chapter 4

1. Estimates made by the authors. Another measure of scale is the size of health expenditure, which is large. See tables included in Chapter 1, suggesting that health expenditure is 4.5 times greater than that on social services.
2. This is clear from the most frequently repeated quotation from Griffiths: 'If Florence Nightingale was carrying her lamp through the corridors of the NHS today, she would almost certainly be searching for the people in charge'.
3. The use of the notion of financial accountability and the designation of 'accountable officers' dates form this reform. There was a perceived need for clarity about who exactly was responsible for overspending when this occurred.

4. They are not, however, the same purchasers as under the internal market (the health authorities), but primary care groups, later to become primary care trusts. These are perceived as purchasing services on the behalf of the local community. See the 1997 white paper, *The New NHS: Modern, Dependable* (DH, 1997).

5. Subsequent work has confirmed these ideas about the pattern of recruitment to the new NHS management. Less than ten per cent of top managers in the new NHS structure are former nurses, whereas more than sixty per cent are former administrative and finance staff. If we add to this sixty per cent the numbers of managers recruited from outside the NHS, it seems very clear that only a minority of the new management of the NHS are former professionals (for a breakdown of the occupational origins of NHS management appointments at the end of the 1980s see Harrison and Pollitt, 1994: 67).

Chapter 5

1. In Scotland similar functions are carried out by nine social services authorities.

2. The largest area for professional employment is services for children and families, with approximately 18,420 qualified field social work staff in area teams, compared with 12,790 staff in adult services in 1997. The number of professional social workers employed in residential services is far lower, with 77 per cent of unit managers of community homes qualified and only 38 per cent of staff below this level (LGMB/CCETSW, 1997).

3. The post war period witnessed a massive expansion in spending on the personal social services in Britain, from about 0.2 per cent in 1955 to about 1 per cent of GNP by 1975 (Evandrou and Falkingham, 1998: 200).

4. This picture conceals a wide variation in organisational forms and structures adopted by SSDs in England and Wales (BIOSS, 1974; Challis, 1990; SSI, 1996; Challis et al., 2001; Whipp et al., 2004). There has been a marked tendency in this sector for periodic re-organisation of services according to shifting logics and rationales. In the 1980s, for example, many SSDs moved towards decentralised (or 'patch') systems of organisation and later to client-based divisions (children and adults) (Challis and Ferlie, 1986). In the 1990s, there were further changes in organisation with moves to establish purchaser-provider structures.

5. The 'administrative' version of care management that was promoted in the UK context might be contrasted with what Huxley (1993) refers to as a 'clinical' model. In the former, the professional adopts the role of a broker (or travel agent), assessing need and organising the purchase of a care package. By contrast, a 'clinical' model emphasised the on-going relationships between the client and professional service provider (the travel companion). Also see Lewis et al. (1997).

Chapter 6

1. The 1996 Housing Act recast housing associations as Registered Social Landlords to account for the way the sector was being changed through stock transfers. We, however, use the traditional term housing association.

References

Abbott, A. (1988) *The System of Professions*, Chicago: University of Chicago Press.

Abbott, P. and Meerabeau, L. (1998) 'Professionalisation and the Caring professions', in Abbott, P. and Meerabeau, L. (eds) *The Sociology of the Caring Professions*, London: UCL Press.

Abbott, P. and Wallace, C. (1996) *An Introduction to Sociology: Feminist Perspectives*, 2nd edn., London: Routledge.

Abbott, P. and Wallace, C. (1998) 'Health visiting, social work, nursing and midwifery: a history', in Abbott, P. and Meerabeau, L. (eds) *The Sociology of the Caring Professions*, London: UCL Press.

Abel-Smith, B. (1964) *The Hospitals: 1800–1948*, London: Heinemann.

Ackroyd, S. (1992) 'Traditional and new management in the NHS hospital service and their effects on nursing', in Soothill, K.L., Henry, C. and Kendrick, K. (eds) *Themes and perspectives in Nursing*, London: Chapman and Hall.

Ackroyd, S. (1995a) *The New Management and the Professions: Assessing the Impact of Thatcherism on the British Public Sector*, Working Paper No. 24, Department of Sociology, Stockholm University ISSN: 1400–4232.

Ackroyd, S. (1995b) 'From public administration to public sector management: understanding contemporary change in British public services', *International Journal of Public Sector Management*, 8, 2, 19–32.

Ackroyd, S. (1996) 'Organisation contra organisations: professions and organisational change in the United Kingdom', *Organisation Studies*, 17, 4, 599–621.

Ackroyd, S. (1998) 'Hospital nurses: beyond bureaucracy or bureaucracy and more?', in Laffin, M. (ed.) *Beyond Bureaucracy: The Professions in the Contemporary public Sector*, Aldershot: Ashgate.

Ackroyd, S. (2002) *The Organization of Business: Applying organizational Theory to Contemporary Change*, Oxford: Oxford University Press.

Ackroyd, S., Hughes, J., and Soothill, K. (1989) 'Public sector services and their management', *Journal of Management Studies*, 26, 6, 603–619.

Ackroyd, S. and Bolton, S. (1999) 'It is not Taylorism: mechanisms of work intensification in the provision of gynaecological services in an NHS hospital', *Work Employment and Society*, 13, 2, 369–87.

Ackroyd, S. and Bolton, S. (2002) 'The management of nurses', *International Journal of Public Sector Management*, 15, 2, 98–106.

AHHRM (Association of Heathcare Human Resource Management) (1997) *Conference Proceedings*, http.www.ahhrm.org.uk.

Alaszewski, A. (1995) 'Restructuring health and welfare professions in the United Kingdom: the impact of internal markets on the medical, nursing and social work professions', in Johnson, T., Larkin, G. and Saks, M. (eds) *Health Professions and the State in Europe*, London: Routledge.

Alaszewski, A. and Manthorpe, J. (1990) 'Literature review: the New Right and the professions', *British Journal of Social Work*, 20, 237–251.

Albourne Associates (2003) *Interim Evaluation of Tenant Participation Compacts*, London: Office of the Deputy Prime Minister.

Andrew, T. and McLean, J. (1995) 'Current working patterns in the personal social services', in Balloch, S., Andrew, T., Ginn, J., McLean, J., Phal, J. and Williams, J. (eds) *Working in the Social Services*, London: NISW.

Andrews, R., Boyne, G.A., Law, J., and Walker, R.M. (2003) 'Myths, measures and modernisation: The comparative performance of English and Welsh local government' *Local Government Studies*, 29, 2, 54–75.

Archer, M. (1995) *Realist Social Theory: The Morphogenic Approach*, Cambridge: Cambridge University Press.

Armstrong, P. (1986) 'Management control strategies and inter-professional competition: the cases of accountancy and personnel management', in Knights, D. and Willmott, H. (eds) *Managing the Labour Process*, Aldershot: Gower.

Ashburner, L. and Fitzgerald, L. (1995) 'Beleaguered professionals: clinicians and institutional change in the NHS', in Scarborough, H. (ed.) *The Management of Expertise*, London: Macmillan.

Audit Commission (1985) *Managing Social Services for the Elderly More Effectively*, London: HMSO.

Audit Commission (1986a) *Managing the Crisis in Council Housing*, London: HMSO.

Audit Commission (1986b) *Improving Council House Maintenance*, London: HMSO.

Audit Commission (1992a) *The Community Revolution: The Personal Social Services and Community Care*, London: HMSO.

Audit Commission (1992b) *Developing Local Authority Housing Strategies*, London: HMSO.

Audit Commission (2000) *Group Dynamics*, London: HMSO.

Audit Commission (2001) *Brief Encounters: Getting the Best from Temporary Nursing Staff*, London: Audit Commission.

Audit Commission (2002a) *A Force for Change: Central Government Intervention in Failing Local Government Services*, London: Audit Commission.

Audit Commission (2002b) *Comprehensive Performance Assessment*, London: Audit Commission.

Audit Commission (2002c) *Learning from the First Housing ALMOs*, London: Audit Commission.

Audit Commission (2002d) *Recruitment and Retention: A Public Service Workforce for the Twenty-First Century*, London: Audit Commission.

Audit Commission (2003) *A Framework for the Review of Housing Inspection and Assessment*, London: Audit Commission.

Audit Commission/Housing Corporation (1997) *House Styles*, London: HMSO/ Housing Corporation.

AC/SSI (1999a) *Getting the Best from Children's Services: Findings from the Joint reviews of Social Services, 1998/1999*, London: Audit Commission.

AC/SSI (1999b) *Making Connections: learning the Lessons from the joint reviews 1998/1999*, London: Audit Commission.

AC/SSI (2001) *Delivering Results: Joint Review Team Fifth Annual Report 2000/1*, London: Audit Commission.

Bach, S. (1999a) 'Europe: changing public service employment relations', in Bach, S., Bordogna, L., Della Rocca, G., and Winchester, D. (eds) *Public Service Employment Relations in Europe: Transformation, Modernisation or Inertia?*, London: Routledge.

Bach, S. (1999b) 'Personnel managers: managing to change?', in Corby, S. and White, G. (eds), *The Public Services: Themes and Issues*, London: Routledge.

Bach, S. (2002), 'Public-sector employment relations reform under Labour: muddling through or modernisation?', *British Journal of Industrial Relations*, 40, 2, 319–339.

Bach, S., Bordogna, L., Della Rocca, G., and Winchester, D. (1999) (eds) *Public Service Employment Relations in Europe: Transformation, Modernisation or Inertia?*, London: Routledge.

Bach, S. and Winchester, D. (2003) 'Industrial relations in the public sector', in P. Edwards (ed.), *Industrial Relations*, 2nd edn, Oxford: Blackwell.

Baggott, R. (1997) 'Evaluating health care reform: The case of the NHS internal market', *Public Administration*, 75, 2, 283–306.

Ball, S.J. (1990) *Politics and Policy Making in Education*, London: Routledge.

Balloch, S., Andrew, T., Ginn, J., McLean, J., Phal, J., and Williams, J. (eds) (1995) *Working in the Social Services*, London: NISW.

Balloch, S., Phal, J., and McLean, J. (1998) 'Working in social services: job satisfaction, stress and violence', *British Journal of Social Work*, 28, 329–50.

Balloch, S., Fisher, M., and McLean, J. (eds) (1999) *Social Services: Working Under Pressure*, Bristol: Policy Press.

Barber M. (1992) *Education and the Teacher Unions*, London: Cassell.

Barker, R., Challen, P., MacLennan, D., Reid, V., and Whitehead, C. (1992) *Competing for Quality in Housing*, London: HMSO.

Bennett, C. and Ferlie, E. (1996) 'Contracting in theory and practice: some evidence from the NHS', *Public Administration*, 74, 1, 49–66.

Berridge, D. and Brodie, I. (1996) 'Residential child care in England and Wales: The inquiries and after', in Hill, M. and Aldgate, J. (eds) *Child Welfare Services: Developments in Law, Policy, Practice and Research*, London: Jessica Kingsley.

Berridge, D. and Brodie, I. (1997) *Children's Homes Revisited*, London: Jessica Kingsley.

Bills, D., Bromley, G., Hey, A., and Rowbottom, R. (1980) *Organising Social Services Departments*, London: Heinemann.

Bilton, K. (1998) 'Child and family social work: organisational context and identity', *Child and Family Social Work*, 3: 197–203.

Bines, W., Kemp, P., Pleace, N., and Radley, C. (1993) *Managing Social Housing*, London: HSMO.

BIOSS (1974) *Social Services Departments*, London: Heinemann.

Black, O., Herbert, R., and Richardson, I. (2003) 'Jobs in the Public Sector, June 2002', *Economic Trends*, No. 598, Sept.

Blau, P.M. and Scott, W.R. (1963) *Formal Organisations: A Comparative Approach*, London: Routledge.

Bolton, S. (2002) 'A bit of a laugh: nurses' use of humour as a mode of resistance', in Dent, M. and Whitehead, S. (eds) *Managing professional Identities: Knowledge, Performativities and the 'New' Professional*, London: Routledge.

Boyne, G.A. (1998) 'Public services under new labour: back to bureaucracy?' *Public Money and Management*, 18, 3, 43–50.

Boyne, G.A., Day, P., and Walker, R.M. (2002) 'The evaluation of public service inspection: a theoretical framework', *Urban Studies*, 39, 7, 1197–1212.

Boyne, G.A., Farrell, C., Law, J., Powell, M., and Walker, R.M. (2003) *Evaluating Public Management Reforms*, Buckingham: Open University Press.

Boyne, G.A., Gould-Williams, J., Law, J., and Walker, R.M. (2000) *The Evaluation Study on Best Value in Wales, Final Report*, Cardiff: Cardiff Business School.

Boyne, G.A., Gould-Williams. J., Law, J., and Walker, R.M. (2002) 'Best Value – total quality management for local government?', *Public Money and Management*, 22, 3, 9–16.

Boyne, G.A., et al. (1999) 'Human Resource Management in the public and private sectors: an empirical comparison', *Public Administration*, 77, 2, 407–420.

Boyne, G.A. and Walker, R.M. (1999) 'Social Housing Reforms in England and Wales: A Public Choice Evaluation', *Urban Studies*, 36, 13, 2237–2262.

Bradley, G. and Manthorpe, J. (1997) *Dilemmas of Financial Assessment: A Practitioner's Guide*, Birmingham: Venture Press.

Braithewaite, B. (1999) 'The harsh language of bureaucracy', *Community Care*, March.

Brint, S. and Karabel, J. (1991) 'Institutional origins and transformations: the case of American community colleges', in Powell, W.W. and DiMaggio, P. (eds) *The New Institutionalism in Organisational Analysis*, London: University of Chicago Press.

Brion, M. (1994) *Women in the Housing Service*, London: Routledge.

Broadbent, J. and Laughlin, R. (2002) 'Public service professionals and the new public management: control of the professions in the public services', in McLaughlin, K., Osborne, S.P. and Ferlie, E. (eds) *New Public Management: Current Trends and Future Prospects*, London: Routledge.

Bryson, C. (2004) 'What about the workers? The expansion of higher education and the transformation of academic work', *Industrial Relations Journal*, 35, 38–57.

Buchan J., Seccombe I., Smith, G. (1997) *Nurses' Work: an Analysis of the UK Nursing Market Developments in Nursing and Healthcare*, Falmer: Institute of Employment Studies.

Buchanan, D., Claydon, T., and Doyle, M. (1999) 'Organisational development and change: the legacy of the nineties', *Human Resource Management Journal*, 9, 2, 20–37.

Bucher, R. and Stelling, J. (1969) 'Characteristics of professional organisations', *Journal of Health and Social Behaviour*, 10, 1, 3–15.

Bull, J. and Hamer, L. (2001) *Closing the Gap: Setting local Targets to Reduce Health Inequalities,* London: Health Development Agency.

Burnham, P. (1999) 'The politics of economic management in the 1990s', *New Political Economy*, 4, 1, 37–54.

Burrage, M. (1992) 'Mrs Thatcher Against Deep Structures: The Ideology, Impact and Ironies of her Eleven Year Confrontation with the Professions', Working paper 92–11, University of California at Berkeley: Institute of Government Studies.

Cabinet Office (1999) *Modernising Government*, Cm 4310, London: Stationary Office.

Cairncross, L., Clapham, D., and Goodlad, R. (1996) *Housing Management: Consumers and Citizens*, London: Routledge.

Cambridge, P. (1999) 'Building care management competence in services for people with learning disabilities', *British Journal of Social Work*, 29, 393–415.

Carey, M. (2003) 'Anatomy of a care manager', *Work Employment and Society*, 17, 1, 121–135.

Carr, F. (1999) 'Local bargaining in the National Health Service: new approaches to employee relations', *Industrial Relations Journal*, 30, 197–211.

Carr-Saunders, A.M. and Wilson, P.A. (1962) *The Professions*, Oxford: The Clarendon Press.

Causor, G. and Jones, C. (1996) 'Management and the control of technical labour', *Work, Employment and Society*, 10, 1, 105–123.

Causor, G. and Exworthy, M. (1999) 'Professionals and managers across the public sector', in Exworthy, M. and Halford, S. (eds) *Professionals and the New Managerialism in the Public Sector*, Buckingham: Open University Press.

Cawson, A. (1982) *Corporatism and Welfare*, London: Heinemann.

Central Housing Advisory Committee (1938) *Management of Municipal Housing Estates*, London: HMSO.

Central Housing Advisory Committee (1959) *Councils and Houses*, London: HMSO.

Central Housing Advisory Committee (1969) *Council Housing: Purposes, Procedures and Priorities*, London: HMSO.

Central Housing Advisory Committee (1971) *Housing Associations*, London: HMSO.

Challis, D., Weiner, K., Darton, R., Hughes, J., and Stewart, K. (2001) 'Emerging patterns of care management: arrangements for older people in England', *Social Policy and Administration*, 35, 6, 672–687.

Challis, L. and Ferlie, E. (1986) 'Changing patterns of fieldwork organisation: I. The headquarters view', *British Journal of Social Work*, 16, 181–202.

Challis, L. (1990) *Organizing Public Social Services*, Harlow: Longman.

Chartered Institute of Housing (1993) *Housing Management Standards Manual*, Coventry: CIH.

Chartered Institute of Housing (2002) *Yearbook*, Coventry: CIH.

Chartered Institute for Personnel Management and Development (2003) *NHS and Local Government Employees are Most Stressed Out Workers*, Press Release (www.cipd.co.uk/press/PressRelease/).

Clapham, D. (1992) 'A women of her time', in Grant, C. (ed.) *Built to Last? Reflections on British Housing Policy*, London: Roof Magazine.

Clapham, D. (1997) 'The social construction of housing management research', *Urban Studies*, 34, 5–6, 761–774.

Clapham, D. and Evans, A. (1998) *From Exclusion to Inclusion. Helping to create successful tenancies and communities*, London: Hastoe Housing Association.

Clare, M. (1988) 'Supervision, role strain and social services departments', *British Journal of Social Work*, 18, 489–507.

Clarke, J. (1993) 'The comfort of strangers: social work in context', in Clarke, J. (ed.) *A Crisis in Care?*, London: Sage.

Clarke, J. (1995) 'After social work?' in Parton, N. (ed.) *Social Theory, Social Change and Social Work*, London: Routledge.

Clarke, J. (1998) 'Doing the right thing? Managerialism and social welfare', in Abbott, P. and Meerabeau, L. (eds) *The Sociology of the Caring Professions*, London: UCL Press.

Clarke, J. and Newman, J. (1997) *The Managerial State*, London: Sage.

Clarke, J., Gerwitz, S., and McLaughlin, E. (2000) 'Reinventing the welfare state', in Clarke, J., Gerwitz, S., and McLaughlin, E. (eds) *New Managerialism New Welfare?*, London: Sage.

Cockburn, C. (1977) *The Local State*, London: Pluto Press.

Cochrane, A. (1993) 'Challenges from the centre', in Clarke, J. (ed.) *A Crisis in Care?*, London: Sage.

Cole, I. and Furbey, R. (1994) *The Eclipse of Council Housing*, London: Routledge.

Collings, J. and Murray, P. (1996) 'Predictors of stress amongst social workers: and empirical study', *British Journal of Social Work*, 16, 3, pp. 375–88.

Colling, T. (1999) 'Tendering and outsourcing: Working in the contract state?', in Corby, S. and White, G. (eds) *Employee Relations in the Public Services*, London: Routledge.

Colling, T. (2001) 'Human Resources in the Public Sector' in Beardwell, I. and Holden, L. (eds) *Human Resource management: A Contemporary Perspective*, 4th edn. London: Pitman.

Collins, R. (1990) 'Changing conceptions in the sociology of the professions', in Torstendahl, R. and Burrage, M. (eds) *The Formation of the Professions: Knowledge, State and Strategy*, London: Sage.

Community Care (2003) 'Rise of the locum', *Community Care*, 16 October.

Conley, H. (2002) 'A state of insecurity: temporary work in the public services', *Work Employment and Society*, 16, 4, 725–737.

Coombs, R. and Cooper, D. (1992) 'Accounting for patients: the implementation of information technology and the NHS', in Loveridge, R. and Starkey, K. (eds) *Continuity and Crisis in the NHS: the Politics of Design and Innovation in Health Care*, Buckingham: Open University Press.

Coote, A. and Appleby, J. (2002) *Five Year Health Check (5) A Review of Government Health Policy, 1997–2002*, London: King's Fund.

Corby, S. and White, G. (1999) 'From the new right to new labour', in Corby, S. and White, G. (eds) *The Public Services: Themes and Issues*, London: Routledge.

Cousins, C. (1987) *Controlling Social Welfare*, Brighton: Wheatsheaf.

Coyle-Shapiro, J. and Kessler, I. (2000) 'Consequences of the psychological contract for the employment relationship: a large scale survey', *Journal of Management Studies*, 37, 7, 903–930.

Craig, G. and Manthorpe, J. (1998) 'Small is beautiful? Local government re-organisation and the work of social services departments', *Policy and Politics*, 26, 2, 189–207.

Crompton, R. (1990) 'Professions in the current context', *Work Employment and Society, Special Edition, A Decade of Change?*, 147–166.

Cully, M., Woodland, S., O'Reilly, A., and Dix, G. (1999) *Britain at Work: As Depicted by the 1998 Workplace Employee Relations Survey*, London: Routledge.

Cutler, T. and Waine, B. (1994) *Managing the Welfare State: Text and Sourcebook*, Oxford: Berg.

Cutler, T. and Waine, B. (2000) 'Managerialism reformed? New Labour and public sector management', *Social Policy and Administration*, 34, 3, 318–332.

Darke, J. and Rowland, V. (1997) 'Are tenants really in control at Kensington and Chelsea?', paper presented to the Housing Studies Association Conference, Housing Organisations and Housing Services: Linking Theory and Practice Cardiff, September.

Daunton, M. (1987) *A Property Owning Democracy?*, London: Faber and Faber.

Davies, C. (1995) *Gender and the Professional Predicament in Nursing*, Buckingham: Open University Press.

Davies, C. and Francis, A. (1976) 'Perceptions of structure in NHS hospitals', *Sociological Review Monograph*, 22.

Davies, H.T.O., Mannion, R., and Marshall, M.N. (2001) 'Treading a third way for quality in health care', *Public Money & Management*, 21, 2, 6–8.

Davies, M. and Niner, P. (1987) *Housing Work, Housing Workers and Education and Training for the Housing Service*, London: Institute of Housing.

Davies, T.O., Hodges, C., and Rundall, T.G. (2003) 'Consensus and contention: doctors' and managers' perceptions of the doctor manager relationship', *British Journal of Health Care Management*, 9, 6, 202–208.

Davis-Coleman, C. (ed.) (2003) *Contract Handbook*, London: CDC Publishing.

Dawson, S., Mole, V., Winstanley, D., and Sherval, J. (1995) 'Management, competition and professional practice: Medicine and the market place', *British Journal of Management*, 6, 3, 169–181.

Dawson, S. and Dargie, C. (2002) 'New public management: a discussion with special reference to UK health', in McLaughlin, K., Osborne, S.P. and Ferlie, E. (eds) *New Public Management: Current Trends and Future Prospects*, London: Routledge.

Day, P. and Klein, R. (1990) *Inspecting the Inspectorates*, London: Joseph Rowntree Foundation.

Deakin, N. and Parry, R. (1998) 'The Treasury and New Labour's social policies', in Brundson, E., Dean, H. and Woods, R. (eds) *Social Policy Review*, 10, London: Social Policy Association.

Denis, J., Langley, A., and Cazele, L. (1996) 'Leadership and strategic change under ambiguity', *Organisation Studies*, 17, 4, 673–699.

Denis, J-L., Lamothe, L., Langley, A., and Valette, A. (1999) 'The struggle to redefine boundaries in health care systems', in Brock, D.M., Hinings, C.R. and Powell, M.J. (eds) *Restructuring the Professional Organisation: Accounting, Health Care and Law*, London: Routledge.

Dent, M. (1993) 'Professionalism, educated labour and the state: hospital medicine and the new managerialism', *Sociological Review*, 41, 244–273.

Dent, M. (1998) 'Hospitals and New Ways of Organising Medical Work in Europe', in Thompson, P. and Warhurst, C. (eds) *Workplaces of the Future*, Basingstoke: Macmillan.

Dent, M. (2003) *Remodelling Hospitals and Health Professionals in Europe: Medicine, Nursing and the State*, London: Palgrave.

Dent, M. and Whitehead, S. (2002) (eds) *Managing professional Identities: Knowledge, Performativities and the 'New' Professional*, London: Routledge.

DfEE: Department for Education and Employment (1999) *Teachers Meeting the Challenge of Change: Technical Document*, London: The Stationary Office.

Department of the Environment (1994) *Education and Training for Housing Management*, London: HMSO.

Department of the Environment/Welsh Office (1995) *Our Future Homes. Opportunity, Choice, Responsibility*, London: HMSO.

Department of the Environment, Transport and the Regions (1999) *Business Planning for Local Authority Housing with Resource Accounting in Place. A Consultation Paper*, London: DETR.

Department of Health and Social Security (1985) *Social Work Decisions in Child Care: Recent Research Findings and their Implications*, London: HMSO.

Department of Health (1979) *Patients First (Consultative Paper)*, London: HMSO.

Department of Health (1992) *Choosing with Care: the Report of the Committee of Inquiry into the Selection, Development and Management of Staff in Children's Homes*, London: HMSO (Warner Report).

Department of Health (1997) *The New NHS: Modern, Dependable*, Cm.3807, London: HMSO.

Department of Health (1998) *White Paper: A First Class Service*, London: HMSO.

Department of Health (2001) *Shifting the Balance of Power within the NHS – Securing Delivery*, London: Department of Health.

Department of Health/LAC (2002) *Fair Access to Care Services: Guidance on Eligibility Criteria for Adult Social Care*, London: Department of Health.

Derber, C. (ed.) (1982) *Professionals as Workers: Mental Labour in Advanced Capitalism*, Boston MA: G.K. Hall.

DiMaggio, P. and Powell, W.W. (1991) 'The iron cage revisited: institutional isomorphism and collective rationality', in Powell, W.W. and DiMaggio, P. (eds) *The New Institutionalism in Organisational Analysis*, London: University of Chicago Press.

Dominelli, L. (1996) 'Deprofessionalising social work: anti-oppressive practice, competencies and postmodernism', *British Journal of Social Work*, 26: 153–175.

Dominelli, L. (1997) *Sociology for Social Work*, London: Macmillan.

Douglas, A. (2002) *Is Anybody Out There? Recruitment and Retention in Social Care in London*, London: Community Care.

Downey, R. (2002) 'Care in the Capital: New Report Reveals Extension of Recruitment Crisis in London', *Community Care*, 18 July.

du Gay, P. and Salaman, G. (1992) 'The [cult]ure of the customer', *Journal of Management Studies*, 29, 5, 615–33.

du Gay, P. (2000) *In Praise of Bureaucracy*, London: Sage.

Dunleavy, P. and Hood, C. (1994) 'From old public administration to new public management', *Public Money and Management*, 14, 3, 9–16.

Eborall, S. (2003) *The State of the Social Care Workforce in England: Summary of the First Annual Report of the Topss England Workforce Intelligence Unit, 2003*, Topss: Leeds.

Edwards, P. and Kenny, D. (1997) *Community Care Trends 1997 Report*, Luton: Local Government Management Board.

Elliott, R. and Duffus, K. (1996) 'What has been happening to pay in the public service sector of the British economy? Developments over the period 1970–92', *British Journal of Industrial Relations*, 34, 1, 51–85.

Esping-Anderson, G. (1990) *The Three Worlds of Welfare Capitalism*, Cambridge: Polity Press.

Etzioni, A. (ed.) (1968) *The Semi Professions and their Organisation*, New York: Free Press.

Evandrou, M. and Falkingham, J. (1998) 'The personal social services', in Glennerster, H. and Hills, J. (eds) *The State of Welfare: The Economics of Social Spending*, Oxford: Oxford University Press.

Evetts, J. (2002) 'New directions in state and international professional occupations: discretionary decision-making and acquired regulation', *Work Employment and Society*, 16, 2, 341–353.

Exworthy, M. and Halford, S. (1999a) 'Professionals and managers in a changing public sector: conflict, compromise and collaboration?', in Exworthy, M. and Halford, S. (eds) *Professionals and the New Managerialism in the Public Sector*, Buckingham: Open University Press.

Exworthy, M. and Halford, S. (1999b) 'Assessment and conclusions', in Exworthy, M. and Halford, S. (1999) (eds) *Professionals and the New Managerialism in the Public Sector*, Buckingham: Open University Press.

Fairbrother, P. and Poyner, G. (2001) 'State restructuring, managerialism, marketisation and the implications for labour', *Competition and Change*, 5, 3, 311–333.

Farnham, D. and Horton, S. (eds) (1996a) *Managing the New Public Services*, London: Macmillan.

Farnham, D. and Horton, S. (eds) (1996b) *Managing People in the Public Services*, London: Macmillan.

Fergusson, R. (2000) 'Modernising managerialism in education', in Clarke, J., Gerwitz, S. and McLaughlin, E. (eds) *New Managerialism New Welfare?*, London: Sage.

Ferlie, E., Ashburner, L., Fitzgerald, L., and Pettigrew, A. (1996) *The New Public Management in Action*, Oxford: Macmillan.

Ferlie, E. and Fitzgerald, L. (2000a) 'Professionals: back to the future', *Human Relations*, 53, 5: 713–739.

Ferlie, E. and Fitzgerald, L. (2000b) 'The sustainability of the new public management in the UK: an institutional perspective'. Symposium paper, American Academy of Management, Toronto, August.

Ferrera, M. (1998) 'The four "social Europes": between universalism and selectivity', in Rhodes, M. and Meny, Y. (eds) *The Future of European Welfare: A New Social Contract?*, Basingstoke: Macmillan.

Fincham, R. (1996) *New Relationships in the Organised Professions: Managers, Professionals and Knowledge Workers*, Avebury: Aldershot.

Flynn, N. (1987) 'Delegating financial responsibility and policy-making within social services departments' *Public Money*, March, 41–44.

Flynn, N. (2000) 'Managerialism in the public services: some international trends', in Clarke, J., Gerwitz, S. and McLaughlin, E. (eds) *New Managerialism New Welfare?*, London: Sage.

Flynn, N. and Strehl, F. (eds) (1996) *Public Sector Management in Europe*, London: Prentice Hall, Harvester Wheatsheaf.

Flynn, R. (1999) 'Managerialism, professionalism and quasi markets', in Exworthy, M. and Halford, S. (eds) *Professionals and the New Managerialism in the Public Sector*, Buckingham: Open University Press.

Foot, M. (1975) *Aneurin Bevan: 1945–1960*, St Albans: Paladin.

Foster, D. and Hoggett, P. (1999) 'Changes in the Benefits Agency: empowering the exhausted worker?', *Work Employment and Society*, 13, 1, 19–39.

Foster, P. and Wilding, P. (2000) 'Whither welfare professionalism?', *Social Policy and Administration*, 34, 2, 143–159.

Franklin, B. (2000) 'Demands, expectations and responses: the shaping of housing management' *Housing Studies*, 15, 907–927.

Franklin, B. and Clapham, D. (1997) 'The social construction of housing management', *Housing Studies* 12, 1: 7–26.

Friedson, E. (1985) 'The reorganisation of the medical profession', *Medical Care Review*, 42, 11–35.

Friedson, E. (1994) *Professionalism Re-born: Theory, Prophesy and Policy*, Cambridge: Polity Press.

Froggett, L. (1998) 'Sustaining tensions in practice supervision', *Social Services Research*, 1, 33–42.

Garrett, P.M. (1999) 'Mapping child-care social work in the final years of the twentieth century: a critical response to the "Looking After Children" system', *British Journal of Social Work*, 29, 1, 27–47.

Geddes, M. (2001) 'What about the workers? Best Value, employment and work in local public services', *Policy and Politics*, 29, 4, 497–508.

Gewirtz, S., Ball, S.J., and Bowe, R. (1995) *Markets*, Choice and Equity in Education, Buckingham: Open University Press.

Giddens, A. (1984) *The Constitution of Society*, Cambridge: Polity.

Gleeson, D. and Shain, F. (1999) 'Managing ambiguity: between markets and managerialism – a case study of "middle" managers in further education', *Sociological Review*, 47, 3, 461–490.

Glennerster, H. (1998) 'New beginnings and old continuities', in Glennerster, H. and Hills, J. (eds) *The State of Welfare: The Economics of Social Spending*, Oxford: Oxford University Press.

Glennerster, H. and Hills, J. (eds) (1998) *The State of Welfare: The Economics of Social; Spending*, Oxford: Oxford University Press.

Goode, W.J. (1957) 'Community within a Community', *American Sociological Review*, 22, 194–200.

Grant, K. (2003) 'Culture Change', *Inside Housing*, 5th December.

Green, F. (2001) 'It's been a hard day's night: the concentration and intensification of work in late twentieth century Britain', *British Journal of Industrial Relations*, 39, 53–81.

Greenwood, E. (1957) 'Attributes of a profession', *Social Work*, 2, 3, 44–55.

Greenwood, R. (1984) 'Incremental budgeting: antecedents of change', *Journal of Public Policy*, 4, 4, 277–306.

Greenwood, R. and Stewart, J.D. (1986) 'The institutional and organisational capabilities of local government', *Public Administration*, 64, 35–50.

Greenwood, R. and Hinings, C.R. (1988) 'Organizational design types, tracks and the dynamics of strategic change', *Organizational Studies*, 9, 3, 293–316.

Greenwood, R. and Hinings, C.R. (1993) 'Understanding strategic change: the contribution of archetypes', *Academy of Management Journal*, 36, 5, 1052–81.

Greenwood, R. and Hinings, C.R. (1996) 'Understanding radical organisational change: bringing together the old and new institutionalism', *Academy of Management Review*, 21: 4, 1022–1054.

Greenwood, R. and Lachman, R. (1996) 'Change as an underlying theme in professional service organizations: an introduction', *Organization Studies*, 17, 4, 563–572.

Greenwood, R., Suddaby, R. and Hinings, C.R. (2002) 'The role of professional institutes in the transformation of institutionalised fields', *Academy of Management Journal*, 45, 1, 58–80.

Greer, A. and Hoggett, P. (1999) 'Public policies, private strategies and local public spending bodies' *Public Administration*, 77, 2, 235–256.

Grey, A. and Jenkins, B. (1997) 'Reinventing professions: changing relationships in public services', paper presented at PSRU conference, Cardiff Business School, March.

Griffiths, R. (1983) *The NHS Management Inquiry*, London: DHSS.

Griffiths, W. (1976) *Local Government Administration*, London: Shaw and Son.

Grimshaw, D. (1999) 'Changes in skills-mix and pay determination among the nursing workforce in the UK', *Work Employment and Society*, 13, 2, 295–328.

Grimshaw, D., Earnshaw, J. and Hebson, G. (2003) 'Private sector provision of supply teachers: a case of legal swings and professional roundabouts', *Journal of Education Policy*, 18, 3, 267–288.

Grimshaw, R. and Sinclair, R. (1997) *Planning to Care: Regulation, Procedure and Practice Under the Children Act 1989*, London: NCB.

Guardian (2002) 'Full text of Tony Blair's speech on public services', 25 January.

Guardian (2003) 'Governing costs. Public Sector productivity', 10 November.

Guest, D. and Conway, N. (2001) *The State of the Psychological Contract*, London: CIPD.

Guest, D. and Conway, N. (2002) *Pressure at Work and the Psychological Contract*, London: CIPD.

Guest, D., Redfern, S., Wilson-Barnett, J., Dewe, P., Pecci, R., Rosenthal, P., Evans, A., Young, C., Montgomery, J., and Oakley, P. (2001) *A Preliminary Evaluation of the Establishment of Nurse, Midwife and Health Visitor Consultants*, www.kcl.ac.uk/depsta/pse/mancen.

Halford, S. and Leonard, P. (1999) 'New identities? professionalism, managerialism and the construction of the self', in Exworthy, M. and Halford, S. (eds) *Professionals and the New Managerialism in the Public Sector*, Buckingham: Open University Press.

Hallett, C. (1982) *The Personal Social Services in Local Government*, London: George Allen and Unwin.

Halmos, P. (1973) *Professionalisation and Social Change*, Keele: Sociological Review Monograph 20.

Hanlon, G. (1998) 'Professionalism as enterprise: service class politics and the redefinition of professionalism', *Sociology*, 32, 1, 43–63.

Harris, J. (1998) 'Scientific management, bureau professionalism, new managerialism: the labour process of state social work', *British Journal of Social Work*, 28, 839–862.

Harris, J. and McDonald, C. (2000) 'Post-Fordism, the Welfare State and the Personal Social Services: A Comparison of Australia and Britain', *British Journal of Social Work*, 30, pp. 51–70.

Harrison, S. (2002) 'New Labour, modernisation and the medical labour Process', *Journal of Social Policy*, 31, 3, 465–485.

Harrison, S. (1997) 'Health – the agenda for an incoming government', *Public Money and Management*, April–June, 27–31.

Harrison, S., Hunter, D.J., and Pollitt, C.J. (1992) *The Dynamics of British Health Policy*, Unwin Hyman: London.

Harrison, S. and Pollitt, C. (1994) *Controlling the Health Professionals: the Future of Work and organisation in the NHS*, Buckingham: Open University Press.

Harrison, S. and Wood, B. (1999) 'Designing health service organizations in the UK, 1968 to 1998: from blueprint to bright idea and "manipulated emergence"', *Public Administration*, 77, 4, 751–768.

Harrison, S. and Ahmad, W.I.U. (2000) 'Medical autonomy and the UK state 1975 to 2025', *Sociology*, 34, 1, 129–46.

Hearn, J. (1982) 'Notes on patriarchy, professionalisation and the semi-professions', *Sociology*, 16, 184–202.

Hebdon, B. and Kirkpatrick, I. (2004) 'Changes in the organization of public services and their consequences for employment relations', in Ackroyd, S., Batt, R., Thompson, P. and Tolbert, P.S. (eds) *The Oxford Handbook of Work and Organisation*, Oxford: Oxford University Press.

Hebson, G., Grimshaw, D. and Marchington, M. (2003) 'PPPs and the changing public sector ethos: case study evidence from health and local authority sectors', *Work Employment and Society*, 17, 3, 481–501.

Heery, E. (1998) 'A return to contract? Performance related pay in a public service', *Work Employment and Society*, 12, 1, 73–95.

Henderson, J. and Karn, V. (1987) *Race, Class and State Housing: Inequality and the Allocation of Public Housing in Britain*, Aldershot: Gower.

Henkel, M. (1991) 'The new evaluative state', *Public Administration*, 69, Spring, 121–136.

Heyes, J. (1996) *An Investigation into the Impact of Change on Social Work after more than a Decade of Ideological Shifts and Legislative Reforms*, Unpublished Research Report – University of Central Lancashire.

Hinings, C.R. and Greenwood, R. (1988) *The Dynamics of Strategic Change*, Basil Blackwell: Oxford.

Hinings, C.R., Brown, J. and Greenwood, R. (1991) 'Change in an autonomous professional organisation', *Journal of Management Studies*, 28, 1, 375–94.

Hoggett, P. (1994) 'The politics of the modernisation of the UK welfare state', in Burrows, R. and Loader, B. (eds) *Towards a Post Fordist Welfare State*, London: Routledge.

Hoggett, P. (1996) 'New modes of control in the public services', *Public Administration*, 74: 1, 9–32.

Holder, A. (1994) *Planning for Housing Management CCT*, Luton: Local Government Training Board.

Home Office (2001) *Diary of a Police Officer – Police Research Series Paper 149*, London: Home Office.

Hood, C. (1991) 'A public management for all seasons', *Public Administration*, 69, 1, 3–19.

Hood, C. (1995) 'The "New Public Management" in the 1980s: variations on a theme', *Accounting Organisation and Society*, 20, 2/3, 93–109.

Hood, C. (1998) *The Art of the State: Culture, Rhetoric and Public Management*, Oxford: Clarendon Press.

Hope, J. (2004) 'March of the NHS Pen Pushers', *Daily Mail*, 6 April.

Hoque, K., Davis, S., and Humphreys, M. (2004) 'Freedom to do what you are told: senior management team autonomy in an acute NHS Trust', *Public Administration*, forthcoming.

Howe, D. (1986) *Social Workers and their Practice in Welfare Bureaucracies*, Aldershot: Gower.

Howe, D. (1992) 'Child abuse and the bureaucratization of social work', *Sociological Review*, 40, 3, 491–508.

Hoyes, L., Lart, R., Means, R., and Taylor, M. (1994) *Community Care in Transition*, York: Joseph Rountree Foundation.

Hugman, R. (1994) *Power in the Caring Professions*, London: Macmillan.

Hugman, R. (1998) 'Social work and deprofessionalisation' in Abbott, P. and Meerabeau, L. (eds) *The Sociology of the Caring Professions*, London: UCL Press.

Hunter, D.J. (1992) 'Doctors as managers: poachers turned gamekeepers?' *Social Science and Medicine*, 35, 4, 557–66.

Hunter, D.J. (1996) 'The changing role of health care personnel in health and health care management', *Social Science and Medicine*, 43, 5, 799–808.

Hunter, D.J. (1998) 'Medicine', in Laffin, M. (ed.) *Beyond Bureaucracy: The Professions in the Contemporary public Sector*, Aldershot: Ashgate.

Huntington, A. (1999) 'Child care social work and the role of state employees', *Child and Family Social Work,* 4, 241–248.

Hutton, W. (2003) *The World We're In*, London: Abacus.

Huxley, P. (1993) 'Case management and care management in community care', *British Journal of Social Work*, 23, 4, 365–81.

Incomes Data Service (2003) *Recruitment and Retention, Pay Levels and the Use of Agency Workers in Local Government*, London: IDS.

Inman, K. (1999) 'Changing roles', *Community Care*, 3–9, June.

Institute of Housing (1985) *Yearbook*, London: Institute of Housing.

Ironside, M. and Seifert, R. (1998) 'Regulating market forces and managing social conservatism: the delivery of public services to the rural poor', paper presented at the Public Services Research Unit annual conference, Cardiff Business School, April.

Isaac-Henry, K. and Painter, C. (1991) 'The management challenge in local government – emerging themes and trends', *Local Government Studies*, 17, 3, 69–90.

Jamous, H. and Peloille, B. (1970) 'Changes in the French hospital system', in Jackson, J.A. (ed.), *Professions and Professionalisation*, Cambridge: Cambridge University Press.

Jepperson, P.K., Nielsen, L.M., and Sognstrup, H. (2002) 'Professions, institutional dynamics and new public management in the Danish hospital field', *International Journal of Public Administration*, 25, 12, 1559–1578.

Jessop, B. (1994) 'Post-Fordism and the state', in Amin, A. (ed.) *Post Fordism: A Reader*, Oxford: Blackwell.

Johnson, N., Jenkinson, S., Kendall, I., Bradshaw, Y., and Blackmore, M. (1998) 'Regulating for quality in the voluntary sector', *Journal of Social Policy*, 27, 3, 307–328.

Johnson, T. (1972) *Professions and Power*, London: Macmillan.

Johnson, T. (1977) 'Professions in the class structure', in Scase, R. (ed.) *Class, Cleavage and Control*, London: Allen and Unwin.

Johnson, T. (1980) 'Work and power', in Esland, G. and Salaman, G. (eds) *The Politics of Work and Occupations*, Milton Keynes: Open University Press.

Johnson, T. (1993) 'Expertise and the state', in Gane, M. and Johnson, T. (eds) *Foucault's New Domains*, London: Routledge.

Jolley, M. 'The Professionalisation of Nursing', in Jolley, M. and Allan, P. (eds) *Current Issues in Nursing*, London: Chapman and Hall.

Jones, C. (1983) *State Social Work and the Working Class*, London: Macmillan.

Jones, C. (1999) 'Social work: regulation and managerialism', in Exworthy, M. and Halford, S. (eds) *Professionals and the New Managerialism in the Public Sector*, Buckingham: Open University Press.

Jones, C. (2001) 'Voices from the front line: state social workers and new Labour', *British Journal of Social Work*, 31, 547–562.

Kearns, A. (1994) *Going By the Board: The Unknown Facts about Housing Association Membership and Management Committees in England*, Glasgow: Centre for Housing Research and Urban Studies, University of Glasgow.

Keat, R. and Abercrombie, N. (1991) (eds) *Enterprise Culture*, London: Routledge.

Keen, L. (1996) 'Organisational decentralisation and budgetary devolution in local government: a case of middle management autonomy', *Human Resource Management Journal*, 5, 2, 79–98.

Keen, L. and Scase, R. (1998) *Local Government Management*, Buckingham: Open University Press.

Kelly, A. (1998) 'Professionals and the changed environment' in Symonds, A. and Kelly, A. (eds) *The Social Construction of Community Care*, Basingstoke: Macmillan.

Kessler, I. and Purcell, J. (1996) 'Strategic choice and new forms of employment relations in the public service sector: developing an analytical framework', *International Journal of Human Resource Management*, 7, 1, 206–229.

Kessler, I., Purcell, J., and Coyle Shapiro, J. (2000) 'New forms of employment relations in the public services: the limits of strategic choice', *Industrial Relations Journal*, 31, 1, 17–34.

Kickert, W. (ed.) (1997) *Public Management and Administrative Reform in Western Europe*, Cheltenham: Edward Elgar.

Kirkpatrick, I. (2000) 'Workplace assimilation and conflict in professional service organisations: the case of university libraries' *Public Policy and Administration*, 14, 4, pp. 71–86.

Kirkpatrick, I. (2003) 'A jungle of competing requirements: management reform in the organizational field of UK social services', *Social Work and Social Sciences Review*, 10, 3, 24–47.

Kirkpatrick, I. (2004) 'Las nuevas formas de organización y gestion de los servicios publicos de asistencia social y sus consequencias: La experiencia del Reino Unido', in Toboso, F. and Ochando, C. (eds) *Organización de Gobiernos y Mercados en las Sociedades Democráticas: un Análisis Transaccional* – forthcoming.

Kirkpatrick, I. and Ackroyd, S. (2003a) 'Archetype theory and the changing professional organization: a critique and alternative', *Organization*, 10, 4, 739–758.

Kirkpatrick, I. and Ackroyd, S. (2003b) 'Transforming the professional archetype?: the new managerialism in UK social services', *Public Management Review*, 5, 4, 511–531.

Kirkpatrick, I. and Hoque, K. (2004) 'A retreat from bureaucracy? Accounting for the rise of agency work in UK social services', paper delivered at the Work, Employment and Society Conference, Manchester, September.

Kirkpatrick, I., Kitchener, M., and Whipp, R. (2001) 'Out of sight, out of mind? Assessing the impact of markets for local authority children's services', *Public Administration*, 79, 1, 49–71.

Kirkpatrick, I., Kitchener, M., Owen, D., and Whipp, R. (1999) 'Un-chartered territory: experiences of the purchaser/provider split in local authority children's services', *British Journal of Social Work*, 29, 707–726.

Kirkpatrick, I. and Martinez-Lucio, M. (eds) (1995) *The Politics of Quality in the Public Sector*, London: Routledge.

Kirkpatrick, I., Whipp, R. and Davies, A. (1996) New public management and professions, in: Glover, I. and Hughes, M. (eds) *The Professional-Managerial Class*, Aldershot: Avebury.

Kitchener, M. (1998) 'Quasi-market transformation: an institutionalist approach to change in UK hospitals', *Public Administration*, 76, 73–95.

Kitchener, M. (1999) 'All fur coat and no knickers': contemporary organizational change in United Kingdom hospitals', in Brock, D.M., Hinings, C.R. and Powell, M.J. (eds) *Restructuring the Professional Organisation: Accounting, Health Care and Law*, London: Routledge.

Kitchener, M., Kirkpatrick, I. and Whipp, R. (2000) 'Supervising professional work under new public management: evidence from an "invisible trade"', *British Journal of Management*, 11, 3, 213–226.

Klein, R. (1989) *The Politics of the National Health Service*, 2nd edn., London: Longman.

Klein, R. (1995) *The New Politics of the NHS*, 3rd edn., London: Longman.

Klein, R. (1998) 'Competence, self regulation and the public interest', *British Medical Journal*, 301, 1740–1742.

Laffin, M. and Young, K. (1990) *Professionalism in Local Government*, Harlow: Longman.

Laffin, M. (1986) *Professions and Policy: The Role of the Professions in the Central-Local Government Relationship*, Aldershot: Gower.

Laffin, M. (1998a) 'The professions in the contemporary public sector', in Laffin, M. (ed.) *Beyond Bureaucracy: The Professions in the Contemporary Public Sector*, Aldershot: Ashgate.

Laffin, M. (1998b) 'Conclusion' in Laffin, M. (ed.) *Beyond Bureaucracy: The Professions in the Contemporary Public Sector*, Aldershot: Ashgate.

Laffin, M. and Entwistle, T. (2000) 'New problems, old professions? The changing national world of the local government professions', *Policy and Politics*, 28, 2, 207–20.

Langan, M. (1993) 'The rise and fall of social work', in Clarke, J. (ed.) *A Crisis in Care*, London: Sage.

Langan, M. (2000) 'Social services: managing the third way', in Clarke, J., Gerwitz, S. and McLaughlin, E. (eds) *New Managerialism New Welfare?*, London: Sage.

Langan, M. and Clarke, J. (1994) 'Managing in the mixed economy of care', in Clarke, J., Cochrane, A. and McLaughlin, E. (eds) *Managing Social Policy*, London: Sage.

Larkin, G. (1995) 'State Control and the Health Professions in the United Kingdom: historical perspectives', in Johnson, T., Larkin, G. and Saks, M. (eds) *Health Professions and the State in Europe*, London: Routledge.

Larkin, G. (1983) *Occupational Monopoly and Modern Medicine*, London: Tavistock.

Larson, M.S. (1977) *The rise of Professionalism: A Sociological Analysis*, London: University of California Press.

Laurence, J. (2001) 'Agencies hold NHS to ransom', *Independent*, 5 September.

Lawler, J. and Hearn, J. (1997) 'The managers of social work: the experiences and indentifications of third tier social services managers and the implications for future practice', *British Journal of Social Work*, 27, 191–218.

Lawson, R. (1995) 'The new technology of management in the personal social services', in Taylor-Goody, P. and Lawson, R., *Markets and Managers: New Issues in the Delivery of Welfare*, Buckingham: Open University Press.

Leach, S., Stewart, J., and Walsh, K. (1994) *The Changing Organisation and Management of Local Government*, London: Macmillan.

Le Grand, J. and Bartlett, W. (1993) *Quasi-markets and Social Policy*, Basingstoke: Macmillan.

Le Grand, J. and Vizard, P. (1998) 'The national health service: crisis, change or continuity?', in Glennerster, H. and Hills, J. (eds) *The State of Welfare: The Economics of Social Spending*, Oxford: Oxford University Press.

Leicht, K. and Fennel, M. (2001) *Professional Work: A Sociological Approach*, London: Blackwell.

Lewis, J. and Glennerster, H. (1996) *Implementing the New Community Care*, Buckingham: Open University Press.

Lewis, J., Bernstock, P., Bovell, V., and Wookey, F. (1996) 'The purchaser/provider split in social care: is it working?' *Social Policy and Administration*, 30, 1, 1–19.

Lewis, J., Bernstock, P., Bovell, V., and Wookey, F. (1997) 'Implementing care management: issues in relation to the new community care', *British Journal of Social Work*, 27, 5–24.

LGEO (2001) *Care to Stay?*, London: Local Government Employer's Association.

Lipsky, M. (1980) *Street level Bureaucracy: Dilemmas of the Individual in Public Services*, New York: Russel Sage.

Llewellyn, S. (2001) 'Two way mirrors: clinicians as medical managers', *Organisation Studies*, 22, 4, 593–624.

Lloyd, C. and Seifert, R. (1995) 'Restructuring in the NHS: the impact of the 1990 reforms on the management of labour', *Work Employment and Society*, 9, 2, 359–378.

Local Government Management Board (1988) *The Development of Senior Managers within Social Services Departments*, London: LGMB.

Local Government Management Board (1994) *Performance Management and Performance Related Pay survey 1993*, London: LGMB.

Local Government Management Board and Central Council for the Education and Training of Social Work (1997) *Human Resources for Personal Social Services*, London: LGMB and CCETSW.

Loveday, B. (1998) 'The police service', in Laffin, M. (ed.) *Beyond Bureaucracy: The Professions in the Contemporary Public Sector*, Aldershot: Ashgate.

Lowndes, V. (1997) 'We are learning to accommodate the mess: four propositions about managing change in local government', *Public Policy and Administration*, 12, 2, 80–94.

Lymbery, M. (1998) 'Care management and professional autonomy: the impact of community care legislation on social work with older people', *British Journal of Social Work*, 28, 863–78.

Lymbery, M. (2001) 'Social work at the crossroads', *British Journal of Social Work*, 31, 369–384.

Mabey, C. and Salaman, G. (1998) *Human Resource Management: A strategic Introduction*, London: Blackwell.

Macdonald, K.M. (1995) *The Sociology of the Professions*, London: Sage.

MacKay, L. (1989) *Nursing a Problem*, Milton Keynes: Open University Press.

Maclennan, D., Clapham, D., Goodlad, R., Kemp., P. Malcolm, J., Satsangi, M., Stanforth, J., and Whitefield, L. (1989) *The Nature and Effectiveness of Housing Management in England*, London: HMSO.

Malpass, P. (2000) *Housing Associations and Housing Policy. A Historical Perspective*, Basingstoke: Macmillan.

Marsh, D. and Rhodes, R. (eds) (1992) *Implementing Thatcherite Policies: Audit of an Era*, Buckingham: Open University Press.

Marshall, T. (1977) *Class, Citizenship and Social Development*, Chicago: University of Chicago Press.

Martin, J.P. (1984) *Hospitals in Trouble*, Oxford: Blackwell.

Martin, S. (2000) 'Implementing Best Value: local public services in transition', *Public Administration*, 78, 1, 209–227.

Martin, S. (2002) 'Best Value: new public management or new direction?', in McLaughlin, K., Osborne, S.P. and Ferlie, E. (eds) *New Public Management: Current Trends and Future Prospects*, London: Routledge.

Martinez-Lucio, M. and MacKenzie, R. (1999) 'Quality management: a new form of control', in S. Corby and G. White (eds) *The Public Services: Themes and Issues*, London: Routledge.

May, T. (1997) 'Social work, professionalism and the rationality of organisational change', Paper presented to the conference on 'Professionalism, boundaries and the workplace', University Of Derby, *Centre for Social Research*, February.

May, T. and Annison, J. (1998) 'The de-professionalisation of probation officers', in Abbott, P. and Meerabeau, L. (eds) *The Sociology of the Caring Professions*, London: UCL Press.

McGrath, M., Grant, G., Ramcharan, P., Caldock, K., Parry-Jones, B., and Robinson, C. (1996) 'The roles and tasks of care managers in Wales', *Community Care management and Planning*, 4, 6, 185–194.

McMahon A. (1999) 'Promoting continuing professional development for teachers: an achievable target for school leaders?', in Bush, T., Bell, L., Bolam, R., Glatter, R., and Ribbins, P. (eds) *Re-defining Educational Management*. London: Paul Chapman Publishing Ltd.

McKinlay, J.B. and Arches, J. (1985) 'Towards the proletarianisation of physicians', *International Journal of Health Services*, 15, 161–95.

McNulty, T. and Ferlie, E. (2002) *Reengineering Healthcare – The Complexities of Organisational Transformation*, Oxford: Oxford University Press.

McNulty, T. (2003) 'Redesigning public services: challenges of practice and policy', *British Journal of Management*, 14, 5, S31–S46.

Means, R. and Langan, J. (1996) 'Charging and quasi-markets in community care: implications for elderly people with dementia', *Social Policy and Administration*, 30, 3, 244–262.

Means, R. and Smith, R. (1998) *Community Care: Policy and Practice*, London: Macmillan.

Melia, V. (1987) *Learning and Working: The Occupational Socialisation of Nurses*, London: Tavistock.

Merritt, S. (1979) *State Housing in Britain*. London: Routledge and Kegan Paul.

Mintzberg, H. (1993) *Structure in Fives: Designing Effective Organisations*, London: Prentice Hall.

Montgomery, K. (1991) 'Professional dominance and the threat of corporatization', *Current Research on Occupations and Professions*, 7, 221–240.

Morgan, P., Allington, N., and Heery, E. (eds) (2000) 'Employment insecurity in the public services', in Heery, E. and J. Salmon (eds) *The Insecure Workforce*, London: Routledge.

MORI/IRIS consulting/Aldbourne Associates (2003) *Large Scale Voluntary Transfers: Staff Impacts and Implications*, London: Office of the Deputy Prime Minister.

Mueller, F., Harvey, C., and Howorth, C. (2000) 'Managers and Clinical Professionals in a Hospital Trust', Paper to the 16th EGOS Conference Helsinki, Finland.

Mullins, D. (1997) 'From regulatory capture to regulated competition', *Housing Studies*, 12: 301–319.

Mullins, D. (1999) 'Managing ambiguity: merger activity in the non-profit housing sector', *Journal of Nonprofit and Voluntary Sector Marketing*, 4, 4.

Mullins, D. (2000) *A Survey of Registered Social Landlord Best Value Activity 1999*. London: National Housing Federation.

Mullins, D., Reid, B., and Walker, R.M. (2001) 'Modernization and change in social housing: the case for an organizational perspective' *Public Administration*, 79, 3: 599–623.

Mullins, D. and Riseborough, M. (2000) *What are Housing Associations Becoming? Final report of Changing with the Times Project*, University of Birmingham, School of Public Policy Housing Research at CURS Series, Number 7.

Murphy, R. (1988) *Social Closure*, Oxford: Clarendon Press.

National Audit Office (2003) *Improving Social Housing Through Transfer*, London: National Audit Office.

National Federation of Housing Associations (1987) *Standards for Housing Management*, London: NFHA.

Newman, J. (2000) 'Beyond the new public management? Modernizing public services', in Clarke, J., Gerwitz, S. and McLaughlin, E. (eds) *New Managerialism New Welfare?*, London: Sage.

Newman, J. and Williams, F. (1995) 'Diversity and change: gender, welfare and organizational relations', in Itzin, C. and Newman, J. (eds) *Gender, Culture and Organisational Change: Putting Theory into Practice*, London: Routledge.

Niskanen, W. (1971) *Bureaucracy and Representative Government*. Chicago: Aldine-Atherton.

Nixon, J. (1993) 'Implementation in the hands of senior managers: community care in Britain', in Hill, M. (ed.) *New Agendas in the Study of the Policy Process*, London: Harvester Wheatsheaf.

O'Connor, J. (1973) *The Fiscal Crisis of the State*, New York: St. Martins Press.

Office for Public Services Reform (2003) *Reforming Our Public Services. Principles into Practice*, London: Office for Public Services Reform.

Oliver, C. (1992) 'The antecedents of deinstitutionalisation', *Organisational Studies*, 13: 4, 563–588.

OECD (1995) *Governance in Transition: Public Management Reforms in OECD Countries*, Paris: OECD.

OECD (1997) *Family, Market and Community: Equity and Efficiency in Social Policy, Social Policy Studies No. 21*, Paris: OECD.

Orme, J. (2001) 'Regulation or fragmentation? Directions for social work under New Labour', *British Journal of Social Work*, 31, 611–624.

Osborne, D. and Gaebler, T. (1992) *Reinventing Government: How the Entrepreneurial Spirit is Transforming the Public Sector*, Reading, Mass: Addison Wesley.

Osborne, S.P. and McLaughlin, K. (2002) 'The new public management in context', in McLaughlin, K., Osborne, S.P. and Ferlie, E. (eds) *New Public Management: Current Trends and Future Prospects*, London: Routledge.

Oxford Brookes University (2002) *Tenants Managing: An Evaluation of Tenant Management Organizations in England*, London: Office of the Deputy Prime Minister.

Pahl, J. (1994) '"Like the job – but hate the organisation": social workers and managers in social services', *Social Policy Review*, 6, 190–210.

Parry, N. and Parry, J. (1976) *The Rise of the Medical Profession: A Study of Collective Social Mobility*, London: Croom Helm.

Parry, N. and Parry, J. (1979) 'Social work, professionalism and the state', in Parry, N., Rustin, M. and Satyamurti, C. (eds) *Social Work Welfare and the State*, London: Edward Arnold.

Parkin, F. (1979) *Marxism and Class Theory: A Bourgeois Critique*, London: Tavistock Publications.

Parsloe, P. (1981) *Social Services Area Teams*, London: George Allen and Unwin.

Parton, N. (1991) *Governing the Family*, London: Macmillan.

Pawson, H. and Fancy, K. (2003) *Maturing Assets. The Evolution of Stock Transfer Housing Associations*, Bristol: The Policy Press.

Payne, M. (2002) 'The role and achievements of a professional association in the late twentieth century: The British association of social workers 1970–2000', *British Journal of Social Work*, 38, 2, 969–995.

Pearl, M. (1997) *Social Housing Management. A Critical Appraisal of Housing Practice*, Basingstoke: Macmillan.

Penna, S., Paylor, I., and Soothill, K. (1995) *Job Satisfaction and Dissatisfaction: A Study of Residential Care Work*, London: NSW and Joseph Rountree Foundation.

Perkin, H. (1989) *The Rise of Professional Society: England Since 1880*, London: Routledge.

Petch, A., Cheetham, J., Fuller, R., MacDonald, C., and Myers, F. (1996) *Delivering Community Care: Initial Implementation of Care Management in Scotland*, London: Statutory Office.

Pinnington, A. and Morris, T. (2002) 'Transforming the architect: Ownership form and archetype change', *Organization Studies*, 23, 2, 182–210.

Pinnington, A. and Morris, T. (2003) 'Archetype change in professional organisations: survey evidence from large law firms', *British Journal of Management*, 14, 1, 85–99.

Pithouse, A. (1989) *Social Work: The Social Organisation of an Invisible Trade*, Aldershot: Avebury.

Pollitt, C. (1990) 'Doing business in the temple? Managers and quality assurance in the public services', *Public Administration*, 68, 4, 435–452.

Pollitt, C. (1993) *Managerialism and the Public Services: The Anglo American Experience*, 2nd edn, London: Macmillan.

Pollitt, C. (2000) 'Is the emperor in his underwear? An analysis of the impacts of public management reform', *Public Management*, 2, 2, 181–200.

Pollitt, C., Birchall, J., and Putman, K. (1998) *Decentralising Public Service Management*, London: Macmillan.

Pollitt, C. and Boukaert, G. (2000) *Public Management Reform: A Comparative Analysis*, Oxford: Oxford University Press.

Postle, K. (2002) 'Working "between the idea and the reality": ambiguities and tensions in care managers' work', *British Journal of Social Work*, 32, 335–351.

Powell, M.J., Brock, D.M., and Hinings, C.R. (1999) 'The changing professional organisation', in Brock, D.M., Hinings, C.R. and Powell, M.J. (eds) *Restructuring the Professional Organisation: Accounting, Health Care and Law*, London: Routledge.

Power, A. (1987) *Property Before People*, London: Allen and Unwin.

Power, M. (1997) *The Audit Society*, Oxford: Oxford University Press.

Pratchett, L. and Wingfield, M. (1996) 'Petty bureaucracy and woolly-minded liberalism? The changing ethos of local government officers', *Public Administration*, 74, 639–656.

Price Waterhouse and Department of Health (1991) *Implementing Community Care: Purchaser, Commissioner and Provider Roles*, London: HMSO.

Proven, B. and Williams, P. (1991) 'Joining the professionals? The future of housing staff and housing work', in Donnison, D. and Maclennan, D. (eds) *The Housing Service of the Future*, London: Institute of Housing/Longman.

Pugh, D.S. (1987) 'The measurement of organisational structures: does context determine form?', in Pugh, D.S. (ed.) *Organisation Theory*, Middlesex: Penguin.

Raelin, J. (1991) *The Clash of Cultures*, Harvard Business School Press.

Rai, D.K. (1994) *Developments in Training in Social Services*, London: NISW.

Redman, T., Snape, E., Thompson, D., and Ka Ching Yan, F. (2000) 'Performance Management in an NHS Hospital', *Human Resource Management Journal*, 10, 1, 48–62.

Reed, M. (1996) 'Expert power and control in late modernity: an empirical review and theoretical synthesis', *Organisation Studies*, 17, 4, 573–597.

Reed, M. (2004) 'Engineers of human souls, faceless technocrats or merchants of morality?: projecting professional futures', paper presented at EURAM Conference, St. Andrews University, 5–8 May.

Reid, B. (1995) 'Interorganizational networks and the delivery of local housing services', *Housing Studies*, 10, 133–150.

Regulatory Impact Unit (2000) *Making a Difference: Reducing School Paperwork*, London: Cabinet Office.

Regulatory Impact Unit (2001) *Making a Difference: Reducing General Practitioner's Paperwork*, London: Cabinet Office.

Rhodes, M. (2000) 'Desperately seeking a solution: social democracy, Thatcherism and the "Third way" in British welfare', in Ferrera, M. and Rhodes, M. (eds) *Recasting European Welfare States*, London: Frank Cass.

Rhodes, R.A.W. (1996) 'The new governance: governing without government', *Political Studies*, XLIV, 652–667.

Rhodes, R.A.W. (1997a) 'Re-inventing Whitehall, 1997–1995', in Kickert, W. (ed.) *Public Management and Administrative Reform in Western Europe*, Cheltenham: Edward Elgar.

Rhodes, R.A.W. (1997b) *Understanding Governance: Policy Networks, Governance, Reflexivity and Accountability*, Buckingham: Open University Press.

Rivett, G. (1997) *From the Cradle to the Grave: Fifty Years of the NHS*, London: King's Fund Publishing.

Rober, M. (1996) 'Germany', in Farnham, D., Horton, S., Barlow, J. and Hondeghem, A. (eds) *New Public Managers in Europe: Public Services in Transition*, London: Macmillan.

Ruef, M. and Scott, W.R. (1998) 'A multidimensional model of organisational legitimacy: hospital survival in changing institutional environments', *Administrative Science Quarterly*, 43, 877–904.

Rushton, A. and Nathan, J. (1996) 'The supervision of child protection work', *British Journal of Social Work*, 26, 357–374.

Saks, M. (1994) *Professions and the Public Interest*, London: Routledge.

Salter, B. (1999) 'Change in the governance of medicine: the politics of self-regulation', *Policy and Politics*, 27, 2, 143–58.

Salter, B. (2001) 'Who rules? The new politics of medical regulation', *Social Science and Medicine*, 52, 871–83.

Sanderson, I. (2001) 'Performance management, evaluation and learning in "modern" local government', *Public Administration*, 79, 2, 297–313.

Satyamurti, C. (1981) *Occupational Survival*, Oxford: Basil Blackwell.

Saunders, P. (1990) *A Nation of Home Owners*, London: Unwin and Hyman.

Savage, M., Barlow, J., Dickens, P. and Fielding, T. (1992) *Property, Bureaucracy and Culture: Middle Class Formation in Contemporary Britain*, London: Routledge.

Scott, W.R. and Meyer, J.W. (1991) 'The organisation of societal sectors: propositions and early evidence', in Powell, W.W. and DiMaggio, P. (eds) *The New Institutionalism in Organisational Analysis*, London: University of Chicago Press.

Seebohm Report (1968) Report of the Committee on Local Authority Allied Personal Social Services (Cmnd 3703), London: HMSO.

Siegrist, H. (1990) 'Professionalism as a process: patterns, progression and discontinuity', in Burrage, M. and Torstendahl, R. (eds) *Professions in Theory and History*, London: Sage.

Shaoul, J. (1999) 'The economic and financial context', in S. Corby and G. White (eds) *The Public Services: Themes and Issues*, London: Routledge.

Shaw, I. (1995) 'The quality of mercy: the management of quality in the personal social services', in Kirkpatrick, I. and Martinez-Lucio, M. (eds) *The Politics of Quality in the Public Sector*, London: Routledge.

Sheppard, M. (1995) *Care Management and the New Social Work: A Critical Analysis*, London: Whiting and Birch.

Sinclair, J., Ironside, M. and Seifert, R. (1996) 'Classroom struggle? Market-oriented reforms and their impact on the teacher labour process', *Work Employment and Society*, 10, 4, 641–661.

Smith (1997) 'The limits of positivism in social work research', *British Journal of Social Work*, 17, 4, 401–16.

Social Care and Health Workforce Group (2003) *Social Services Workforce Survey 2002* (Report 31), London: Employers Organisation.

Social Exclusion Unit (2000) *National Strategy for Neighbourhood Renewal: A Framework for Consultation*, London: Cabinet Office.

Social Services Inspectorate (1986) *Inspection of the Supervision of Social Workers in the Assessment and Monitoring of Child Care When Children Subject to a Care Order Have Been Returned Home*, London: DHSS.

Social Services Inspectorate (1994) *Inspection of Assessment and Care Management Arrangements in Social Services Departments, October 1993–March 1994*, London: Department of Health.

Social Services Inspectorate (1995) *Partners in Caring: The 4th Annual Report of the Chief Inspector*, London: Department of Health.

Social Services Inspectorate (1996) *Organization of Children's Services Project*, Interim Report, London: Department of Health.

Social Services Inspectorate (1997) *Better Management, Better Care: The Sixth Annual Report of the Chief Inspector*, London: Department of Health.

Social Services Inspectorate (1998) *Someone Else's Children: Inspections of Planning and Decision Making for Children Looked After and the Safety of Children Looked After, Social Care Group*, London: Department of Health.

Social Services Inspectorate (1999) *Meeting the Challenge: Improving Management for the Effective Commissioning of Social Care Services for Older People*, London: Department of Health.

Social Services Inspectorate (2001) *Modernising Social Services: A Commitment to Deliver: The 10th Annual Report of the Chief Inspector of Social Services*, London: Department of Health.

Social Services Inspectorate (2002) *Modernising Services to Transform Care: Inspection of how Councils are managing the Modernisation Agenda in Social Care*, London: Department of Health.

Soothill, K., MacKay, L., and Webb, C. (1995) *Interprofessional Relations in Health Care*, London: Edward Arnold.

Stationery Office (2001) *Public Expenditure: Statistical Analysis 2001–2002* (Cm 51a), London: Stationery Office.

Stevenson, O. (1994) 'Social work in the 1990's: empowerment – fact or fiction?', *Social policy Review*, 6, London: Social Policy Association.

Stewart, J. (1988) *A New Management for Housing Departments*. Luton: Local Government Management Board.

Stoker, G. (1989) 'Creating a local government for a Post-Fordist society: the Thatcherite project?', in Stewart, J. and Stoker, G. (eds) *The Future of Local Government*, London: Macmillan.

Stone, D. (1996) *Capturing the Political Imagination: Think Tanks and the Policy Process*, London: Frank Cass.

Strauss, A. Schatzman, L., Ehrlich, D., Butcher, R., and Shashin, M. (1963) 'The hospital and it's negotiated order', in Friedson, E. (ed.) *The Hospital in Modern Society*, London: Free Press.

Swenarton, M. (1981) *Homes Fit for Heroes*, London: Heinemann.

Symon, P. and Walker, R.M. (1995) 'A consumer perspective on performance indicators: the local authority reports to tenants regimes in England and Wales', *Environment and Planning C: Government and Politics*, 13, 2, 195–216.

Syrett, V., Jones, M., and Sercombe, N. (1997) 'Implementing Community Care: the Congruence of Manager and Practitioner Cultures', *Social Work and Social Sciences Review*, 7, 3, 154–69.

Taylor-Gooby, P., Sylvester, S., Calan, M., and Manley, G. (2000) 'Knights, knaves and gnashers: professional values and private dentistry', *Journal of Social Policy*, 29, 375–395.

Thomas, P. (1998) 'Environmental Health', in Laffin, M. (ed.) *Beyond Bureaucracy? The Professions in the Contemporary Public Sector*, Aldershot: Ashgate.

Thomas, R. and Dunkerley, D. (1999) 'Janus and the bureaucrats: middle management in the public sector', *Public Policy and Administration*, 14: 1, 28–41.

Thomas, R., Hardy, S. and Davies, A. (2000) 'Gender, restructuring and new public management: changing managerial identities in three public service organisations', paper presented at the British Academy of Management Annual Conference, 13–15 September, University of Edinburgh.

Thomas, R. and Davies, A. (2004) 'Theorising the micro-politics of resistance: discourses of change and professional identities in UK public services', *Organisation Studies* – forthcoming.

Thompson, N., Stradling, S., Murphy, M., and O'Neill, P. (1996) 'Stress and organisational culture', *British Journal of Social Work*, 26, 5, 647–66.

Thornley, C. and Winchester, D. (1994) 'The remuneration of nursing personnel in the United Kingdom', in Marsden, D. (ed.) *The Remuneration of Nursing Personnel*, Geneva: I.L.O.

Timmins, N. (1996) *The Five Giants*, London: Fontana.

Timmins, N. (1998) *NHS 50th Anniversary: A History of the NHS*, London: National Liaison Steering Group.

Tonge, R. and Horton, S. (1996) 'Financial management and quality', in Farnham, D. and Horton, S. (eds) *Managing the New Public Services*, London: Macmillan.

Torstendahl, R. (1990) 'Introduction: promotion and strategies of knowledge-based groups', in Torstendahl, R. and Burrage, M. (eds) *The Formation of the Professions: Knowledge, State and Strategy*, London: Sage.

Townley, B. (1997) 'The institutional logic of performance appraisal', *Organisation Studies*, 18, 2, 261–285.

UNISON (2000) *Against the Odds: Delivering Local Services – Report of an NOP Survey of UNISON Local Government Members*, London: UNISON.

UNISON (2001) *Making a Difference Under Pressure: UNISON Members Delivering Local Services 2001*, London: UNISON.

Waine, B. (2000) 'Managing performance through pay', in J. Clarke, S. Gerwitz and E. McLaughlin (eds) *New Managerialism New Welfare?*, London: Sage.

Walby, S. and Greenwell, J. (1994) *Medicine and Nursing: Professions in a Changing NHS*, London: Sage.

Walker, R.M. (1991) *Housing Co-operatives: Routes to Tenant Control and Satisfaction?* Unpublished PhD thesis, University of Reading.

Walker, R.M. (1998) 'New public management and housing associations: from comfort to competition', *Policy and Politics*, 22, 1, 71–87.

Walker, R.M. (2000) 'The Changing Management of Social Housing: The Impact of Externalisation and Managerialisation', *Housing Studies*, 15, 2, 281–299.

Walker, R.M. (2001) 'How to abolish public housing: Implications and lessons from public management reform', *Housing Studies*, 16, 5, 676–696.

Walker, R.M. (2003) *Continuous Improvement for Housing Associations: A Discussion Paper Prepared for the Housing Corporation*, Cardiff: Cardiff University.

Walker, R.M. and Enticott, G. (2004) 'Using Multiple Informants in Housing Studies: Methodological Issues and Prescriptions for Research', Paper Presented at the Asia-Pacific Network for Housing Research, Hong Kong, February.

Walker, R.M. and Jeanes, E. (2001) 'Innovation in a regulated service: the case of English housing associations', *Public Management*, 4, 4, 525–550.

Walker, R.M., Jeanes, E., and Rowlands, R. (2001) *Managing Public Services Innovation: The Experience of English Housing Associations*, The Policy Press: Bristol.

Walker, R.M. and Smith, R.S.G. (1999) 'Regulator and organisational responses to restructured housing association finance in England and Wales', *Urban Studies*, 36, 4, 737–754.

Walker, R.M. and Williams, P.R. (1995) 'Implementing Local Government Reorganisation in the Housing Service: The Case of Wales', *Local Government Studies*, 21, 3: 483–508.

Walsh, K., Deakin, N., Smith, P., Spurgeon, P., and Thomas, N. (1997) *Contracting for Change: Contracts in Health, Social Care, and Other Local Government Services*, Oxford: Oxford University Press.

Walton, R. (1975) *Women and Social Work*, London: Routledge and Kegan Paul.

Ward, H. (ed.) (1997) *Looking After Children: Research into Practice*. London: HMSO.

Ward, S. (1974) *Tenants in Control*, London: Architectural Press.

Webb, A. (1980) 'The personal social services', in Bosanquet, N. and Townsend, P. (eds) *Labour and Equality: A Fabian Study of Labour in Power, 1974–79*, London: Heinemann.

Webb, A. and Wistow, G. (1987) *Social Work, Social Care and Social Planning: The Personal Social Services Since Seebohm*, London: Longman.

Webb, J. (1999) 'Work and the new public service class', *Sociology*, 33, 4, 747–766.

Webb, S.A. (2001) 'Some considerations on the validity of evidence-based practice in social work', *British Journal of Social Work*, 31, 57–79.

Whipp, R., Kirkpatrick, I., and Kitchener, M. (1998) *The External Management of Local Authority Children's Homes*, London: Department of Health.

Whipp, R., Kirkpatrick, I., and Kitchener, M. (2004) *The Management of Children's Residential Care: A Managed Service?*, London: Palgrave.

White, G. and Hutchinson, B. (1996) 'Local government', in Farnham, D. and Horton, S. (eds) *Managing People in the Public Services*, London: Macmillan.

White, G. (1999) 'The remuneration of public servants: fair pay or new pay?', in Corby, S. and White, G. (eds) *The Public Services: Themes and Issues*, London: Routledge.

Whitfield, D. (2001) *Public Services or Corporate Welfare? Rethinking the Nation State in the Global Economy*, Streling VA, London: Pluto Press.

Wilcox, S. (1999) (ed.) *Housing Finance Review 1999–2000*, London: Chartered Institute of Housing and Council for Mortgage Lenders.

Wilding, P. (1982) *Professional Power and Social Welfare*, London: Routledge and Kegan Paul.

Wilding, P. (1992) 'The British welfare state: Thatcherism's enduring legacy', *Policy and Politics*, 20, 2, 201–11.

Wilding, P. (1997) 'The welfare state and the Conservatives', *Political Studies*, 45, 4, 716–26.

Wilensky, H.L. (1964) 'The professionalisation of everyone?', *American Journal of Sociology*, 70, 137–58.

Winchester, D. and Bach, S. (1995) 'The state: the public sector', in Edwards, P. (ed.) *Industrial relations*, Oxford: Blackwell.

Winchester, D. and S. Bach (1999) 'Britain: the transformation of public service employment relations', in Bach, S., Bordogna, L., Della Rocca, G., and Winchester, D. (eds) *Public Service Employment Relations in Europe: Transformation, Modernisation or Inertia?*, London: Routledge.

Wistow, G., Knapp, M., Hardy, B., Forder, J., Kendall, J., and Manning, R. (1996) *Social Care Markets*, Milton Keynes: Open University Press.

Witz, A. (1992) *Professions and Patriarchy*, London: Routledge.

Witz, A. (1994), 'The challenge of nursing', in Gabe, J., Kelleher, D. and Williams, G. (eds) *Challenging Medicine*, London: Routledge.

Young, K. (1997) *Portrait of Change 1997*, London: Local Government Management Board.

Younghusband, E. (1978) *Social Work in Britain 1950–1975, Volumes I and II*, Surrey: George Allen and Unwin.

Index